Concealment and Revelation

Concealment and Revelation

ESOTERICISM IN JEWISH THOUGHT AND ITS
PHILOSOPHICAL IMPLICATIONS

Moshe Halbertal
Translated by Jackie Feldman

PRINCETON UNIVERSITY PRESS
PRINCETON AND OXFORD

Published by Princeton University Press, 41 William Street, Princeton,
New Jersey 08540

In the United Kingdom: Princeton University Press, 3 Market Place,
Woodstock, Oxfordshire OX20 1SY

Library of Congress Cataloging-in-Publication Data
Halbertal, Moshe.
   [Seter ve-gilui. English]
   Concealment and revelation: esotericism in Jewish thought and its philosophical
implications / Moshe Halbertal; translated by Jackie Feldman.
      p. cm.
   Includes bibliographical references and index.
   ISBN-13: 978-0-691-12571-8 (hardcover: alk. paper)
   ISBN-10: 0-691-12571-6 (hardcover: alk. paper)
   1. Mysticism—Judaism. 2. Cabala—History. 3. Judaism—History—Medieval and early
modern period, 425-1789. I. Title.
   BM526.H34513 2007
   296.7'12—dc22   2007001212

British Library Cataloging-in-Publication Data is available

This book has been composed in Sabon

Printed on acid-free paper. ∞

pup.princeton.edu

Printed in the United States of America

10 9 8 7 6 5 4 3 2 1

For my daughters Nomi, Racheli and Shira

Contents

Acknowledgments

THIS BOOK was written with the generous support of the Shalom Hartman Institute in Jerusalem and the Institute for Advanced Studies at the Hebrew University. The community of scholars at the Hartman Institute has been an ongoing source of intellectual inspiration and companionship, and I wish to thank David and Donniel Hartman, the directors of the institute, for their support. The last section of the book was written at NYU School of Law, and a draft of it was presented at the Colloquium in Legal, Political and Social Philosophy at NYU. I have learned a great deal from the attentive and insightful comments I received from my colleagues Thomas Nagel and Ronald Dworkin, and the other participants at the Colloquium.

I owe gratitude to my friends Yonathan Garb, Melila Helner, Stephen Holmes, Moshe Idel, Mattias Kumm, Yair Lorberbaum, Menachem Lorberbaum, Adi Ofir, Elchanan Reiner, Guy Stroumsa and the late Israel Ta-Shma, who read parts of the manuscripts and shared with me their most valuable comments. I wish to thank Fred Appel my editor at Princeton Press for his wise and encouraging advice and support, Nathan Carr of the Princeton Press for his dedicated treatment of the production process, and the copy editor Eric Schramm for his patient reading and valuable comments.

A Note on Editions Used

MISHNA AND Babylonian Talmud: *The Babylonian Talmud*. Ed. Isidore Epstein and Judah Slotki. London: Soncino Press, 1948–1952.

Tosefta: *The Tosefta*. Ed. Jacob Neusner. New York: Hendrickson Publishers, 1977–1986.

Palestinian Talmud: *The Talmud of the Land of Israel*. Ed. Jacob Neusner. Chicago: University of Chicago Press, 1982–1994.

Midrash Rabbah: *Midrash Rabbah*. Ed. H. Freedman and Maurice Simon. London: Soncino Press, 1961.

Hekhalot: *Übersetzung der Hekhalot Literatur*. Ed. Peter Schäfer in Zusammenarbeit mit Hans-Jürgen Becker. Tübingen: J. C. B. Mohr, 1987–1995.

Ibn Ezra: Abraham Ibn Ezra. *Commentary on the Torah*. Ed. Asher Weiser. Jerusalem: Mossad Harav Kook, 1977.

Maimonides: Moses Maimonides. *The Guide of the Perplexed*. Trans. with an introduction and notes by Shlomo Pines. Chicago: University of Chicago Press, 1963.

Naḥmanides: *Ramban's (Naḥmanides) Commentary on the Torah*. Ed. and trans. Charles Chavel. 5 vols. New York: Soncino Press, 1971–1976.

Concealment and Revelation

Introduction

ESOTERIC TEACHINGS FORM a body of knowledge whose dissemination is severely restricted. These restrictions are meant to carefully filter the listening public in the case of oral transmission, and to impose limits on copying and circulation, and later on the printing, of the written word. As a result of these restrictions, complex strategies of encoding and double speech and writing were developed, which enabled the transmission of secret information to the worthy elect, without preliminary filtering of the congregation of listeners or readers. Esotericism as a general attitude, in distinction from actual esoteric practice, is a tendency to view canonical texts, social phenomena, or even individual behavior as a form of coded manifestation that intentionally conceals something deeper and more meaningful that only the few can decipher. In that respect esotericism as an interpretative outlook reflects a consciousness of the existence of something concealed and hidden, whose knowledge or experience is of decisive or even redemptive import; this consciousness is expressed through a wide variety of conceptions. What the variations of esoteric consciousness have in common is the assumption that, behind what is revealed, there exists a purer, deeper, and truer level of meaning. Consequently, esoteric teachings express varying levels of alienation from the surface of existence, from revealed religion or from the external aspects of human behavior. At the most alienated pole of the esoteric conception stands the Gnostic position, which sees human beings as hostages of an evil, scheming demiurge; it offers esoteric knowledge of the existence of a foreign and pure god, external to the universe. This knowledge liberates humans from their bondage. While not all esoteric structures create such a severe tension between the revealed and the hidden, the basic position of distance and alienation is common to all of them. Opposed to the alienated, Gnostic esotericism, we find positions that view the esoteric not as a substitute for the domain of the revealed, but as a kind of deeper understructure for it, which endows the revealed surface with meaning. In these conceptions, the revealed surface of existence, the sacred scriptures, and, sometimes, human behavior as well become symbolic structures that designate and signify something concealed that lies beneath them.

The esoteric mentality is embodied in various forms of thought. It appears in theological and magical contexts, in which hidden knowledge of the godhead and the universe are transmitted, or else as a method of exegesis of canonical works disclosing an encoded level of meaning. Esotericism also has a secular form, in which it serves as the basis for sociopolitical explanations, which assume that nothing is as it appears, and that society is, in fact, governed by secret organizations pulling on hidden strings. In its political contexts, the esoteric mentality is a breeding ground for a multitude of conspiracy theories, which assume hidden centers of power behind what appear to be individual, unrelated actions. The psychoanalytic conception, which maintains that a repressed, guarded region of consciousness guides people's actions, is also a complex instance of the esoteric conception.

The remarkably varied structure of esoteric knowledge includes multiple complex techniques for approaching the hidden: the adoption of a precise and strict method of thought in order to penetrate the deep metaphysical structure of being, entering alternative states of consciousness to facilitate insights from other planes, the use of various magical techniques, the interpretation of dreams and their analysis for the purpose of revealing the repressed level of the self in order to overcome internal censorship, and many, many others.

Some theories on the universe or on society are extremely remote from the revealed surface of things. Examples include modern physics, which postulates the existence of particles which have never been observed, or Marxism, which maintains that the ideological and economic structure of society is determined by the level of development of the means of production. Yet the enormous gap between these theories and what is revealed on the surface is not sufficient for them to be considered esoteric teachings. In addition to the existence of such gaps, esoteric conceptions claim that the existence of the esoteric is dependent on intentional concealment and camouflage (which does not hold true, for example, in the case of modern physics), or that essentially the esoteric may only be expressed through indirect symbols. We might say that what is common to all types of esotericists is the metaphor of the key. Esotericists do not understand, interpret, and explain; rather, they open, decipher, liberate or expose.[1]

Naturally, strictly esoteric traditions were not written down at all. Oral transmission enables control over the identity of the receivers and constant supervision over what is revealed and clarified through the medium of conversation. Writing, even if in veiled form, is a relaxation of the strictest restrictions of esotericism. One who writes down his words seeks to transcend the gaps of space and time between himself and his readers, who are not his immediate conversational partners. Once the words have been committed to writing, he may no longer restrict access to them, unless he took care to write in a veiled or hidden fashion.[2] The Midrash utilizes the distinction between the written and the spoken in the context of the anti-Christian polemic, in order to explain the existence of the Oral Law:

> Rabbi Yehuda bar Shalom said: Moses requested that the Mishna too be given in writing, but the Holy One, blessed be He, foresaw that the nations would translate the Torah and read it in Greek and say, "We are Israel." The Holy One, blessed be He, said to Moses, "I shall write him most of my Torah," and thus "they shall be considered as strangers" (Hosea 8:12). Why should He do this? Because the Mishna is the *mysterion* of the Holy One, blessed be He, and the Holy One, blessed be He, divulges his *mysterion* to the righteous alone, as it is written (Psalms 25:14), "The secret of God is for those who fear Him." (Midrash Tanḥuma, Vayera, 5)

The translation of the Written Torah is described in this passage as an act of usurpation of an exclusive relationship—a kind of theological and literary theft committed by Christianity. Avoidance of writing down the Mishna, which is called "The Holy One, blessed be He's *mysterion*," ensures the exclusivity of Israel as God's chosen ones and confidants. Besides the link forged by the Midrash, between esotericism and oral transmission, this passage illustrates another important element of esotericism—the link between esotericism and status.[3] The restrictions on the dissemination of knowledge, and the relation between knowledge, status, and power give esotericism an important role in determining social stratification.[4] Esotericism is, among other things, a means of protecting the privileged position of a group in the society by limiting the dissemination of the knowledge that endows it with its status.[5]

For many of its devotees, esotericism is as well a way of protecting the multitude or the uninitiated from the destructive power of truth. At the root of the elitist political esoteric outlook, as Leo Strauss developed it, is the idea that social order will collapse under complete conditions of transparency.[6] Plato's *Seventh Letter* is the foundational text of the esoteric obligation on the philosophers. The letter represents an argument against the explicit and clear writing of philosophical matters which ought to be restricted only to the initiates. If philosophy is the love of truth as a way of life, it must go underground since it poses a serious threat to the social order which is inherently established on myth. The harsh lesson that was drawn from the fate of Socrates is that the Polis would not tolerate public undermining of its accepted myths, and the philosopher is advised to carve a hidden space in which he can pursue truth without undermining the social structure and without endangering himself. The problem of transparency extends beyond the political structure and institutions to the self. It might be argued that not only social order and institutions will collapse under complete conditions of transparency, but the self will be undermined if it becomes completely transparent to itself. After all, repression and its relative self-deception are necessary forms of self-maintenance. It is no wonder that Freud draws on the analogy between censorship in the social and political context, and the workings of the internal censor who blocks from consciousness distressful mental material. After explicating the function of the internal censor in distorting the wishful contents of dreams, Freud makes the following claim:

> A similar difficulty confronts the political writer who has disagreeable truths to tell to those in authority. . . . A writer must beware of the censorship, and on its account he must soften and distort the expression of his opinion. According to the strength and sensitivity of the censorship he finds himself compelled either merely to refrain from certain forms of attack, or to speak in allusions in place of direct references, or he must conceal his objectionable pronouncement beneath some apparently innocent disguise; for instance, he may describe the dispute between two Mandarins in the Middle Kingdom, when the people he really had in mind are officials in his own country.[7]

Veiling is therefore a constant, necessary feature of our limited and imperfect social and psychological condition. It is no wonder that in the history of esoterically minded ideologies, redemption is conceived to be the achievement of transparency, both within mystical tradition, but also within psychoanalytic conception of health and harmony. (It is worthwhile noting that the word *apocalypse* means *unveiled* or *revelation*.)

This book seeks to achieve a dual aim: the first is historical and cultural, and the second conceptual and philosophical. The historical and cultural focus aims to examine the phenomenon of esoteric teaching in Jewish medieval tradition in the twelfth and thirteenth centuries in its cultural and social contexts. The attention devoted to this particular period through the prism of esotericism is no accident, since the idea of the esoteric in Jewish tradition blossomed in this period. The main streams in Jewish thought in this period—philosophy, Kabbalah, astrology, and magic—presented their positions as the expression of the authentic Jewish esoteric tradition. The major writings of this period were consecrated to expounding the esoteric level of Jewish tradition; as such, they too were written as texts of an esoteric nature, and so concealed, to some extent, their internal meaning. The second focus of this book, the conceptual and philosophical, aims to extrapolate from the wealth of the historical material a taxonomy of the esoteric phenomena, and structural features and paradoxes that are implicit in it. Disclosing these features will help to illuminate esotericism as a general philosophical concern as it stands at an interesting intersection of hermeneutics and political theory. The relevance of esotericism to hermeneutics and political theory stems from both its presumed role in reading and interpreting texts, and from its reflecting a basic mode of power and its relationship to truth.

In line with these dual aims, the first (and larger) portion of the book is devoted to a detailed analysis of the medieval Jewish case of esotericism, while the latter portion deals with the conceptual structures that can be drawn from the historical case. The historical analysis is guided by the following questions: What are the internal justifications that esoteric traditions provide for their own existence, especially in the Jewish world, in which, apparently, the democratization of knowledge was of great importance? How do esoteric teachings co-exist with the revealed tradition, and what is the relationship between the various esoteric teachings that compete with that revealed tradition? How does the idea of esotericism influence the development of elites and secondary elites and the category of the masses? How does the disclosure of esoteric teachings take place, and what happens once those teachings are revealed? Is there any common ground between the esoteric traditions that claim that revealed religion has a deep structure, which constitutes the climax of religious drama? Answers to these questions will enable a closer examination of the conceptual and philosophical concerns of esotericism.

We may rightly call the twelfth and thirteenth centuries the age of esotericism and its disclosure. The rise of esotericism in the twelfth century is not restricted to any single movement within the Jewish world. Esotericism appeared as a central element in works of different and sometimes opposing orientations—in *Sefer Habahir*, in Rabbi Abraham Ibn Ezra's commentary on the Torah, and in Maimonides' *Guide of the Perplexed*. This tendency continued throughout the thirteenth century, for example in the early compositions of the Ḥasidim of Ashkenaz and in the writings of Naḥmanides. In that century, however, and especially in the fourteenth century, the boundaries of the esoteric began to be tested and cracked, partially as a result of the composition of dozens of commentaries on the hidden levels of the esoteric canon in the twelfth and thirteenth centuries. The rise of esotericism in these centuries is a phenomenon that demands explanation. Why did esoteric teachings flower in this period, and what is the dynamic that led to their disclosure?

The history of esotericism in these centuries embodies the tension between concealment and disclosure intrinsic to the esoteric idea. We may state at the outset that the act of announcing the existence of the esoteric is the beginning of its disclosure. A guarded secret, by its very nature, is one whose very existence, and not just content, remains unknown to all but those directly concerned. But, as we shall see, the esotericists of the Middle Ages felt it important to guard the esoteric while at the same time announcing its existence. Consequently, in this period, esoteric teaching is marked by an unresolved tension between concealment and exposure.

The analysis of the various positions of Jewish esoteric teaching comprises the majority of research into medieval Jewish thought, both in quantity and in quality. The major movements in this thought presented themselves as the esoteric core of Jewish tradition and as its internal, deep meaning. Nonetheless, the phenomenon of esotericism—independent of its particular content—has been little discussed. The pioneering work of Leo Strauss dealt with esotericism as a substantive element in the relation between philosophy and society; recently, Sarah Klein-Breslavy systematically analyzed the concept of esotericism in Maimonides.[8] Several scholars have dealt with this concept in the kabbalistic tradition: Gershom Scholem has published and analyzed, among other texts, the important epistle of Isaac the Blind on the dissemination of the Kabbalah. Yosef Dan has described and analyzed the esoteric tradition in Ashkenaz and its dissemination by Rabbi Eleazar of Worms. Moshe Idel has identified important elements of esotericism in the Kabbalah in general, and in the Kabbalah of Nahmanides in opposition to the kabbalists of Gerona. Yehuda Liebes and Elliot Wolfson have analyzed the doctrine of esotericism in the *Zohar*. My own study of the medieval Jewish sources will be conducted in a dialogue with the previous scholarship.

My initial focus on the medieval history of the phenomenon of esotericism as such, rather than on the particular doctrines of the esotericist, serves the dual aim of this book. It is probably right to claim that every systematic picture of the world is created by elites, yet in most cases such elites address the community as a whole. With esotericism, which prohibits dissemination of its material and transmits its knowledge through hints only to the initiates, a completely new dimension emerged in which doctrines were not only created by the elites, they were also addressed only to the elites. It might be the case that capable readers of revealed teachings form an elite as well, since they have been selected by virtue of their knowledge and education. Even when the revealed teachings were already aimed to the elite, esoteric teachings were addressed to an elite within the elite. Nahmanides' commentary on the Torah, for example, has been widely available from the end of the thirteenth century onward. In this popular text, Nahmanides inserted cryptic comments concerning concealed layers of the Torah, introducing them with the formula "by way of truth." Many of his readers, even the immensely learned among them, have no way to understand such hints, and so skip these lines. Like Nahmanides' esoteric commentary, the great corpuses of medieval Jewish thought, such as Maimonides' *Guide of the Perplexed* and the esoteric layers of Ibn Ezra's commentary on the Torah, were created by the elites for a narrow group of elites. The actual doctrines produced by these elites were completely different from one another. The relationships between philosophers, kabbalists, and astrologists were complex and sometimes full of rivalry and tension. Yet the unity of their esoteric structure points to something deep which they shared in facing the community at large. Exploring and uncovering the reason why in the medieval period the Jewish elites did not address the community regarding major dimensions of their doctrines, but rather limited their doctrines to a narrow circle of initiates, contributes to a deeper understanding of medieval Jewish thought and its crisis.

Exploring the full scope of the medieval obsession with the concealed exposes the paradoxical features of the esoteric phenomena. Among other things, the uncovering of the presence of esotericism within a range of contradictory movements and teachings such as philosophy, Kabbalah, and astrology reveals a far more complex and subtle phenomenology of esotericism than what Leo Strauss understood. The rich historical material therefore enables a closer examination of the structural and phenomenological dimensions of esotericism. These phenomenological features will be developed as our inquiry proceeds with the historical material, and they will become sharper and clearer in the last, conceptual section of the book. Since the book aims to achieve a dual goal, it may also have a dual readership. The reader who is interested in the general problem of concealment and transparency in philosophy and political theory but is not particularly interested in medieval Jewish thought will naturally shift his focus to the last section of the book, which can be read independently. Yet since I take the historical material as an enlarged, complex experiment in esotericism that highlights many of its structural features, such a reader may want to join me and other readers through a detailed journey through the history of medieval esotericism. The journey into the depth of the esoteric imagination has to begin with the examination of the early features of the esoteric idea in Jewish tradition, as found in talmudic sources and in the earliest layer of esoteric writings—the Hekhalot literature.[9]

CHAPTER 1

The Paradox of Esotericism:
"And Not on the Chariot Alone"

THE CLASSICAL FOUNDATIONAL text for the existence of a realm of secret knowledge within Jewish tradition is the Mishna in the tractate Ḥagiga 2:1:

> The [subject of] forbidden sexual relations may not be expounded before three persons, nor the work of creation before two, nor [the work of] the chariot before one alone, unless he is a sage and understands of his own knowledge. (p. 59)

More than any other source, this Mishna—which dates to the second century, though it might reflect earlier traditions—granted legal authority to the claim that there is a secret dimension to the Jewish tradition. It is small wonder that many esotericists called their teachings *ma'ase merkabah* (the work/vision of the chariot). An analysis of this Mishna yields several important insights. The area of knowledge for which the group of students must be filtered and access restricted is related to certain specified portions of Scripture. "The work [vision] of the chariot" and "the work [narrative] of creation" deal with the opening chapters of Genesis and Ezekiel, respectively, as is evidenced in another passage of the Mishna.[1] The exposition of these passages is proscribed outside closed, restricted contexts. The secret whose dissemination is prohibited by the Mishna is not located in the hidden exegetical level of the biblical text as a whole, but in certain specified chapters.[2] At this point, we may already state that the idea that all of Scripture has a hidden esoteric level, which runs parallel to its external meaning—an idea of profound import in the Middle Ages—finds no expression in talmudic literature. Moreover, it seems that the exegesis of passages of Genesis and Ezekiel is not understood as the employment of a unique technique of interpretation, revealing esoteric levels of these passages. The Mishna mentions a dispute as to whether the chapters of Ezekiel dealing with the chariot may be read in public, but according to all opinions, they may not be expounded, even if the method of exposition is the same as that used for other chapters of Scripture.[3] Thus, the Bible has no esoteric meaning which must be restricted to those with occult wisdom; rather, Scripture possesses certain passages which may not be expounded, even before a limited audience.[4]

Whereas the Talmud formulates esotericism as a restriction on the study of certain texts, the medieval concept treats esotericism as an exegetical level of Scripture in its entirety; this distinction demonstrates the extremely innovative character of the medieval concept as an approach that is hermeneutic in nature.

The idea that the text possesses a level of hidden meaning, and the development of ramified exegetical techniques for exposing it, radically changed the concept of Torah. This idea first appears in a magical text called *Ma'ayan Ḥokhmah*, which is a kind of introduction to a work entitled *Shimushei Torah*. This source, discussed by Idel and dated to the eighth or ninth centuries,[5] is an expansion of the *aggadah* in the tractate Shabbat (88b) that describes the ascent of Moses to the heavens to receive the Torah. There follows a dispute before God between the angels and Moses over his right to receive the Torah, which is designated as "a hidden treasure." Moses overcomes the angels and receives the Torah, and they, according to the *aggadah*, become his admirers: "Immediately, each and every one became his admirer and gave him something, as it is written, 'You went up to the heights, you took captives, to take tribute for men'" (Psalms 68:19). The anonymous author of the introduction to *Shimushei Torah* specifies what the angels gave him: 'and all the ministering angels became his lovers, and each and every one gave him a technique of healing and a secret of the names which are contained within each and every passage and all their uses, as it is written, 'you went up to the heights, you took captives, to take tribute for men.'"[6] Thus, within each and every passage lies concealed an esoteric level containing names of God which can be used in magic, and these secrets were transmitted to Moses by the angels. The secret of God's essence is encrypted in the Holy Scriptures, and the knowledge of these secrets grants man possession of magical powers.

The idea that Scripture contains meanings that can be unveiled through unconventional means of exegesis is already present in pre-medieval midrashic literature. According to certain midrashic conceptions, Scripture encrypts meanings that are not apparent in its direct reading. These conceptions, however, do not assert that Scripture possesses an esoteric level dealing with the godhead's internal life and essence, alongside the primary layer of textual meaning. The Torah, according to certain midrashic conceptions, has a semantic fullness; thus it must be treated as a text that has no lacunae or superfluities, and which does not speak in the language of humans. Exposition of prepositions and conjunctions such as *et* and *gam*, which are attributed to Rabbi Akiba and his school, are an expression of the semantic fullness of the text. The matters derived from these exegetical techniques, however, are on the same level of meaning as those derived from the revealed levels. For example, let us analyze the following expository passage, in which *et* is an untranslatable preposition marking the relationship between a verb and its direct object, and *v'* is a conjunctive prefix meaning "and": " 'Honor (*et*) thy father and (*v'et*) thy mother.' '(*et*) thy father'—that is your father's wife. '(*et*) thy mother'—that is your mother's husband. The extra letter *vav* [in *v'et*] comes to include your older brother" (Ketubot 103a). From the preposition *et* that precedes the honor of the mother, the rabbis derive that a son is obligated to honor his mother's husband even if he is not his own father. Honoring the husband of the mother is an extension of the honor granted to the mother, and it is accordingly derived from the *et* that is juxtaposed to the mother. The same technique is applied by the Talmud to extend the obligation to the father's wife. The exegesis of the words *et* and the additional letter *vav* is based on the conception that nonconventional exegetical criteria must be applied to the sacred scriptures, since the text possesses absolute semantic fullness. The meanings derived from such exegesis, however, have no special relation to the realm of the secret or the sublime, the magic or the divine. The laws derived from these types of exposition are of the same status as other laws; in our example, they deal with the organization of authority relations within the family. The most appropriate metaphor for this midrashic conception of Scripture is not the multileveled text of the esoteric conception, but rather the full, dense text. The exposition of *et* does not reveal an accompanying deeper level, but rather fills out all possible gaps within the text itself.

We have thus identified two concepts of esotericism—passages that may not be interpreted and a hidden exegetical level. This distinction is crucial for the history of the esoteric idea. The passage in Mishna Ḥagiga 2:1, however, contains a linguistic ambiguity that opens possibilities to an entirely different understanding of the text. Whether this understanding is true or not, the very raising of the possibility points to an internal tension within the esoteric idea, a tension that will break forth at later stages in its development. The accepted reading of the Mishna is that it sets maximal conditions for the exegesis of certain passages. One may teach the passages on incest only among two people and no more, the work of creation to no more than one student, while the work of the chariot may not be taught even to a single student, unless the student is of exceptional capacities. According to this reading, the verb *dorshin* (to expound) means "to teach," whereas the expressions *bishlosha*, *bishnayim*, and *b'yaḥid* mean "before three," "before two," and "before one." The title "a sage and understands of his own knowledge" applies to the qualities of the individual student, before whom one may expound the work of the chariot.

There is, however, an opposing way of reading the Mishna. In this reading, the Mishna establishes minimal rather than maximal criteria: it is prohibited to investigate the work of the chariot alone. It must be studied with another person unless the learner is a sage who understands of his own knowledge. Thus, we should read the Mishna as follows: "Nor the work of the chariot alone"—but two may do so. The verb *lidrosh* (to expound) in rabbinic language does not require that there be an audience; rather, it refers to investigation and commentary which may take place before students or in public, but not necessarily so.[7] Thus, the Mishna does not direct its rules to the teacher, but to the learner. If the Mishna established mimimal criteria, we should not understand the word *beyaḥid* as meaning in front of a single person, and the word *dorshin* is not to teach but rather to interpret. Furthermore, *ḥakham umevin mida'ato*— "a sage who understands of his own knowledge"—is not a title ascribed to the student, but to the learner/interpreter.[8] According to this reading, study of the work of the chariot requires at least two, but if a person is a sage and understands of his own knowledge, he may study this topic alone. This reading of the Mishna is rejected, however, by the text of the Tosefta: "The [passage on] forbidden relations may not be expounded (*dorshin*) before three, but it may be expounded before two; the work of creation may not be expounded before two, but it may be expounded before a single person; the chariot may not be expounded even before one, unless he is a sage and understands on his own" (Tosefta Ḥagiga 2:1, p. 380).[9] It may be that the Tosefta's additions to the words of the Mishna—"but it may be expounded before two . . . but it may be expounded before a single person"—were designed to alter its meaning. Indeed, some scholars view our second suggested reading as the original meaning of the Mishna.[10]

The reason for such a minimal requirement is explained in the passage cited by Rabbi Yehuda of Barcelona, at the beginning of the twelfth century, in his commentary on *Sefer Yetzira*:

We have found in a text of the early scholars as follows: When our forefather Abraham was born the ministering angels said before the [Holy One] blessed be He: Creator of the universe, you have a beloved one in the world, and yet you conceal something from him? Immediately, the Holy One, blessed be He, said: would I conceal something from Abraham? He consulted the Torah and said to her: my daughter, come and let us betroth you unto my beloved Abraham. She replied to him: no, not until the humble one [Moses] comes and will betroth humility. Immediately, the Holy One, blessed be He, consulted *Sefer Yetzira* who said: yes. He transmitted it to Abraham who sat alone and studied it, but he could not understand a thing. Finally, a voice (*bat kol*) came from heaven and said to him: do you wish to compare yourself to me? I am One and I created the *Sefer Yetzira* and studied it, and you cannot understand it alone; choose a friend and investigate it together and you shall understand it. Immediately, Abraham went to Shem his

teacher, and sat and studied with him three years, and they investigated
and knew how to create the world. And to this day there is no man
who can understand it alone, only two wise men [together]; and they
cannot comprehend it in less than three years, and when they comprehend it, they can do anything their heart desires. When Abraham understood it, he acquired great wisdom and apprehended the entire Torah.
Rabba also wanted to comprehend it on his own and Rabbi Ze'ira said
to him: behold it is written, "A sword is upon the boasters, and they
shall become fools"—a sword upon the enemies of the scholars, who sit
and study the Torah alone. If so, let us go and study *Sefer Yetzira*. They
sat together and studied it for three years and understood it, and they
created a calf and slaughtered it, and feasted with it at the termination of
a tractate. And when they slaughtered the calf, they forgot it all. They sat
together for an additional three years and recovered their knowledge.[11]

This passage is of great importance for understanding the history of
the magical use of *Sefer Yetzira*.[12] In addition, it raises an interesting
question relating to esoteric teaching. As Yehuda Liebes has noted,[13] this
passage teaches us that the Scriptures on creation may only be studied by
a certain minimum number of people, because of the presumptuousness
and the dangers of solitary study.[14] As I make clear below, the realm of
magic is esoteric because of the danger of transmitting creative powers to
those unworthy of them. Consequently, there are severe restrictions on its
teaching, which restrict the number of learners in order to prevent uncontrolled dissemination of magical knowledge. This passage teaches us,
however, that overly strict esotericism can achieve the opposite result.
Solitary study carries with it risks no less severe than irresponsible dissemination of esoteric ideas. In both cases, there is no control over the
learning process. The double reading of the Mishna, as a rule regulating
either minimal or maximal requirements, exposes the tension that we
may designate as the esoteric paradox, a tension that will surface repeatedly in the history of esotericism. The justification for esotericism reflects
an attempt to preserve particular knowledge in a state of purity, without
fault or distortion, as a protected, well-guarded realm. Because, however,
the esoteric realm is a closed one, it cannot be effectively controlled. An
esotericist may claim that a new body of knowledge is actually the transmission of an ur-ancient esoteric Jewish tradition. In response to those
who dispute him, claiming that they had never heard of such a teaching
in Jewish tradition, he will claim: "This knowledge was kept secret; consequently, it left no trace in the traditions known to you." Thus the most
guarded realm is also the least restricted. This paradox leaves its surprising marks at the stage at which the esoteric idea reaches its peak of development—in the Jewish works of the Middle Ages.

CHAPTER 2

The Hidden and the Sublime:
Vision and Restriction in the Bible
and in Talmudic Literature

THE MISHNA in Ḥagiga that we have studied does not tell us why there is
a need to restrict the number of students. With respect to the restrictions
on exegesis of matters of incest, many suggestions have been raised and
the issue is still a mystery. The restriction on the study of the chariot is explained by the Jerusalem Talmud as follows: "'Nor the chariot before
one alone'—is this also according to Rabbi Akiba? It is the opinion of all.
So that one will know how to render proper respect to the honor of his
Creator" (JT Ḥagiga 2:1, 77a). Public exposition of the passages dealing
with the chariot constitute a violation of the honor of God, and, as such,
according to the Jerusalem Talmud, it is forbidden even in the opinion of
Rabbi Ishmael, who permits public exposition of the passages on the work
of creation and incest. This explanation, which links secrecy to honor,
has a basis in tannaitic literature. Rabbi Yoḥanan ben Zakkai praises his
student Rabbi Elazar ben Arakh for proper exegesis of the work of the
chariot: "He stood up and kissed him upon his head, and said, blessed be
the Lord, God of Israel, who granted to our father Abraham a son who
knows how to understand and expound on the honor of his father in
heaven" (Tosefta Ḥagiga 2:1, p. 380). It is possible to explain the offense
to the honor of God as a result of a metaphysical error which may be
committed by those who are unworthy. Since the interpretation of the
chariot vision deals with speculation on the essence of God, distortions
and errors in these matters by such people are an offense to His honor.
This explanation was popular in the Middle Ages, and this motive is apparently present in talmudic literature on the exegesis of the work of creation and the work of the chariot, especially in sources that link the
investigation of certain questions with Gnostic matters.[1] I would like to
focus on another, more direct explanation, linked to the particular nature
of the vision of the chariot in talmudic sources.

Exposition of the chariot includes an attempt at visual representation
of God and His chariot throne, through explanation of the chariot vision
in Ezekiel, a vision with explicit plastic properties. The state of consciousness of one who exposits the chariot, who deals with an internal

visual image, is explained in the Tosefta: "A blind person may say the blessings before and after the *Shema* and may serve as translator. Rabbi Yehuda said, 'Whoever has never seen the lights of the firmament in his lifetime, should not recite the blessings before and after the *Shema*.' They said to him: 'Many have expounded the chariot, though they have never seen it'" (Tosefta Megilla 3:28). In their reply to Rabbi Yehuda, the Sages say: just as one who interprets the chariot can provide himself with an internal image of the chariot, even though he never saw it, so too the blind man with respect to the lights of the firmament.[2] Furthermore, we find in talmudic literature descriptions of direct visions of God and His chariot throne that are not restricted to the internal image of the mind's eye, as Saul Lieberman has described.[3] The fear of violating the honor of God is linked to internal or actual vision that arises from examination of the details of the chariot and the God who rides upon it. Such observation results in violation and offense to the honor of God if done in a disrespectful manner or by one who is unworthy. The core of the requirement of esotericism in dealing with the chariot vision is not the fear of error, but reticence toward the exposure inherent in the visual image. Seeing is a kind of intimacy restricted to the elect few who know how to peek with a cautious, fleeting glance.

The image of "visual trespass" linked to the chariot appears in the story of entering *pardes*. This story, in its many details, has engendered mountains of commentary, and I have no desire to add my own explanation to the ever-growing collection of interpretations. I will focus on the link between esotericism and looking, by examining the verbs dealing with vision in the passage and in related sources: "Four entered the garden (*pardes*): Ben Azzai, Ben Zoma, the Other, and Akiba. One peeked and perished, one peeked and was smitten, one peeked and cut down sprouts, and one ascended in peace and descended in peace" (Tosefta Ḥagiga 2:3; p. 381). Peeking is a fleeting and modest look, which is the goal of those entering *pardes*, even if it involves substantial risk. Not everyone is worthy of a peek at the face of the King, and certainly not of seeing Him.[4] The parallel passage in the Tosefta brings a parable from the realm of the ethics of vision: "Rabbi Akiba ascended in peace and descended in peace. About him, the Scripture says, 'Draw me after you, let us make haste (the king has brought me into his chambers).' To what should we compare this? To a royal garden with an upper room built over it. What is the (guard's) duty? To look, but not feast his eyes upon it" (Tosefta Ḥagiga 2:5; p. 381). The lingering of the gaze to the point of pleasure and satiation is opposed to the glance, and is a desecration and violation of the holy.

We could dismiss the focus on the various forms of looking as merely an overly literal reading of a metaphor, for we are dealing here, after all, with a parable.[5] In talmudic literature, however, we find the expression *hazanat ha'ayin*—the nourishment of the eye—in the exposition of a direct experience of the vision of God. This exegesis deals with the vision of God by the elders of Israel at Mount Sinai:

> "And Moses and Aaron and Nadav and Abihu and seventy of the elders of Israel went up. And they saw the God of Israel and under his feet was like a paved work of sapphire stone and like the very heaven for clearness. And upon the nobles of the children of Israel He laid not His hand, and they beheld God and did eat and drink" (Exodus 24:9–11). From this, said R. Pinḥas, it may be inferred that they deserved to have a hand laid upon them. For R. Hoshaya said: Did provisions go up with them to Sinai, that you should be able to say "and they beheld God and did eat and drink" (Exodus 24:10)? No, but it teaches you that they fed their eyes upon the *Shekhina* as a man looks upon his neighbor while in the act of eating and drinking. R. Yoḥanan says: They derived actual nourishment; as is proved by the citation, "In light of the king's countenance is life" (Proverbs 16:15). The text, said R. Tanḥuma, teaches us that they uncovered their heads, became presumptuous and fed their eyes on the *Shekhina*. R. Yehoshua of Sikhnin in the name of R. Levi observed: Moses did not feed his eyes on the *Shekhina* and derived benefit from the *Shekhina*. He did not feed his eyes upon the *Shekhina*, as it says, "And Moses hid his face" (Exodus 3:6). And he derived benefit from the *Shekhina*, as it says, "Moses knew not that the skin of his face sent forth beams" (Exodus 34:29). As a reward for "And Moses hid his face" he attained to the privilege of "And the Lord spoke unto Moses face to face" (Exodus 33:11). As a reward for "He was afraid" (Exodus 3:6) he attained to the privilege of "They were afraid to approach him" (Exodus 34:30). As a reward for "afraid to look" (Exodus 34:30) he attained to the privilege of "and the similitude of the Lord he beholds" (Numbers 12:8). Nadav and Abihu, however, fed their eyes on the *Shekhina* and did not derive benefit from the *Shekhina*, as may be inferred from the following: "And Nadav and Abihu died before the Lord" (Leviticus 3:4). (Leviticus Rabbah 20:10, pp. 465–467; *Midrash Rabbah* 4:261–262)

The elders of Israel ascended Mount Sinai in peace and descended in peace, but deserved to die for having nourished their eyes. Indeed, Nadav and Abihu were punished for that reason. A presumptuous and pleasurable look, to the point of satiating the eye, is a terrible sin and a violation of the honor of God. The expressions *hetzitz* (peeked) and *hezin et 'enav* (nourished his eyes) are not metaphors but verbs of actual vision, which designate the poles of looking—from the modest peek to the voracious gaze.[6]

Esotericism thus depends on the relation between honor and concealment, rather than on the relation between dissemination and error, as is
mentioned in the famous passage cited in the Jerusalem Talmud as justification for esotericism: "It is the glory of God to conceal a thing."[7] The
link between esotericism and God's glory is also conveyed by an additional midrash on the secrets of the Torah, whose content is linked not to
vision, but to public dissemination:

> R. Huna quoted in Bar Kappara's name (an exegesis of Psalms 31:19):
> "Let the lying lips be dumb": this means, let them be bound, made
> dumb, and silenced. . . . "Which speak arrogantly (*'atak*) against the
> righteous," meaning, against the Righteous One, who is the Life of all
> worlds, on matters which he has withheld (*he'etik*) from His creatures.
> "With pride"—in order to boast and say, "I discourse on the creation
> narrative!" (*ma'asei Bereshit*). "And contempt": to think that he dis-
> graces My Honor! For R. Yosi beRabbi Ḥanina said: Whoever elevates
> himself at the cost of his fellow man's degradation has no share in the
> World to Come. How much more then [when it is done at the expense
> of] the honor of God! . . . In human practice, when an earthly monarch
> builds a palace on a site of sewers, dunghills, and garbage, if one says,
> "This palace is built on a site of sewers, dunghills and garbage," does
> he not discredit it? Thus, whoever comes to say that this world was
> created out of *tohu* and *bohu* and darkness, does he not impair [God's
> honor]? R. Huna said in Bar Kappara's name: If the matter were not
> written, it would be impossible to say it: "God created Heaven and
> earth"; out of what? Out of "now the earth was *tohu* and *bohu*"
> (Genesis 1:2). (Bereshit Rabbah 1:1, pp. 2–3 [trans. modified])

One who expounds the creation narrative in public does not cause
error or heresy; rather, he reveals things that the Holy One, blessed be
He, has hidden because of their defects, such as the creation of the world
from *tohu* and *bohu*. The King has indeed built His palace upon the sew-
ers and garbage, but this matter should not be made public.[8]
The first motive of esotericism is thus related to the relationship between concealment and honor, and, in the case of the restrictions on
viewing the chariot—the ethics of vision. Asymmetry in the possibilities
of vision give rise to a relation of authority and sublimity. The more powerful partner may survey the one standing opposite him from head to toe,
whereas the weaker one averts his glance, hesitating to create eye contact.
The more a person may see others, without being seen by them, the further
his status is elevated; the inverse is also true. Social status is expressed
through varying degrees of privacy, for example, through the expanse of
space surrounding a person, in which access to others is restricted. A person's status rises in direct proportion to the size of the personal space

allotted him. This conception, which links secrecy with sublimity, found its most radical political expression in the Persian kings' custom of covering their faces, even in their portraits on coins. This is the basic biblical intuition behind the distinction between hearing God and seeing Him. God's invisibility from human eyes does not derive from His essential formlessness, but rather results from the fact that the exposure of God's form to the human eye blemishes his sublimity. The tension between nearness and distance, which typifies the Scriptural personality of God, is expressed through the possibility of speech and description of God, on the one hand, combined with the restriction on seeing, sculpting, or drawing Him on the other. This primary motive of concealment places a severe limitation on the attempt to bridge the fundamental biblical gap between the heard deity and the visible deity. The esoteric is not a body of knowledge that may not be diffused. It is, first and foremost, the creation of a realm that no eye may behold, neither in actuality nor in its *imagination*. It is the hidden realm in the most literal sense of the word.

The Ethics of Gazing: The Attitude of Early Jewish Mysticism Toward Seeing the Chariot

THE RELATION THAT we find in talmudic literature between the vision of the deity and the restriction of looking at Him is linked to the nature of early Jewish mysticism in general. It is reflected in the Hekhalot literature, whose epitome is the crossing of the border of heaven and the vision of God in all his beauty and splendor. We do not know the identity of the circles in which this early level of Jewish mysticism originated; the date and place of composition, as well as the degree of unity of the works of Hekhalot literature, are also disputed among scholars. It seems clear that this mystical literature is connected to the broader phenomenon of Gnosticism, and it might represent a particular strand of Jewish Gnosticism.[1] Some date these writings as early as the second or third centuries C.E., whereas others place them as late as the seventh or eighth centuries. The affinity of the Hekhalot literature to the world of the talmudic Sages is also a matter of dispute.[2] In spite of these substantial problems, we may discern a link and a tension between talmudic literature and the Hekhalot literature, with respect to esotericism and its nature. We will now turn to Hekhalot literature, where scholarly research has identified two distinct loci of activity, each with its own logic of esotericism.[3]

The first locus is the mysticism of ascending and vision. One who ascends to the chariot embarks on a dangerous voyage in the upper Hekhalot (palaces). On his way, he encounters angels who guard each of the gates of the Hekhalot; if he is deemed worthy and passes these fearsome guards, he arrives at the peak of his journey—the seventh hekhal, where he views the Throne of Glory and the Lord enthroned upon it. The voyage is accompanied by descriptions of divine sublimity, of the immense, terrifying dimensions of the angels, the seraphs and the holy beasts who stand before the Lord to serve Him, and especially the songs and praises to the high and mighty God. This focus of the Hekhalot literature is the most impressive source of descriptions of divine sublimity and hymns of angels glorifying God and His chariot to be found in all of Jewish literature.

The second focus of Hekhalot literature deals with the names of God rather than His image. The heroes of this literature are Rabbi Akiba, Rabbi Ishmael, and Rabbi Neḥunya ben Hakanah. They obtain knowledge of the names of God that bear His essence and strength, and through which they can perform magical actions, especially in the area of attainment of Torah insights. In the compositions of the Hekhalot literature in which this motive is prominent, as in *Hekhalot Zutarti*, and in the passage entitled *Sar Hatorah* in *Hekhalot Rabbati*, we find a list of the names of God and His angels, whose use enables almost unlimited action in the world. The question of the relation between these two foci of Hekhalot literature, the mystic and the magic, both as concerns the textual redaction of the works of Hekhalot literature, whether it be their date of composition or their significance within the overall corpus of Hekhalot literature, is a matter of dispute among scholars. The two foci are, however, intertwined on many levels. Part of the technique for ascending to the seventh hekhal requires a certain magical knowledge. Those who descend to the chariot pass the gates of each hekhal by uttering the proper formula at the appropriate place and after showing the guard seals with names—a kind of laissez-passer to the interior of the hekhal. In addition, an important part of the viewing of God's image, especially in the *Shi'ur Komah* literature, is the vision of the names written on the various parts of God's body; sometimes the revealed nature of God consists of names alone. These names, which designate the essence of God and His bodily parts, are powerful magical tools.[4] Mystical ascension and magic are inextricably bound up with each other. Whatever the relationship between these two foci in Hekhalot literature, each reflects a different logic of esotericism, as we will proceed to demonstrate.

Let us begin with the ethics of vision. In the mystical approach of the Hekhalot literature, the impulse to see God is dominant.[5] The goal of the perilous heavenly journey is the view of God. Thus, the Hekhalot literature fixes *as its peak religious goal* the crossing of the boundary between the heard and the seen divinity. In one of the tendencies in biblical tradition, all vision of God is completely obscured. This approach places this boundary as the *outer limit* between humans and God, and, consequently, prohibits the making of sculptures and images. God preserves His sublimity and separateness, not because He has no image, but because it has never been seen. The realm of contact between humans and God is hearing rather than vision. Moses, who yearns to see the Glory of God, is told, "For no man may see Me and live" (Exodus 33:20). The cost of vision is life itself. The esoteric, in this sense, is reflected not only through the precise characteristics of God's nature, but also through piercing the fearsome veils in order to arrive at the experience of the vision of the hidden God. The desire for vision dominates the Hekhalot literature, which is interested in making the speaking and heard God into the visible and viewed one. If our claim is correct, that in their writings, restricting the expounding of the chariot and guarding God's honor, the talmudic Sages understood esotericism as the placement of limitations on the encounter with God and His visible image, then the Hekhalot literature constantly seeks to test and perhaps even contest the limits set by talmudic literature. The desire to see and view dominated the religious imagination and traversed the restrictions that limited peeking to the one who understands of his own knowledge.

Nonetheless, Hekhalot literature established severe restrictions on who was worthy of ascending to the chariot. The restrictions demand, first and foremost, strict observance of the requirements of institutional revealed religion:

> To what can we compare this measurement? To a person who has a ladder in his house. To anyone who descends to the chariot, who is clean and free of idolatry and incest and bloodshed and evil talk and false oaths and rudeness and gratuitous hatred and observes all positive and negative commandments. Rabbi Ishmael said in the name of Rabbi Nehunya: "Son of haughty ones! Blessed be he and blessed be the soul of one who is clean and free of these eight measures, for ShTWTRKhY'L, God, and SWRYA, His privy servant detest them. He descends and sees the amazing pride and the extraordinary majesty, the pride of the heights and the majesty of grandeur." (Schäfer, sec. 199, p. 86)

At the entrance to the sixth hekhal, the guardian warns the one who descends to the chariot:

> And Dumiel would say to him: "I attest and warn you about two things that are before you. Whoever descends to the chariot only descends there if he possesses the following two attributes: he has read the Torah, the Prophets, and the Writings, has learned Mishna, midrash, halakhot and aggadot, and has understood the meaning of the positive and negative laws. He has fulfilled all that is written in the Torah, and has kept all the warnings of the laws and ordinances and judgments which were transmitted to Moses on Mount Sinai." (Schäfer, sec. 234, p. 102)

The requirement to fulfill perfectly the standards of the revealed religion, as a preliminary condition for entering the concealed, esoteric realm, may be well understood against the background of the deviance of this action from the values of the revealed tradition. Similarly, in their own consciousness, the esotericists see themselves as a select group, whose traits and authority far surpass that of the institutional religious charisma. The self-consciousness of the descenders to the chariot is described in the opening passage of *Hekhalot Rabbati*:

> His exceeding greatness is in that he sees all the deeds of mankind that they do even in their innermost chambers, whether they be worthy or

dishonorable deeds. If a man fornicates, he knows it and discerns it. If a man kills another, he knows it and discerns it. If a man is suspected of having sexual relations with a menstruating woman, he knows it and discerns it. His exceeding greatness is in that he knows and discerns all those who know sorcery. His exceeding greatness is in that anyone who raises a hand against him is clothed with leprosy and bedecked with macula. His exceeding greatness is in that anyone who speaks evil of him, he is cast down and afflicted with all types of wounds, injuries, and running sores from which pustulent boils develop. His exceeding greatness is in that he stands apart from all men, and because of all his attributes, he is feared and respected by all, high and low. And to all who cause him to stumble, great, evil, difficult afflictions are cast upon him from heaven, and to all who stretch out their hand toward him to do evil, the heavenly court of justice takes hold of him and annihilates him from the world. . . . His exceeding greatness is in that all who treat him rudely, the light of their eyes is dimmed. His exceeding greatness is in that all who mock him, leave behind neither root nor branch, and have no descendants. (Schäfer, secs. 83–91, pp. 40–44).

Those who descend to the chariot are a distinct sect, who, after fulfilling all the requirements of institutional religion, have acquired titles, powers, and attributes, which distinguish them from the routine authority of the Sages.

Beyond the preliminary conditions for entering the sect, the esoteric component is strengthened through the oft-repeated description of the terrifying perils that await those who ascend before the proper time as well as the dangers linked to the vision of the face of God:

A measure of bravery, a measure of holiness, a measure of terror and panic. A measure of trembling. A measure of sweat. A measure of trepidation. A measure of division. Of ZHRRY'L YHW-H of Hosts God of Israel, who is crowned and comes to His holy throne and (the crown) is everywhere engraved inside and out with the name YHW-H YHW-H, and the eyes of all creatures cannot look upon Him, neither the eyes of flesh and blood, nor the eyes of His servants. And one who looks upon Him or peeks at Him and sees, visions take hold of him and (are transmitted) to the pupils of his eyes, and the pupils of his eyes emit torches of flame and they scorch him and burn him up. (Schäfer, sec. 102, p. 48)

The passage continues:

Whoever looks upon Him, is immediately torn to bits, and whoever peeks at His beauty is poured out like a jug. Those who serve Him today, shall not serve Him tomorrow. Those who serve Him tomorrow shall not serve Him again, for their strength is exhausted and their faces have darkened, their hearts go astray, their eyes grow dim from the majesty of the splendor of the beauty of their King. (Schäfer, sec. 159, p. 70).

These sections, which are but a few of many, strengthen the barriers impeding the vision of God. The angels, seraphs, and holy creatures, which are close to God and bear His throne, are not permitted to see Him. God is surrounded by an immense and fearsome bureaucracy, who are at His service, even though they never see His face:

Immediately, they all stand in fear and trepidation and trembling, in holiness and truth and humility, and they cover their faces with their wings so that they do not discern the image of God who dwells in the chariot. (Schäfer, sec. 183, p. 80)[6]

This conception meshes well with the sublime nature of God the King as it is formulated in the Hekhalot literature. More than in any other literature, the God of the chariot lacks any dimension of immanence, and the fearsome sense of sublimity accompanies each and every line of this literature.

The nature of Hekhalot literature cannot, however, be entirely subsumed under its esoteric dimension. Paradoxically, the very corpus which extols the infinite majesty of God contests the absoluteness of the limits of the esoteric, as fixed by the talmudic literature. After Rabbi Nehunya ben Hakanah specifies the attributes that prepare a person to descend to the chariot, Rabbi Ishmael complains to him:

Rabbi Ishmael said: "When my ears hear this warning, my strength fails." I said to him: "Rabbi, if so, there is no end to it, for you cannot find any person whose soul dwells within him, who is clean and free of these eight measures." He answered me: "Son of the haughty, if that be the case, stand up and bring before me all the mighty ones of the circle and all the great ones of the academy, and I will speak before them the secrets and concealed and hidden things." . . . Rabbi Ishmael said: "Immediately, I arose and gathered all the scholars of the Great and Small Sanhedrins to the third entrance of the House of God. . . . There came Rabbi Shimon ben Gamliel, Rabbi Eliezer Hagadol, Rabbi Elazar ben Dama, Rabbi Eliezer ben Shamua, Yohanan ben Dahavai, Hananya ben Hakhinai, Yonatan ben Uzi'el, Rabbi Akiba ben Yosef, and Rabbi Yehuda ben Bava. We all came and sat before him, and many students stood on their feet. . . . Rabbi Nehunya ben Hakanah sat and set out before them all the things that deal with the chariot, the descent to it and the ascent from it, how the descender descends and how the ascender ascends" (Schäfer, secs. 201–203, pp. 86, 88).

The description of the Sages and the multitude of scholars who assemble to hear in public the secrets of the chariot from Rabbi Neḥunya completely shatters the limits of esotericism as set in talmudic literature. Rabbi Neḥunya ben Hakanah, faced with a lack of adept people, increases their number through widespread dissemination of the technique of ascending and descending, to enable protection from the dangers awaiting those who are not entirely worthy. Thus the Hekhalot literature becomes a kind of mystical guide even for those who are not exceptional and who are not sages who understand of their own knowledge.

Hekhalot Rabbati supports the contestation of the esoteric limits with a daring theological idea, which may well be the most astonishing and unique idea in this entire literature. In addition to the desire of the mystic to cross over into the realm of the hidden and see God, there is the desire of God to be seen:

> All those who descended to the chariot ascended unharmed. They would see the entire portion and descend in peace and return and stand and testify and tell of the fearsome and terrifying vision, something that does not exist in any palace of kings of flesh and blood. They bless, praise, laud, adorn, extol, glorify and give honor, glory, and greatness to TWTRWSY'Y, God the Lord of Israel, who rejoices in those who descend to the chariot, and He would sit and await each and every person in Israel, when shall he descend in awesome glory and exceptional majesty, in the glory of the exalted and the majesty of grandeur. (Schäfer, sec. 216, p. 92)

The sublime God sits and awaits those who descend to the chariot; not only the select few, but each and every one of Israel. The longing of God to make Himself seen appears in other sources as well:

> TWTRWSY'Y, God, the Lord of Israel desires and waits in the measure that He awaits the redemption and the time of salvation which is prepared for Israel for the day of vengeance after the destruction of the last Temple: when will the descender descend to the chariot, when shall he see the pride of the heavens, when shall he hear of the end-time of salvation, when shall he see what no eye has seen, when shall he ascend and speak of it to the seed of Abraham, my beloved? (Schäfer, sec. 218, p. 94).

Furthermore, God adjures those who descend to the chariot to publicize what they have seen:

> The punishment of heaven is upon them (=you) descenders to the chariot, if you do not remember and tell what you have heard, and if you do not testify to what you have seen before the face of exaltation and might and pride and grandeur. (Schäfer, sec. 169, p. 74).

God has, so to speak, a fear of anonymity. Thus, he demands that the sublime vision be disseminated in public. Vision is a kind of contact, like hearing, and contact with loved ones is a source of pleasure. In one of the passages of *Hekhalot Rabbati*, we find expressed the immense satisfaction of God when he establishes real eye contact with Israel:

> Blessed by heaven and earth, be you who descend to the chariot, if you tell and inform my children what I do during the morning prayer, and during the afternoon prayer and evening prayer, and each and every day and each and every hour when Israel recites before me "Holy." Teach them and tell them, lift up your eyes to heaven above the place of the house of your prayer at the hour when you recite "Holy" before Me. Teach them, that I have no pleasure in all the world I have created, except for that hour when your eyes are raised to Mine, and my eye looks into your eyes at the time when you say "Holy" before Me. (Schäfer, secs. 163–164, p. 72)

The God of the Bible longs to escape His sublime loneliness and be heard. But the distance between Him and mankind is zealously guarded in the Bible, so that He is rarely seen, though He may be heard. It is only in the Hekhalot literature, which created the most intense image of sublimity, that God's desire to be seen is expressed in a unique manner. This literature, which is interested in eliminating the distance created by the distinction between hearing and vision, adds to the human motivation to peek at the mysteries, the desire of God to be revealed and be seen. The Holy One, blessed be He, has, so to speak, a "sight deficiency," and his desire for contact with mankind pushes Him to a contact more all-embracing than speech. God wishes to be liberated from His invisibility, and he sits and awaits the time when each and every one of Israel will see Him.

The most fascinating text on the new relation to vision in the Hekhalot circles appears in another midrash, *Midrash Mishlei*, which manifests influences of Hekhalot literature. This passage is an expansion of the talmudic saying that in the heavenly court, a person is asked if he studied Torah:

> One who possesses Talmud learning comes, and they ask him: "Since you occupied yourself with Talmud study, did you see the chariot, did you see the glory?" For there is no pleasure in My world other than the hour when the learned Sages sit and study Torah, and they peek and look and glance and meditate much over this teaching: how does My throne of glory stand? . . . How does the ḥashmal stand. . . . Greatest of all, how am I from my toenails to the top of my head. What is the dimension of my palm, and how large are my toes? . . . This is my greatness, this is the majesty of my beauty, that my children discern my glory by this measure. (*Midrash Mishlei*, pp. 66–67)[7]

The Holy One, blessed be He, has pleasure in His world only when He is seen, and not with a fleeting glance. The midrash increases the experience of vision through a series of verbs of seeing that steadily widen in scope and duration: "They peek and look and glance." Beyond the desire to be seen and the satisfaction that results from it, this passage clearly expresses the reversal of values—from respect and concealment to vision and greatness. The esotericism of vision claims that the glory of God is his invisibility, whereas the midrash proclaims: "This is My greatness, this is the majesty of My beauty, that My children discern my glory by this measure."

We should mention that in this matter, God and the angels have conflicting interests. God is trapped in the fearsome bureaucracy of angels who guard his distance from mankind. The angels do not see God Himself and refuse to permit this to their human competitors. They zealously guard the distance of the King, even if He Himself wants His admirers to see Him:

> For the guardians of the gateway to the sixth hekhal would destroy those who descended to the chariot; not [only] those who descended to the chariot without permission. They would command them harshly and beat them and burn them, and put others in their place. And even the other (guardians) who remained in their places would act in the same way. They do not fear and dare to say, why are we burning? What pleasure do we have from destroying those who descend to the chariot, other than those who descend to the chariot without permission? Nevertheless, such is the behavior of the guardians of the gateway to the sixth hekhal. (Schäfer, sec. 224, pp. 96–98)

In their extreme care for the glory of God, and in their jealousy toward men who might succeed in seeing Him, the guardians of the hekhal injure even those descenders to the chariot who are worthy of God's proximity, although they may be punished for this act. Rabbi Akiba describes the Holy One, blessed be He, as the one who saved him from the angels who wished to prevent him from seeing the chariot: "Rabbi Akiba said: 'When I ascended to the heavens, I gave more signs at the entrance of the *rakia* than at the entrance to my own house. And when I reached the veil, the angels of destruction came out to destroy me. The Holy One, blessed be He, said unto them: "Let this elder be, for he is worthy to look upon My glory'" (Schäfer, sec. 673, p. 248).[8] Those who descend to the chariot attain a degree of intimacy that even God's close servants cannot attain. In *Pirkei deRabbi Eliezer*, a composition that displays influences of Hekhalot literature, this tension is described as a violent altercation between the angels and Moses that took place when Moses requested to see God:

> The ministering angels said to the Holy One, blessed be He, behold, we serve before you day and night and we may not see your glory; yet this

creature, born of a woman, wishes to see your glory?! And they stood in anger and panic, ready to kill him, and his soul reached the point of death. What did the Holy One, blessed be He, do? He revealed Himself to him in a cloud, as it is written, "And God came down in the cloud" . . . and the Holy One, blessed be He, covered him with His palm so that he not die, as it is written, "and when my glory passes, I shall place you in the cleft of the rock and cover you with my hand." (*Pirkei deRabbi Eliezer*, chap. 46)

This gap between those who descend to the chariot and the angels is revealed at the peak of the mystical voyage, when God appears in his full beauty before the mystic: "and the holy beasts cover their faces, and the cherubim and wheels turn their faces away, and he enters and stands before the throne of His Glory" (Schäfer, sec. 250, p. 110).

The literature of the most pronounced sublimity and loftiness in all of Jewish tradition created the idea of the traversing of the final barrier of intimacy of vision. This is remarkable, even if it does possess its own interior logic. This literature formulated its concept of vision, not only as the aim of a selected religious elite, but also as the desire of God to be seen; thus, the clear limits of the esoteric, which it established for itself, were traversed time and time again. According to this tendency in the Hekhalot literature, the guarding of the honor of God, which is expressed in talmudic literature through the restriction of vision, enshrines a distance that God wishes to annul. This is esoteric literature, and yet it seeks to contest the mystery that it posited. As if the idea of the sublime leads to its own dissolution by imposing on God an isolation and solitude that in turn gives rise to His urge to be seen. It is of no wonder, then, that in the heart of the most sublime literature, the deep hunger for intimacy emerges.

The ambivalence of Hekhalot literature toward the limits of the esoteric is clearly expressed in the opening portion to the work *Hekhalot Zutarti*:

If you wish to distinguish yourself in the world, so that the secret of the world and the hidden wisdom will be revealed to you, learn this Mishna, and be careful with it until the day of your departure. Do not try to understand what is behind you, and do not research the words of your lips. Understand what is in your heart and be silent, so that you become worthy of the beauty of the chariot. Take heed of the glory of your Creator, do not go down toward Him, and if you go down toward Him, do not take pleasure from Him. And if you did take pleasure, you will be driven out of the world. "It is the glory of God to conceal a thing," so that you not be driven from the world. (Schäfer, sec. 335, p. 142)

This passage is an adaptation of the warnings on esotericism mentioned in the Talmud. The warning "Take heed of the honor of your Creator" is, of course, the text of the Mishna (Ḥagiga 2:1). The restriction "Do not seek to understand what is behind you" is a repetition of the prohibition to look "at what is before you and what is behind you," which is in the same Mishna. The command "Understand what is in your heart and be silent" is, in fact, a reconstruction of the saying in the Jerusalem Talmud, "If [you are investigating what happened] before the world was created, learn and contemplate it in your heart. If [you study what happened] after the world was created, you may go and your voice may resound from one end of the world to the other" (Ḥagiga 2:1, 77c). The sequence of warnings, "Do not go down toward Him, and if you go down toward Him, do not take pleasure from Him. And if you did take pleasure, you will be driven out of the world," is related to the eye's nourishment from the *Shekhina*. It reminds us of the sequence found in a parable in *Avot de-Rabbi Natan*, "He [Ben Zoma] would say: 'Do not peek into a man's vineyard, and if you peeked, do not go down into it; and if you went down into it, do not look; and if you looked, do not touch; and if you touched, do not eat; and if a man eat from it, he will have destroyed his soul both from the life of this world and from that of the World to Come.'"[9]

This redaction of the classic collection of warnings from talmudic literature, as they appear in *Hekhalot Zutarti*, is preceded by a sentence which alters the tenor of the esoteric approach: "If you wish to distinguish yourself in the world, so that the secret of the world and the hidden wisdom will be revealed to you, learn this Mishna." This formula introduces other texts in Hekhalot literature as well, and determines that all persons in Israel should repeat this Mishna until it becomes a daily liturgical reading.[10] This esoteric Mishna is not destined for those individuals who understand of their own knowledge. The opposite is the case—it is the constant repetition of this Mishna which transforms the reader into an exceptional individual.

CHAPTER 4

Concealment and Power: Magic and Esotericism in the Hekhalot Literature

IN THE HEKHALOT LITERATURE, as we mentioned earlier, there is one focus that deals not with the image of God, but with His names; this theme has its own esoteric logic. The esotericist transmits the names designating the essence of God and His powers. Through the proper enunciation or writing of these names, one may activate the creative power of the godhead or of the angels. These names were transmitted to Rabbi Akiba: "This is the name that was revealed unto Rabbi Akiba, as he was gazing at the vision of the chariot, and Rabbi Akiba descended and taught it to his disciples. He said to them, 'My sons, take heed of this name, for it is a great name, a holy name, a pure name, and all who employ it with awe, with fear, with purity, with holiness and with humility, his seed will be multiplied and he shall succeed in all his ways'" (Schäfer, sec. 337, p. 144). The dissemination of this magical knowledge is accompanied by severe warnings of esotericism:

> Rabbi Akiba said: "Anyone who wishes to learn this Mishna, and to expound the Name as it is, should sit and fast for forty days, and place his head between his knees until the fast dominates him, and whisper to the earth and not to the heavens, that the earth may hear and not the heavens . . . and if he tell it to his fellow, he should tell him one letter of the first name and one letter of the last name, and not pair the two [letters], lest he err and destroy the world, the world of the Holy One, blessed be He. And if he wish to test him, he should test him but once, and not twice, and be scrupulous when he tests him, so that he not err and destroy the world of the Holy One, blessed be He" (Schäfer, sec. 424, p. 180).

Later in the text, we find a severe warning against the dissemination of such knowledge: "Rabbi Ishmael said, SWRYA, the privy servant spoke to me saying that I had revealed all to you, and anyone who reveals this to one who is unworthy, is banished from this world and relegated to the lowest rank of Gehenna" (Schäfer, sec. 425, p. 182).

Magic is a kind of power that may not be entrusted to one who is unworthy, and as such, it is transmitted esoterically. There is a parallel passage on the esotericism of magic in the Talmud:

> Raba bar bar Khannah said in the name of Rabbi Yoḥanan: "The four-letter Name, the sages confide to their students once in seven years."

Some say, twice in seven years. Rabbi Naḥman bar Yitzḥak said: "Reason supports the view that it was once in seven years, as it is written: 'This is my name forever' (le'olam). It is written le'alem (to keep secret)." Raba intended to lecture on it in public, but a certain old man said to him: "It is written le'alem (to keep secret)." Rabbi Abina opposed [two verses]: It is written "this is my name"; but it is also written, "And this is my memorial"! The Holy One, blessed be He, said: "I am not called as I am written: I am written with *yod he,* but I am read *alef, daled.*" Our rabbis taught: "At first, the twelve-letter name would be entrusted to all people. When unruly men increased, it was confided to the pious of the priesthood, and these 'swallowed it' during the chanting of their brother priests." It was taught: Rabbi Tarfon said: "I once ascended the dais after my mother's brother, and I inclined my ear to the High Priest, and heard him swallowing the Name during the chanting of his brother priests." Rav Yehuda said in the name of Rav: "The forty-two lettered Name is entrusted only to him who is pious, meek, middle-aged, free from anger, sober and not insistent on his rights. And he who knows it is heedful thereof and observes it in purity, is beloved above and envied below, his fear lies upon mankind, and he inherits two worlds, this world and the next world" (Kiddushin 71a, pp. 361–362 [trans. modified])[1]

Similar restrictions and warnings are frequently repeated in magical literature. This esotericism is designed to establish a relation between esotericism and power.[2] These traditions of esotericism, at least in the view of their transmitters, contain divine powers, and the gap between the power given to man and his personal stature threatens the existence of the world. In the modern context, we may compare this to knowledge of nuclear secrets. The attempt to control their dissemination, if it bears a moral meaning and not merely a political one, is linked to this fear. An interesting analogy between nuclear secrets and magical secrets can be found in the restriction on magical experiments, lest they go out of control: "If he seeks to experiment with [the Name], he may do so once, but not twice. And he should be very scrupulous with it when he experiments with it, lest he err and destroy the world of the Holy One, blessed be He" (Schäfer, sec. 424, p. 180). The esotericism of power is common to talmudic writings and to magical literature in general. There is, however, in the Hekhalot literature one composition that demonstrates a fascinating exception to these esoteric conventions.

This composition is part of *Hekhalot Rabbati,* and some scholars, who see this section as an independent literary unit, have designated it as *Sar Hatorah.* The literary framework for this unit is the story of the builders of the Second Temple. The builders wish to learn Torah as they toil, but request a technique that will enable them to perform their study without the usual toil and effort that it normally demands. They claim that they do not possess sufficient strength for both tasks at once. In the storehouse of the Holy One, blessed be He, there is a secret that was not revealed to Moses and has been kept for this generation, which ensures that the Temple builders will be able to know the entire Torah without effort, and will even enjoy the superior status that ensues from this knowledge:

> You are happy, but my servants are sad, for this secret, one of the secrets, has departed from my storehouse. From now on the sound of your sitting and learning will be contented as grazing calves; you shall no longer learn by struggle and effort, but by the Name of this seal and the mention of My crown. . . . Riches and money will come mightily over you, the great ones of the world will cleave to you, the families you marry into will be surrounded with lofty lineage on all sides, will be blessed by you and will be exalted through you; you will be called vindicators of the many, you will be called the benefactor of creatures, you will determine the new moons and the intercalation of the years from the shrewdness of your wisdom. (Schäfer, secs. 289–290, p. 128).

The sad angels in this passage are opposed to the transfer of the seal, just as they were opposed to the giving of the Torah to Moses. The reason for their opposition is directly related to the relation of esotericism to status:

> This secret must not leave your storehouse, and the secret wisdom not leave your treasure house. Do not make flesh and blood like unto us, and do not equate us to mankind through our Torah. Let them struggle with the Torah in the way that they struggled throughout all the generations until now; let them fulfill it with great effort and much pain. For it is your glory and it is your splendor. When they praise and pray repeatedly before you, they will call with all their hearts and entreat you with longing souls: let what we have acquired remain with us, let what we have learned endure in our hands, let what our ears have heard abide, let our hearts retain the paths of the teaching that we have heard from the mouths of our masters, and they will honor each other. If this secret be revealed unto your children, they will equate large and small, the fool and the wise, this is the answer of His servants. (Schäfer, sec. 292, pp. 128–130)

This passage is fascinating because of the reversal of the esoteric structures in it. The angels entreat God not to reveal the secrets of the Torah, because the Torah is to be acquired through struggle and effort. The disclosure of the secret will blur the differences between the wise and the fool, as the seal promises total equality of knowledge: "And if you are worthy of this great seal, to utilize the fearsome crown, there shall be no ignorant ones among you ever, neither will there be any fool or unwise ones among you" (Schäfer, sec. 288, pp. 126–128). The angels view this situation, in which "the little shall be equal to the great, and the fool to the wise" as a threat to the hierarchical structure of the status of the Sages. The transfer of a means for understanding the Torah without effort will totally undermine their status and honor. In spite of the opposition of the angels, the magical tool was placed in the hands of the Temple builders.

The anonymous author of these passages describes a social utopia, in which an esoteric magical tool given to all eliminates the existing gaps in the distribution of knowledge and the hierarchy that results from such gaps. In a society in which the dominant good is the knowledge of the Torah, and social status in many realms derives from the possession of such a good, the equal distribution of knowledge has radical consequences. The author of *Sar Hatorah* amplifies the revolutionary nature of the disclosure of the secret by describing in full, colorful detail the glory and splendor of the scholars, which will then become the lot of all. Esotericism changes its nature completely. Under normal conditions of esotericism, magical knowledge is the most extreme instrument of stratification. The status of the esotericists who know the Names is far beyond that of the scholars who struggle in the study of Torah. The *Sar Hatorah* composition, however, eliminates the stratification whose source is revealed knowledge, with the aid of magical knowledge that becomes common property. Although we do not know the identity of the circles that authored this utopian idea of the distribution of knowledge, it seems evident that these circles were never assimilated into the establishment of Torah scholars. Halperin, in his interesting analysis of this passage, suggested that it derives from circles of unlettered magicians.[3] Yosef Dan identified the source of this work among the scholars of the Land of Israel, who attempted to foresee the end of Babylonian hegemony.[4] The great difference between these two *identifications* demonstrates just how little we know about the social context of the passage. In any case, it remains a fascinating, singular example of the complex relationship between esotericism and status.

Early sources of esotericism outline two concepts of esotericism, which derive from disparate areas of religious activity. The first concept dwelt on the link between sublimity and esotericism and tests the boundary between vision and desecration. The second concept, which concerns magical knowledge, sees esotericism as a kind of regulation of power. Both concepts of esotericism may be found in the variant manuscripts of a single talmudic text describing the attempt of the angels to harm Rabbi Akiba: "And Rabbi Akiba too the ministering angels sought to thrust away. The Holy one, blessed be He, said to them: 'Let this elder be, for he is worthy to make use of (*l'hishtamesh*) my glory'" (Ḥagiga 15b). The verb *l'hishtamesh* in this context has a clear magical significance. Thus the restrictions determine who is worthy of magical power. Rabbenu Ḥananel, on the other hand, preserves a variant of this passage that reads, "Let this elder be, for he is worthy to *look upon* (*l'histakel*) my glory."[5] This reading deals with the restrictions on disclosure and vision and is tied to visual mysticism. The alternative readings *l'hishtamesh/l'histakel* (to make use of/to look at) present the two foci of esotericism whose boundaries are tested in the Hekhalot literature.

The phenomenon of the transgression of the boundaries of the esoteric and the dissemination of its traditions accompanies the esoteric idea throughout the course of its development. The very proclamation that there exists a realm of knowledge whose dissemination is restricted invites the transgression of those limits. Absolute esotericism can only be achieved, as we mentioned earlier, when no one hears of the existence of the secret, other than those who guard it. The concealment of esoteric content, when not accompanied by the concealment of the very fact of its existence, is a breach in the armor of secrecy. The violation of the framework of esotericism which we exposed in our discussion of Hekhalot literature typifies a model that surfaces repeatedly in cases of the transgression of the esoteric code; it is linked to the consciousness of a crisis, or else of redemption. The passage describing how Rabbi Neḥunya ben Hakanah expounded his chariot teachings before the Sages, without restricting it to those individuals who understand of their own knowledge, is preceded by the following description: "Rabbi Ishmael said: 'When Rabbi Neḥunya ben Hakanah saw that evil Rome had taken counsel to destroy completely the mighty ones of Israel, he stood up and revealed the secret of the world' " (Schäfer, sec. 198, p. 86). A severe historical crisis threatening the continued existence of the circle of esotericists led to the decision to diffuse the secrets. In such a situation, the esotericist must decide between the extinction of the esoteric tradition and the certainty of its preservation through forbidden dissemination of its contents.

The consciousness of a crisis resulting from the inability to continue to transmit the esoteric tradition under its normally restrictive conditions characterizes various occasions of disclosure; one possible consequence may be the committing of esoteric oral traditions to writing. Hundreds of years after the composition of the Hekhalot literature, in the early thirteenth century, Rabbi Eleazar of Worms acted under similar perceptions of crisis. He justified the writing down of the esoteric traditions of the Ḥasidim of Ashkenaz, contrary to the custom of his teacher Rabbi Yehuda Heḥasid:

> I was not fortunate with my only son, who received all the secrets, for he departed this world at half the normal life-span . . . and I did not

merit to teach the chapters to others, for the men of deeds are no more, and the hearts have become too narrow to comprehend how the Talmud is derived from the Books of the Pentateuch, as I will explain in detail in the following chapters. And I shall write them down, and reveal a drop of the sea, and write adjacent passages in brief, as one who gleans stalks. Perhaps they shall increase their learning and will understand from the force of their own intelligence.[6]

The fundamental unit for the transmission of esoteric oral knowledge is the family. According to the testimony of Rabbi Eleazar of Worms, the termination of his family line, as a result of the early death of his son and combined with the diminution of his students, moved him to commit the secrets of the Torah to writing. The fear of the loss of the secret as a result of the diminution of the line of transmission justified the writing down of the secret; thus, the knowledge could be passed on without relying on the continuous chain of oral transmission.[7]

The opposite circumstance, the messianic, could also lead to the breaking of the esoteric codes. The desire to remove the veil of secrecy at the end of days is expressed in Hekhalot literature, in the mouth of God who awaits the coming of the age of redemption: "TWTRWS'Y, God, the Lord of Israel, awaits and desires in the measure that He longs for the redemption and the time of salvation which is prepared for Israel. . . . When shall He who descends to the Merkabah descend? When shall he see the Glory of the Most High? When shall he hear of the end time of salvation? When shall the eye see what no eye has seen? When shall he ascend and tell it to the seed of his beloved Abraham?" (Schäfer, sec. 218, p. 94). The messianic age is one of complete transparency, in which the gap between the concealed and the revealed shall disappear.[8] Messianic revivals are often accompanied by the opening of the gates of secrecy. An interesting case of this is the messianic justification for the dissemination of the *Zohar*, which was raised during the dispute over its printing in the sixteenth century.[9] In the Hekhalot literature, we thus find a link between the weakening of the limits of secrecy and the two opposing poles of historical consciousness—severe crisis and redemption. This relationship is a first expression of a commonly recurring theme in the history of esotericism, as we shall explain further below.

CHAPTER 5

Esotericism and Commentary:
Ibn Ezra and the Exegetical Layer

THE EARLIEST SOURCE dealing with the attitude of rabbinic authorities to the Hekhalot literature is the discussion in the tenth century between Rav Shrira Gaon and his son Rav Hai Gaon and the community of Fez on the nature of the composition *Shi'ur Komah*. Rav Shrira Gaon and Rav Hai Gaon were the heads of the academy in Pumpedita in Babylonia at the tenth and the beginning of the eleventh centuries. In their capacity as the authoritative rabbinic leaders of the era they corresponded with the vast Jewish diaspora concerning legal and theological matters. In a question addressed to Rav Shrira and Rav Hai, the people of Fez expressed their confusion over the status of the work: "We need to know if Rabbi Ishmael transmits what he heard from his teacher, and that his teacher received from his teacher, going back to the law transmitted to Moses on Mount Sinai, or whether he said this of his own authority. And if it be the case that he spoke this of his own authority, is it not written: "Whoever does not take care to preserve the honor of his Maker, it were better that he had never come into the world? May our master please clarify this matter to us with perfect clarity" (*Otzar Hageonim, Ḥagiga* 11). The responsum of the *geonim* is a crucial turning point in the history of esotericism:

> We cannot explain this matter with perfect clarity, but only along general lines. God forbid that Rabbi Ishmael say these things of his own authority! How could a man conceive such things of his own mind? Furthermore, our Maker is too lofty and exalted to have bodily parts and dimensions as [might be understood] from the literal understanding of the words, for who can be compared unto God, and what image can resemble Him? Yet, these are indeed words of wisdom (that conceal understandings greater and higher than the highest of mountains, and very wondrous indeed, and these *words* are their hints, and their secrets and their concealed, hidden things), which may not be transmitted unto every man, but only unto those who possess the proper attributes that have been transmitted to us. . . . And we tell you this, for you are very dear to us, but we cannot discuss such matters in writing, and not even orally, except to those who are worthy. (*Otzar Hageonim, Ḥagiga*, p. 12)

Rav Shrira and Rav Hai do not deny the sacred status of the *Shi'ur Komah*. Nevertheless, the great distance between their view and the worldview of the book gives rise to a paradoxical claim that the book is a tradition obtained by Rabbi Ishmael, rather than something transmitted of his own authority. They argue that the apparent, indecipherable meaning of the book and its bizarre nature prove that Rabbi Ishmael could not have transmitted it of his own authority: "From whence shall a man speak of such matters on his own authority? Furthermore, our Maker is too lofty and exalted to have bodily parts and dimensions in the literal sense of those words." Rav Shrira and Rav Hai reject the anthropomorphic religious position, and consequently attribute a secret, hidden meaning to the book: "Yet, these are indeed words of wisdom that conceal understandings greater and higher than the highest of mountains, and are very wondrous indeed, and these words are their hints, and their secrets and their concealed, hidden things." According to Rav Shrira and Rav Hai, the mystical vision of the dimensions (*shi'ur Komah*) of God, including His bodily parts and His names, is but the symbol of deeper matters, secrets which may not be revealed in public. The composition *Shi'ur Komah* is esoteric because on the surface level it is meaningless, but it contains a hidden layer of meaning. The responding rabbis focused on the esoteric level of meaning, because the plain meaning of the words raises a severe problem of anthropomorphism. Rav Shrira and Rav Hai thus transformed the *Shi'ur Komah* from an esoteric work into a work that contains a layer of esoteric meaning. Through this change, they neutralized the anthropomorphic nature of the book. This responsum of the *geonim* is the earliest example of a new idea of esoteric exegesis. The esoteric text is no longer a text that may not be studied and disseminated, but rather a text containing an encrypted layer of meaning.

The concept of the esoteric as the hidden layer of meaning of a sacred work became a central idea in medieval Jewish thought. Rabbi Abraham Ibn Ezra, in the first half of the twelfth century, was the first medieval commentator and thinker to make extensive use of this conception. Born in Toledo in 1089, Ibn Ezra was one of the greatest products of Judeo-Arabic culture. He was a poet, astronomer, and physician who had an immense impact on Jewish culture, mainly through his magnificent commentary on the Bible. Among other achievements, by inserting into his biblical commentary a layer of hints relating to a concealed meaning of the text, he created a work that marks a turning point in the esoteric idea within Jewish tradition. An examination of the esoteric idea in the writings of Ibn Ezra lays bare the major features that exemplify the great blossoming of esotericism in the twelfth and thirteenth centuries. A striking expression of the esoteric concept that the text bears a double meaning may be found in Ibn Ezra's commentary on the plural form in the expression "my commandments (*mitzvotai*) and my teachings (*torotai*)": "The reason for the plural form in *mitzvotai* and *torotai* is that all the commandments and teachings are undoubtedly true in their apparent meaning, yet they contain secrets concerning matters of the soul, which only the instructed may understand; thus each commandment is double" (Exodus 16:28; Weiser 2:107). The esoteric is thus a level of meaning that transforms the basic structure of the text to one bearing a double meaning. The idea of the esoteric, which accompanies substantial portions of the text, endows the concept of esotericism with an entirely new meaning. According to the previous understanding of esotericism, that of the Hekhalot and tannaitic literature, the vision of the chariot which might not be expounded was an extremely marginal case, which remained adjunct to the tradition and which must be approached with care. In tannaitic and talmudic literature, the esoteric did not influence the larger structure of the tradition, nor did it change its meaning or essential nature. In a striking contrast to the medieval esotericism, scriptural interpretations which reveal encoded meanings in the sacred text are absent from the Hekhalot literature. Esotericism became a hermeneutical project from the twelfth century onward and ushered in a major transformation of Jewish tradition as a whole. In the Middle Ages, the esoteric realm acquired its exclusive significance, as a deep-structural layer that ran parallel to many of the revealed portions of the canon; this layer endowed all of religious activity with a new meaning—from basic principles of faith to the performance of the commandments. From Ibn Ezra's day on, the esoteric realm serves as an answer for a basic, fundamental question relating to the wider meaning of Jewish tradition, and became a level of meaning casting its influence over the entire surface of the religious framework.

This concept, that esotericism separates the meaning of the text into several levels, created an important new dimension in the esoteric idea in the Middle Ages—the stratification of the learning public. The esoteric levels could be understood only by the instructed, while the other learners would have to suffice with the revealed levels of the text. The medieval esotericist is not one who knows how to expound Ezekiel or Genesis; rather, he reads the very same text in an entirely different manner than the other learners. The stratification of the learning public into an enlightened community and one that is unenlightened is no less significant than the splitting of the meaning of the text. From this point on, the learning public is no longer seen as a single organic unit, as opposed to the unlettered (*amei ha'aretz*); rather, that public is itself divided into the instructed and the uninstructed.

Ibn Ezra expresses the idea of addressing two separate publics by splitting a verse in two: "I am the Lord your God, who took you out of the land of Egypt" (Exodus 20:2): "for [Scripture] tells the instructed

'I am the Lord,' and adds 'who took you out,' so that both the instructed and the uninstructed shall understand" (Exodus 20:1; Weiser 2:132). The words of Ibn Ezra are given as in response to the question of Rabbi Yehuda Halevi, who asked, "Why is it not written, 'I am the Lord your God, who created the heavens and the earth'?" According to Ibn Ezra, for the instructed, the words "I am the Lord your God" suffice, for his faith is based on knowledge of nature and the structure of the universe:

> He whose heart leads him to acquire wisdom . . . will recognize the works of God in metals and plants, in animals and in the very body of man . . . and will raise his heart to know the matters of the celestial spheres . . . and he will know all of these with completely discernment, that knows of no doubt, and through the ways of God, the instructed shall know God. For behold, the glorious God mentions in the First Commandment, "I am the Lord your God." And this can only be understood by one who is exceedingly wise. (Exodus 20:1; Weiser 2:132)

The historical level of religion, as expressed in the second part of the verse, is directed toward those who are uninstructed, that is, the believer who lacks the ability to base his faith upon investigation of creation, and requires miracles to uphold his faith. For this uninstructed reader, one must add to the words "I am the Lord" the visible miracle: "who took you out of the land of Egypt." According to the commentary of Ibn Ezra, the division of the verse indicates that the esoteric level of the text hints at the causal and fixed aspects of the universe, as opposed to the revealed level, which deals with the historical miraculous dimension. This position is a hallmark of the esoteric conception throughout the Middle Ages, as will become clearer when the full scope of the esoteric medieval project will be unraveled.

This passage may serve as a starting point for our investigation as to who is an instructed one, how a selected public of readers is formed within the larger community, and what characterizes this privileged community. Ibn Ezra describes the instructed in other contexts as well: "For if I desired to reveal this secret, I could not write it in the same manner I write throughout my commentary on this book, for he who has not learned geometry and the secrets of astronomy will not understand" (Exodus 28:6; Weiser 2:187). In still another place, he writes: "And the men endowed with the knowledge of geometry understood these secrets" (Genesis 1:1; Weiser 1:13). The determination of who is instructed is of central importance in our understanding of the role of the esoteric idea in the Middle Ages. The instructed person is acquainted with scientific discourse—in the case of Ibn Ezra, Greek and Arabic geometry and astrology—and through this scientific discourse he comes to understand the secrets of the Torah.[1] Ibn Ezra is aware that this knowledge is not derived directly from the study of the Torah, but is acquired from the surrounding culture. Indeed, the astrological hermetic picture was transmitted to Ibn Ezra through a long Arabic tradition. Astrological teachings began to enter the Islamic world in the ninth century and they left their deep impression upon authors and groups such as al-Kindi and his student, the greatest of Arabic astrologers, Abu Ma'shar al-Balkhi, the Brethrens of Purity, al-Biruni, and others.[2] Ibn Ezra expressed the external source of such knowledge in his commentary: "There are great sages, steeped in the two Torahs, who have not delved into the wisdom of nature. Thus, I cannot explain these blessings, unless I mention some of these teachings" (Exodus 23:25; Weiser 2:163).[3] The public that is acquainted only with the surface level of the text is not made up only of the unlettered. The public of listeners or readers is divided between sages proficient in the Written and Oral Law, and those who have delved into the study of nature and other forms of wisdom. The internal stratification is determined by the differing contexts of knowledge brought to the text by the reader and the understandings facilitated by these forms of knowledge.[4]

The gap between the two parts of the public is formed not only as a result of the question of interpretation. According to Ibn Ezra, the community of esotericists is a religious elite that realizes the supreme telos of religious existence. The stratification runs so deep that it creates an essentially separate religious elite. This is stated forcefully by Ibn Ezra in his response to the question as to why the Torah does not mention the rewards of the World to Come:

In my opinion, the Torah was given to all, not to one alone. Matters concerning the World to Come can be understood only by one in a thousand, for they are deep. The reward in the World to Come depends on matters of the soul. For it is reward for the service of the heart, whose work is the contemplation of the deeds of God, for they are the ladder by which one may ascend to attain the degree of the knowledge of God, which is the essence. For the Torah also explained to the instructed person the matter of the tree of life. For there is a power that can defeat the cherubim [guarding the entrance to the Garden of Eden]. For he who eats of the tree of life lives forever like the ministering angels, as we find in the Psalm to the sons of Koraḥ: "Hear this all nations" (Psalms 49:2), for the secret is "for the Lord shall redeem my soul from She'ol, for He shall take me, Selah" (49:16). Furthermore, "after honor, shall He take me" (73:24). For the verb "to take" (lekiḥa) is mentioned in both verses, just as it is mentioned in the cases of Enoch and Elijah . . . and the instructed person (maskil) shall understand. (Deuteronomy 32:39; Weiser 3:318).

The instructed esotericists are those who understand what the World to Come is. Furthermore, they are the only ones to merit the World to Come. As Ibn Ezra says in his commentary on the verse "that a man do them and live with them": "To explain that they [the commandments] provide for those who observe them in both worlds. For he who understands their secret, the Life of the World shall sustain him so that he never die, as it is written, 'I am the Lord your God,' as I explained" (Leviticus 18:4; Weiser 3:54). In a more extreme formulation, we may say that the only ones who acquire eternal life as individuals are those who cleave to God through their knowledge, whereas all others, excepting the instructed person, may achieve eternal life as part of the human species, as this species will never die out. The instructed person maintains an unmediated, direct relationship with God as an individual, unlike other human beings: "Since Adam saw that he was to die, he gave birth to a son so that the species might be preserved; thus, he received a special status through the collective. Consequently, Eve said: 'For I have purchased the Lord through a man' (Genesis 4:1). But the sons of the prophets would isolate themselves, in the hopes that each would receive according to his own capacities" (Exodus 3:15; Weiser 2:34–35). This idea appears in an extremely abbreviated form in Ibn Ezra's words on the promise of long life: "For the days shall be lengthened for all upon the earth, and for the individual in the World to Come" (Deuteronomy 6:30; Weiser 3:234).[5] The two levels of reading of the text reflect far more than different exegetical possibilities. They present the internal religious life and the possibility of the existence of a religious elite of a status fundamentally different from that of other readers. It is they who realize the inner telos of religion.

Even before we deal with the unique elements in Ibn Ezra's concept of esotericism, his definition of the instructed esotericist may teach us a fundamental principle of the function of esotericism in the Middle Ages. The instructed person is, as we mentioned, one who bears a particular scientific knowledge, which is the key to the internal understanding of the text, which, in the case of Ibn Ezra, deals with the astrological-hermetic worldview, which then becomes the inner meaning of Judaism. Consequently, the esoteric idea becomes a powerful tool for the integration and internalization of external cosmological and theological views into the tradition. Thus, in the Middle Ages, under the cloak of esotericism, astrological, hermetic, Aristotelian, Neoplatonic, Gnostic, and other positions found their way into the heart of Judaism. Through the realm of the esoteric, an encounter took place between the particularistic Jewish tradition and its surroundings, and doctrines of high cultural status were incorporated into the Jewish tradition.

This phenomenon, which was vigorously expounded during the Middle Ages, became possible as a result of two fixed structural elements within esoteric teaching. The first and simpler element was the exegetical range that the esoteric idea grants to the canon of sacred scripture. The addition of an esoteric level expands the text's "receptive capacity to meaning" to almost infinite dimensions. What can be read into it becomes far more varied and extreme. The esoteric idea provides a new and powerful tool to exegesis as a means of receiving ideas and transforming them into an integral part of the tradition. Thus, Ibn Ezra could claim that the astrological worldview, which is apparently completely alien to the surface meaning of the text, is in fact the internal meaning of that text. Ibn Ezra was of course not the only one to make such radical use of the exegetical opportunities offered by the idea of the existence of an esoteric level; he did, however, clear new paths by making the esoteric realm into a systematic method for absorbing the scientific worldview from the broader surrounding culture.

The second element of esoteric teaching is far more complicated and more significant; it derives from the unregulated nature of the esoteric realm. The presentation of radical views as traditional Jewish esoteric teachings became possible because, in esotericism, there is no revealed tradition that may be employed to critique the suggested esoteric teaching. A possible critic of the hermetic-astrological esoteric teaching of Ibn Ezra cannot employ the argument that these elements are not part of the tradition. To this argument, the esotericist may respond that the surface level of the tradition cannot serve to contradict his claims, for after all, the entire realm was hidden and secretive. Small wonder, then, that during the Middle Ages, various thinkers proposed esoteric teachings that were radically opposed to one another, and the contents of the esoteric realms became widely varied and unregulated. Could there be, in the entire history of Jewish thought, two writings that differ from each other more than the *Zohar* and *Guide of the Perplexed*? Yet both are canonical works, and both claim to be revelations of Jewish esoteric teachings. Esotericism is thus a powerful tool for the reception of a variety of teachings, none of which can claim priority through reference to other written texts or to the revealed tradition. Here we see the paradox of esotericism that we discussed above cast in sharp relief: the esoteric realm, which was defined as esoteric to enable close guard, regulation, and the continuity of a fixed and pure tradition, became the most unregulated and diverse field of all for those very reasons!

It may be worthwhile to mention that the absorption of widely varied teachings into Jewish tradition through the medium of esotericism lent them not only legitimacy, as part of the canonical text, but also primacy. When such doctrines are understood as esoteric and enshrouded with the aura of secrecy, they become accepted as the inner meaning of Judaism, so that they penetrate to the most influential levels of meaning of the tradition.

Medieval Jewry was characterized by a tradition of unusual intellectual flexibility, as a result of the medium of esotericism. Through this medium, it could digest the worldviews surrounding it, and these worldviews, with all their resultant ramifications, became the inner and deepest meaning of Judaism in the eyes of its defenders.

A telling example of the paradox of esotericism discussed here is the attitude expressed by Ibn Ezra in his commentary on the verse "which the Lord your God divided among all the nations" (Deuteronomy 4:19). This verse that refers to the heavenly bodies seems to imply that while Israel is controlled by God, the stars were allotted to the nations as forces that will control their fate. In order to avoid such a possible recognition of the divine power of the stars, the Septuagint translation of the text changes the meaning of the verse by adding that God divided the stars in order to give light to the nations. The stars accordingly do not have a power of control; they just provide light. Ibn Ezra, following his basic belief in the astrological power of the planets, affirms the direct and simple meaning of the verse: "Know that all the plants and living things in the land, and all the birds and cattle, wild animals and creeping things and all humans are linked to the forty-eight forms of the spheres, and this is what the Lord your God divided among all the nations. And those who add the word *l'ha'ir* (to give light to) are mistaken. Perhaps they knew this and did not wish to reveal the secret and the evidence to Ptolemy and did not share it with them" (long commentary to Exodus 33:21).[6] As Shlomo Sela has shown, this obscure passage is based on the tradition in the Talmud dealing with the Septuagint translation of the Pentateuch into Greek:

> It happened that King Ptolemy gathered seventy-two wise men and placed them in seventy-two houses and did not reveal to them why he gathered them. He then came to each one of them individually and said to them, write me the Law of your teacher Moses. The Holy One, blessed be He, placed His counsel in the hearts of every one of them and they all were of exactly the same mind. And they wrote him . . . "that the Lord your God divided to give light to all the nations." (Megilla 9b)

The translators of the Pentateuch added the word *l'ha'ir* (to give light to); this addition, as many commentators have explained, was made in order to avoid the erroneous understanding that the heavenly hosts have power and mastery. The word *l'ha'ir* diminishes the importance of the stars and constellations and demotes them from lords to servants. Ibn Ezra, on the other hand, maintained that the change introduced in translation was not to avoid possible error, but rather to conceal an important fact—the influence of the stars upon the nations. As he writes in his commentary in Deuteronomy: " 'for he divided': it is a known thing, that each and every nation has its star and constellation, and that each and every town has its own constellation." According to the astrological conception of Ibn Ezra, stars dominate the political fate of nations, and even influence the condition of towns and states. It was this very fact that the translators attempted to conceal from Ptolemy; thus, they added the word *l'ha'ir*. The secret is the astrological structure of reality. Shlomo Sela identified the scientific-astrological context of this concealment. King Ptolemy, who in the Arabic tradition—and, consequently, in the Jewish tradition as well—was seen as one of the founders of the science of astrology, recognized that the sages of Israel possessed incredibly accurate astrological knowledge. The translation of the Pentateuch was one of Ptolemy's attempts to get a hold of these secrets. According to Ibn Ezra, the wise men changed the meaning of the text in order to hide from Ptolemy the existence of Jewish astrological positions, and thus the astrological knowledge possessed by the sages of Israel.

Ibn Ezra's claim, that the earlier wise men of Israel possessed astrological knowledge, was linked to the concept *sod ha'ibur* (the secret of intercalation) mentioned in the Talmud, and the understanding that took root in the tenth century, that there is a secret tradition for calculating the calendar, called "the calculation of Rav Ada bar Abba," which differs from the revealed tradition, "the calculation of Shmuel," mentioned in the Talmud.[7] This concept is also expressed by Abraham bar Ḥiyya, a contemporary of Ibn Ezra who wrote at the beginning of the twelfth century, and another thinker who internalized the astrological worldview and planted in the heart of Judaism:

> I read in one of the ancient books as follows: "I asked, my teachers, why was the calculation of Rav Ada done in private?" They told me, "Because all that happens in the world, famine or plenty, death or life, depends on the moon's renewal and the season, and the sages feared that an immoral man might arise and destroy the world; and I accept this with all my heart, and know that this matter is true."[8]

Ibn Ezra, who, contrary to the view of Abraham bar Ḥiyya, did not believe that Rav Ada's calculation is based on magical knowledge, believed that Rav Ada's calculation aids in knowing the future, and consequently must be kept secret: "In my opinion, [Rav Ada's calculation] was transmitted in private lest anyone who wished to know would know all that would come to pass in the land through the sages' knowledge of the laws of the zodiac."[9]

The esoteric conception in astrological matters of Abraham bar Ḥiyya and Ibn Ezra continues the esoteric tradition dealing with the magical names in Hekhalot literature, and essentially creates a controlled distribution of power.

The accepted position in the twelfth century on ancient astrological knowledge possessed by the sages of Israel demonstrates the flexibility of the esoteric idea. Since, a priori, we cannot know what the secret of intercalation or the secret of Rav Ada were, all of astrological knowledge can be linked to it. The esoteric realm is, by its very nature, sealed; thus a variety of teachings, including the science of astrology, with its Greek, hermetic, and Arabic contents, may be projected onto it. Moreover, the issue of translation raised by Ibn Ezra in his comments on the concealment of knowledge from Ptolemy raises the issue of what might be called the ambivalence of influence. Translation is a medium of cultural influence, and this is certainly the view that Ibn Ezra had of the Septuagint. Influence and recognition are signs of the success of a tradition, and Ptolemy showed interest in the Torah of Israel and recognized its importance and supremacy. Too much and too wide success, however, poses a threat to the uniqueness of the tradition. The secret that is not transmitted in translation is what preserves the unique status of the tradition, even under extreme conditions of intercultural transmission and influence. In a reality characterized by such widespread cultural links, secrecy has a double function: it facilitates integration on a tremendous scale, while also creating consciousness of separation and isolation.

CHAPTER 6

Concealment and Heresy:
Astrology and the Secret of the Torah

A MORE DETAILED examination of the concept of esotericism in the writings of Ibn Ezra can illuminate another essential element of the esoteric idea in the Middle Ages. In Ibn Ezra's commentaries, as we have seen, the esoteric refers to astrological and magic knowledge that elucidates the inner level of the text. This knowledge is the key to understanding various aspects of the commandments and of ritual, and also helps us comprehend miracles. This layer, does not, however, merely exist alongside the revealed level of meaning. This deeper layer is in profound tension with the revealed level; the crux of the tension is the magical explanations of Torah passages, whose plain meaning expresses the voluntary action of a personal deity. The astral explanations impinge upon the meaning of ritual and the essence of miracles, and Ibn Ezra himself is aware that they are in tension with the understandings of the larger body of the faithful of Israel. This awareness is made explicit when Ibn Ezra provides a talismanic explanation for the Temple. According to this explanation, the location and structure of the Temple were determined by the positions of the stars, so that the Temple is an instrument for attracting forces, according to the magic astral conception:

> We know that the glorious Name has informed us that His glory fills the entire world, yet there are places where the power of God is made more manifest than in others, depending on two factors: The first is the qualities of the nature of the receiver. The second is the extent of heavenly powers which are (bestowed) upon the head of the receiver. Based on these, a place was chosen for the Temple. If the Lord has placed wisdom in your heart, you will understand the secret of the ark and the mercy-cover and the cherubim which spread their wings; and outside the veil, the candelabrum and the altar of incense and the table [of the shew-bread]; and outside the entrance to the sanctuary, the altar of sacrifice and all its vessels, and the laver and its base—all these things are the glory of God. Thus, I have only hinted of these things to you, for there are in our generation men who are wise in their own eyes, who may otherwise mock my words. (Exodus 28:40; Weiser 2:177)

The fear of those who are "wise in their own eyes" is a reason for concealment. By contrast, the instructed person understands the profundity of the matter: "This is the rule: each cherub was made to receive heavenly powers, in order that the instructed person may learn, and there is no need to discuss this at length" (Exodus 28:40; Weiser 2:177). Furthermore, Ibn Ezra employs the hierarchy of space to explain other Torah matters, such as the Land of Israel or the concept of holy place in general.[1] The astrological position is accompanied by a hermetic magical idea of the attraction and reception of divine power, a position clearly demonstrated through the research on Ibn Ezra and his followers undertaken by Moshe Idel and Dov Schwartz.[2] The talismanic conception explains the breastplate, the bronze serpent, the sin of the golden calf, the sacrifices,[3] and many other issues in Scripture. Ibn Ezra clearly reveals his astrological views, although in places where he employs this view as a key to understanding ritual, he does so in hints; this later posed no small difficulty for his exegetes.

The realm of the esoteric is not only a means for internalizing wider cultural contexts, but also a shelter for positions that appear unorthodox or heretical. We may say of all medieval esoteric doctrines that, as a rule, each one of them deeply undermines the structure of revealed faith as it appears in Scripture and in the Midrash. The esoteric has a subversive aspect, which effectively precludes any decisive formulation of principles of faith, which might serve as a kind of Jewish dogma. The multiplicity of contradictory esoteric positions makes the formulation of Jewish theology an impossible mission. The esoteric is a wide field, which enables apparently heretical positions to thrive. Through the esoteric, questions arise with respect to the basic concepts of revealed religion. We should be reminded that, because of the preferential status of the esoteric, heretical positions acquire a status as the inner core of religion and even as the loftiest pinnacle of religious life. As in the example of Ibn Ezra, the penetration of astrology and magic is not merely the incursion of "foreign" sources at the boundary of tradition; esotericism transforms these elements into the holy of holies of the Jewish experience.

Another area that Ibn Ezra considered as esoteric dealt with the secret of the Name and the concept of miracle. Here too, as in the concept of ritual, esotericism was linked to a causal magical conception, which precipitates changes in the theology of will and personality. Ibn Ezra explains his doctrine of names in his extensive commentary on the expression "I am what I am" (Exodus 3:14). The name of God (YHWH) is the personal name of God, which refers to His essence, whereas the names *adonai* and *elohim* are adjectives, describing powers dependent on God; thus they are expressed in plural form. These names refer to the angels that establish the astrological order of the universe. Humans, whose source is in the upper worlds, may transcend the astrological constellation and perform miracles through his relation to the glorious Name of YHWH: "For the soul of man is of their type, and it receives heavenly power through the constellation of the servants, and each servant stands *opposite* the great [heavenly] host at the hour of his creation. And if the soul becomes wise, it may receive the secret of the angels and receive great power from the heavenly powers that it receives through the light of the angels. Then it shall cleave unto (*davek*) the glorious Name." Later on in his commentary, Ibn Ezra describes two reactions to death: "When Adam saw that he was to die, he gave birth to a son so that the species might be preserved, and so he received power and privilege as part of the collective . . . but the sons of the prophets would isolate themselves, in the hopes that each would receive [power], each according to his own capacities. Thus, through this Name, signs and wonders could be introduced into the world, as it was said to him (Moses), 'This is the glorious Name, ask for signs and wonders'" (Exodus 3:15; Weiser 2:34–35).

The natural astrological constellation guarantees the existence of species in the world. Among the human species, the few instructed persons transcend the limits of the causal astrological framework by cleaving (*d'vekut*) to the Name, through which signs and wonders are performed in the world. In his commentary on the verse "And I appeared unto Abraham, Isaac, and Jacob through El Shaddai, and my name, YHWH, I did not make known to them" (Exodus 6:3), Ibn Ezra describes his conception of the names and the miraculous powers linked to knowing them as the inner core of the entire Torah: "For this is the secret of the entire Torah" (Exodus 3:15; Weiser 2:47). The differences in the capacities of members of the elect to liberate themselves from the astrological constellation and perform changes is a function of the level of their cleaving to God (*d'vekut*): "For the forefathers did not reach the same level of cleaving to the Name (*d'vekut*) as Moses, whom God knew face to face. Thus, Moses could change the nature of the inferior world and effect signs and wonders, which the forefathers could not achieve" (Exodus 3:15; Weiser 2:47). The miracle is no longer a free expression of God's will. It takes place through the human ability to transcend the astral system and receive power from the name YHWH Himself.

Ibn Ezra frequently repeats that the comprehension of miracles is an esoteric matter—for example, in his commentary on the sin of Moses and Aaron at the waters of Meribah: "The correct explanation, I will reveal in hints. Know that when the part knows the all, it will cleave unto the all, and renew in the all signs and wonders. For in truth, God said to Moses 'and you shall speak,' yet they did not speak as a result of the people's argument with Moses. And thus the part remains part. So, he hit the rock and no water emerged until he hit it a second time" (Numbers 20:8;

Weiser 3:171). The miracle depends upon the "part" knowing the "all" and cleaving unto it. The expression "the all" (*hakol*) in Ibn Ezra refers to God and the name YHWH: "For God is one and He is the creator of all and He is the all, and I may explain no further" (Genesis 1:26; Weiser 2:19).[4] Moses, who is the "part," was to perform the miracle through his cleaving (*d'vekut*) to the glorious Name, but in the heat of the dispute with the people, he was obliged to hit the rock. The secret of the Name, which is part of astrological-magical knowledge, explains the miracle in the framework of a causal conception; as such it is similar to the esoteric teaching on the understanding of law and ritual in Ibn Ezra's writings.[5]

Ibn Ezra, in one of his general comments about his esoteric teachings, identified these two areas—the concept of ritual and the concept of miracle—as the realms of the esoteric: "For in truth, within the words of the Torah, we must investigate the names of the glorious and awesome God, and profound secrets in the commandments and laws as well, which no fool's eye has beheld, and which are known only to the instructed. And if God help me that I may accomplish my vows, I shall explain some of them" (alternate interpretation to Genesis, Weiser 1:139). There are two esoteric matters common to the esoteric level of ritual and the secret of the Name. In both of them, the understanding of this level is reserved for the instructed alone, as it is dependent on the internalization of a wider scientific astrological-magical understanding. Thus, the public of readers is divided in two—the ignorant and the instructed. This stratification is typical of the esoteric teaching of Ibn Ezra in particular and medieval scholars in general. Furthermore, the esoteric level provides a causal picture underlying the revealed level of the text. Deep beneath the surface of the biblical text lies a systematic natural picture which only the instructed can identify, as only he can integrate the biblical words into a Greek and Arabic scientific worldview. This esoteric picture claims that God and the world are linked in a causal system, and ritual activates this causal framework. Regardless of its particular standpoint, the very idea of a full causal translation stands in opposition to the biblical heritage that assumes an interpersonal will that acts in the world within a covenantal relational framework. In such traditional understanding, ritual is not designed to activate God, but to please Him.[6] The esoteric level is thus not merely an addition of depth to the surface level. In its bold transformation of the basic understanding of God and the world the esoteric is in fact an actual reversal of the surface level. In the writings of Ibn Ezra, the first commentator to make systematic use of the idea of an esoteric level of Scripture, we find the basic traits that characterize medieval esotericism: the double text, the stratification of the reading public, the transformation of the esoteric realm into a medium for integrating central positions of the wider cultural context; finally, the possibility that the esoteric realm offers for the penetration of positions that might be considered as bordering on heresy into the holy of holies of the Jewish tradition. Consequently, the esoteric realm, which was designed to be sealed and guarded, became, for this very reason, unguarded and threatening.

CHAPTER 7

Double Language and the Divided Public in *Guide of the Perplexed*

THE BASIC ELEMENTS of the esoteric structure in the conception of Ibn Ezra are found in the writings of Maimonides as well. Maimonides' works are the most important esoteric teachings of the philosophical movement in the Middle Ages. He was born in approximately 1135 and grew up in Cordova before being forced to immigrate to North Africa, and was thirty years old when Ibn Ezra died. He was the crown of the last generation of the great Jewish Andalusian tradition, which produced Ibn Ezra as well. As one of the most renowned legal authorities in the Jewish medieval world, Maimonides' authority as a towering talmudist gave great weight as well to his philosophical achievements. His stature as a philosopher and talmudist and the centrality of his esoteric themes in his writings made concealment a vital cultural concern and a conflicting source of identification, suspicion, and upheaval. Maimonides, like Ibn Ezra, was of the opinion that the elite that held the keys to the esoteric were the *maskilim*, the instructed, the possessors of broad cultural knowledge. Maimonides, however, rejected completely the astrological-magical conception of Ibn Ezra, and belonged to a completely different philosophical movement in the Greek and Arabic world. The instructed, according to Maimonides, belonged to the Aristotelian movement, especially as understood through the writings of al-Farabi. For both Ibn Ezra and Maimonides, the esoteric facilitated broad cultural integration, by absorbing a metaphysical-scientific worldview, and defining it as the esoteric meaning of the Torah. The particular worldview that Maimonides absorbed through the esoteric and expressed through his teaching was completely different, however, and relied on opposing metaphysical-scientific paradigms current in the medieval world. Although there is a huge difference in their metaphysical and scientific worldviews, the division of the learning public into the instructed and the multitude is even more pronounced for Maimonides, as is the idea that the instructed form a distinguished religious elite, who are able to realize the loftiest elements of religious existence.[1]

His treatise, *Guide of the Perplexed*, whose aim is the explication of the secrets of the Torah, is designated for the instructed alone: "My speech in the present Treatise is directed, as I have mentioned, to one who has philosophized and has knowledge of the true sciences. . . . As for those who never even once see a light, but grope about in their night . . . the truth . . . is entirely hidden from them. . . . They are the vulgar among the people. There is no occasion to mention them here in this treatise" (Introduction to *Guide*, pp. 10, 7–8). The group of the instructed does not include scholars competent in the matters of the Talmud and its laws, as Maimonides makes perfectly clear at the outset: "It is not the purpose of this Treatise to make its totality understandable to the vulgar or to beginners in speculation, nor to teach those who have not engaged in any study other than the science of the Law—I mean the legalistic study of the Law. For the purpose of this Treatise and all those like it is the science of Law in its true sense" (5). According to Maimonides, one must distinguish between the halakhic knowledge of the Talmud scholars and the true knowledge of the Torah. Thus, Maimonides sets up a tension, not only between the ignorant multitudes and the instructed, but also between the traditional scholarly elite and the esotericists.[2]

The concept that the learning public is divided by a great gap between the instructed and the uninstructed is accompanied, as in Ibn Ezra, by the concept of a double language, which Maimonides develops in his introduction to *Guide of the Perplexed*. Maimonides links the esoteric to his concept of language in general; thus, he raises the issue of esotericism to a higher level of sophistication. Maimonides defines the content of *Guide of the Perplexed* as the explanation of equivocal names and the parables of Scripture: "The first purpose of the Treatise is to explain the meanings of certain terms occurring in books of prophecy. Some of these terms are equivocal; hence the ignorant attribute to them only one or some of the meanings in which the term in question is used" (Introduction to *Guide*, p. 5). Further on he states: "This treatise also has a second purpose: namely, the explanation of very obscure parables occurring in the books of the prophets, but not explicitly identified there as such. Hence an ignorant or heedless individual might think that they possess only an external sense, but no internal one" (6). An equivocal term is one that designates two different objects or refers to two disparate meanings. Maimonides is aware that there is no one-to-one correspondence between an expression in language and an object or the content that it is supposed to refer to. He sees this as a significant source of metaphysical error. For example, verbs like *alah* ("to ascend") or *yarad* ("to descend") refer to movements in space, but they also have a borrowed meaning referring to social status, as in *alah b'dargah* ("ascended in rank") or *yarad min'khasav* ("descended from [=lost] his worldly goods"), which refer to social space rather than to change of position in physical space. The inability to distinguish which meaning is used in expressing movement in biblical language and the confusion between literal and borrowed meanings give rise to profound errors, which distort the understanding of reality, as transmitted by language. It is, however, this very element of language, its fundamental opacity, which facilitates its use as a political tool. The equivocal word, like the parable, can be directed toward two publics simultaneously.

The nontransparent nature of language is a source for great metaphysical errors but an opportunity as well for concealment and camouflage. This essential feature of language as an esoteric medium was highlighted in a completely different esoteric outlook—that of psychoanalysis. Freud pointed out the effective nature of the linguistic medium as a means for concealment, in which unconscious mental material in disguise passes the inner censorship and appears camouflaged to the conscious mind:

> There is no need to be astonished at the part played by words in dream-formation. Words, since they are the nodal points of numerous ideas, may be regarded as predestined to ambiguity; and the neuroses (e.g., in framing obsessions and phobias), no less than dreams, make unashamed use of the advantages thus offered by words for purposes of condensation and disguise. (*Interpretation of Dreams*, p. 456)

In Maimonides' words the ambiguous nature of language is of great political value: "That which is said about all this is in equivocal terms so that the multitude might comprehend them in accord with the capacity of their understanding and the weakness of their representation, whereas the perfect man, who is already informed, will comprehend them otherwise" (Introduction to *Guide*, p. 9). The parable and the equivocal word enable the prophet, who is the political leader, to address diverse strata of the public with the same linguistic expressions. The concept that the Torah has an esoteric level of exegesis is linked to a much wider conception— both of human language and of the divided nature of the political public.

In his esoteric conception, Maimonides continued tendencies in the Greek and Muslim world that viewed the realm of metaphysical and scientific knowledge as a realm that must be hidden.[3] In *Guide of the Perplexed* Maimonides himself explicates the link between the esoteric philosophical tradition and the secrets of the Torah:

> Do not think that only the divine science should be withheld from the multitude. This holds good also for the greater part of natural science. In fact we have repeatedly set down for you our dictum: "The Account of the Beginning ought not to be taught in the presence of two men." This is not only the case with regard to people adhering to the Law, but also with regard to the philosophers and learned men of the various communities in ancient times. For they concealed what they said about the first principles and presented it in riddles. (I:17, pp. 42–43)

Esotericism is, as we have discussed, a powerful tool for integrating worldviews into the heart of the Jewish tradition. Moreover, investigation of the esoteric conception of Maimonides reveals that the very concepts of esotericism, as well as its limits and supporting arguments, are drawn from the very same cultural background that Maimonides integrates into his esoteric teaching. That is, Maimonides sees esoteric doctrine as an instrument bridging tradition and the Arabic Aristotelian surroundings; furthermore, his entire esoteric idea and its justification in Jewish tradition are understood in terms of the philosophic tradition.

The supporting arguments for esotericism in the Arabic philosophical tradition, as expressed in the writings of al-Farabi, Ibn Bajja, Ibn Sina, and Ibn Rushd, are fundamentally linked to the tension between truth and society, as expressed with varying emphasis in the writings of these philosophers. The esoteric concept of Maimonides and its relation to philosophical esotericism has been discussed by Leo Strauss, and at length recently in Sarah Klein-Breslavy's book, which deals with philosophical esotericism in Maimonides' writings.[4] Based on these studies, I analyze the main justifications for esotericism as found in the thought of Maimonides, and the various components of the tension between truth and society. Aside from guarding and justifying the boundaries of secrecy, Maimonides' works repeatedly test the limits of esotericism. Maimonides builds and breaches the walls of secrecy simultaneously. I believe that the discussion of this tension, which is typical of the esoteric tradition of the Middle Ages, can fundamentally change the conception of esotericism, as understood by Strauss. This is the focus of our discussion in the following chapter.

Esotericism is intended, first and foremost, to protect the philosopher and philosophy from the mockery of the multitudes that cannot fathom it. More important, it protects the philosopher from the iron fist of the religious or political authorities, who see the philosopher as a dangerous subversive, seeking to undermine the political order or religious doctrine. Thus, Maimonides justifies the esoteric nature of *Guide of the Perplexed*, which is made up of fragments and chapter headings, as follows:

A sensible man thus should not demand of me or hope that when we mention a subject, we shall make a complete exposition of it, or that when we engage in the explanation of the meaning of one of the parables, we shall set forth exhaustively all that is expressed in that parable. An intelligent man would be unable to do so even by speaking directly to an interlocutor. How then could he put it down in writing without becoming a butt for every ignoramus who, thinking that he has the necessary knowledge, would let fly at him the shafts of his ignorance? (Introduction to *Guide*, p. 6)

Esotericism is thus a precondition for the existence of philosophy as an independent and unrestricted domain. The philosopher protects his freedom of thought through concealment, and in order to transmit his views to those who are worthy of receiving them, he develops sophisticated instruments of writing and speaking in double language. Furthermore, esotericism is not only designed to protect the philosopher and philosophizing, but the multitudes as well. The exposure of the multitudes, or anyone who has not yet undergone the scientific educational process, to philosophical content will lead him to a loss of faith, since he will be incapable of understanding the truth and consequently will distort it: "If, however, he begins with the divine science, it will not be a mere confusion in his beliefs that will befall him, but rather absolute negation" (*Guide* I:33, p. 71). He continues: "These true opinions were not hidden, enclosed in riddles, and treated by all men of knowledge with all sorts of artifice through which they could teach them without expounding them explicitly, because of something bad being hidden in them, or because they undermine the foundations of the Law, as is thought by ignorant people who deem that they have attained a rank suitable for speculation. Rather have they been hidden because at the outset the intellect is incapable of receiving them" (*Guide* I:33, p. 71).[5] For example, the argument that attributes of quantity and quality do not apply to the deity will lead to denial of the very existence of God, as the multitudes are dominated by the imaginative faculty, and cannot conceive of the existence of an abstract entity. The exposure of philosophical contents like these before the multitudes will lead to the undermining of the very belief in God's existence.

Aside from the threat posed by the truth to the faith of the multitudes, the philosopher is aware that truth also undermines the social order and the authority of law. The philosophical conception rejects the understanding of God as a personality, and thus endangers the multitude's faithfulness to the law. Philosophical doctrines that describe prophecy as a process of apprehension based also on the imaginative faculty of the prophet—as opposed to the traditional anthropomorphic image, in which the sovereign God commands the law to his prophet—subvert the authority of the law as the command of a sovereign God. Moreover, the Maimonidean conception of providence holds that the evildoer is abandoned to the vagaries of chance and is not supervised at all, and that punishment results from the destructive forces intrinsic to a life of sin. This conception threatens the multitude's loyalty to the law, as this loyalty is based on fear of punishment and expectation of rewards. The subverting of the anthropomorphic conception of God, as a commanding sovereign who supervises, punishes, and rewards, endangers the very existence of society as it enfeebles discipline and obedience to the law, which depends on the belief that there is a judge and a higher judgment and that the evildoer will get his just deserts, even if he evades the ever-watchful eye of the worldly sovereign at the time that he commits the sin. Thus, Maimonides includes under the secrets of the Torah not only the creation narrative and the chariot vision, in their restricted sense, but also prophecy, providence, and knowledge dealing with the relationship of God to the world:

> And as for the . . . discussion concerning His creation of that which He created, the character of His governance of the worlds, the "how" of His providence with respect of what is other than He, the notion of His will, His apprehension, and His knowledge of all that He knows; and likewise for the notion of prophecy and the "how" of its various degrees,[6] and the notion of His names, though they are being indicative of one and the same thing—it should be considered that these are obscure matters. In fact these are truly the mysteries of the Torah and the secrets constantly mentioned in the books of the prophets and in the dicta of the Sages, may their memory be blessed. They are the matters that ought not to be spoken of except in chapter headings, as we have mentioned, and only with an individual such as has been described. (*Guide* I:35, pp. 80–81)

In his aim of guarding the structure of social authority, Maimonides expresses concern not only for the integrity of society, but also for the existence of philosophy itself. The philosopher requires an orderly society and a division of labor as is practiced in states, for the existence of philosophy as the highest human endeavor depends on its being hidden from the multitudes. The philosopher's dependence on society is described in stark terms in Maimonides' introduction to his commentary on the Mishna:

> For if all humankind were learned philosophers, the world would be destroyed, and man would be wiped out within a short time. For man is in need of many things, and he would have to learn to plow and reap and thresh and grind and cook, to make vessels and so on, before he could get his food . . . and the lifetime of Methuselah would not suffice to learn all the trades that man necessarily requires in order to exist. And, if so, when shall he learn wisdom and understand science? Thus, all these things are necessary to do the work that the world needs, whereas the learned man learns for his own sake.[7]

Maimonides was of the opinion that the existence of the multitude was an unalterable fact. Among other limitations, such as lack of time and training, there exists also a natural limitation of ability, which will always exist. Consequently, esotericism becomes a permanent political fact. This passage demonstrates, however, a convergence of interests between the interests of the philosopher and the apparently unfortunate situation of the existence of the multitude. Esotericism facilitates a division of labor, which is a prerequisite for the activity of the philosopher. The democratization of knowledge or the universalization of the philosophical ethos would bring destruction on the world; thus, to ensure the continued existence of the philosopher and philosophy, this ethos ought to remain restricted to esotericists alone.

In addition to the tension between truth and society in the Greek and Arabic tradition, we find the idea that the social order is based on the dissemination of myths, which are called necessary and useful beliefs. This idea, which played an important role in Plato's *Republic*, in the works of al-Farabi, and in Maimonides' thought, exercised decisive influence in medieval political thought on the relation between philosophy on the one hand and religion and politics on the other. According to this approach, the legislator or ruler should instill in his subjects a worldview beneficial to the existence of the state, without regard for the question as to whether it is true or false. In his comments on the views that the Torah imparts to the community, Maimonides distinguishes between true views, which are designed to bring man to utmost perfection, and necessary beliefs, which contribute toward the proper functioning of society:

> Among the things to which your attention ought to be directed is that you should know that in regard to the correct opinions through which the ultimate perfection may be obtained, the Law has communicated only their end. . . . In the same way the Law also makes a call to adopt certain beliefs, belief in which is necessary for the sake of political welfare. Such, for instance, is our belief that He, may He be exalted, is violently angry with those who disobey Him and that it is therefore necessary to fear Him and to dread Him and to take care not to disobey. (*Guide* III:28, p. 512)

At the end of that chapter, he writes:

> Sum up what we have said concerning beliefs as follows: In some cases a commandment communicates a correct belief, which is the one and only thing it aims at—as for instance the belief in the unity and eternity of the deity and in His not being a body. In other cases, the belief is necessary for the abolition of reciprocal wrongdoing or for the acquisition of a noble moral quality, as for instance, the belief that He, may He be exalted, has a violent anger against those who do injustice, according to what is said: "And my wrath shall wax hot, and I will kill" and so on, and the belief that He, may He be exalted, responds instantaneously to the prayer of someone wronged or deceived: "And it shall come to pass, when he crieth unto Me, that I will hear; for I am gracious."[8] (*Guide* III:28, pp. 513–514)

The true views were presented in abbreviated form and in chapter headings, because broad scientific knowledge and natural intellectual capabilities are necessary for their comprehension. By contrast, the useful views on providence and divine recompense appear in the Bible at length and in their entirety, as they are useful tools for the foundation of the social order, and are, as such, intended for the multitude.

Myth functions not only to strengthen the political structure of society, but also to uproot contrary myths. Maimonides was of the opinion that the rule of idolatry over the multitude was linked to promises and threats addressed to man's primal fears. Rational arguments, which prove that pagan myth consists of idle threats and vain promises, cannot suffice to uproot pagan practices. In order to displace a myth, a contrary myth must be presented. Thus Maimonides argues, for example, that in order to combat the threat made by the pagan priesthood, that whoever does not make his children pass through the fires of Moloch, his children will be harmed, the Torah poses a contrary threat: namely, that whoever *does* make his children pass through the fires of Moloch, his family would be exterminated.

> Now it is known that it is in the nature of men in general to be most afraid and most wary of losing their property and their children. Therefore the worshippers of fire spread abroad the opinion that the children of everyone who would not make his son or daughter to pass through the fire would die. And there is no doubt that because of this absurd belief everybody hastened to perform this action because of the strong pity and apprehension felt with regard to children. . . . Therefore the Law is strongly opposed to this action, an opposition that is affirmed in such terms as are not used with regards to other kinds of idolatrous practices. . . . Thereupon the truthful one makes known in the name of God, may He be exalted, and says: Whereas you perform this action so that the children stay alive because of it, God will cause him who performs it to perish and will exterminate his descendants: he says: "Then I will set My face against that man and against his family" and so on. (*Guide* III:37, p. 546)

Myth, in the sense of fabrication, is a necessary element of the political order.

In addition to political esotericism, we find in Maimonides' writings a position that sees esotericism as an essential characteristic of metaphysical language. In this conception, metaphysical matters cannot be expressed through language, so that all we can do is hint at them through symbols:

> Know that whenever one of the perfect wishes to mention, either orally or in writing, something that he understands of these secrets, according

to the degree of his perfection, he is unable to explain with complete clarity and coherence even the portion that he has apprehended, as he could do with the other sciences whose teaching is generally recognized. Rather there will befall him when teaching another that which he had undergone when learning himself. I mean to say that the subject matter will appear, flash, and then be hidden again, as though this were the nature of this subject matter, be there much or little of it. For this reason, all the Sages possessing the knowledge of God the Lord, knowers of the truth, when they aimed at teaching something of this subject matter, spoke of it only in parables and riddles. (Introduction to *Guide*, p. 8)[9]

The distinction between political esotericism and essential esotericism engenders different understandings of the biblical text. Political-social esotericism understands Scriptural parables as allegory, whose hidden contents may be expressed in direct conceptual language. Essential esotericism sees the Scriptural parable as symbol rather than allegory. The symbol does not hide contents that could otherwise be expressed directly through concepts, but points and directs us to what cannot be expressed directly. Under this conception, the esoteric structure of language is not the result of a strategy adopted by philosophy in its relation toward society, but is part of the essence of the philosophical realm.[10]

The explanation for essential esotericism is formulated differently in the introduction to *Guide of the Perplexed* than in the chapters dealing with the negative attributes. In the introduction to his book, Maimonides argues that the understanding of truth in the area of the divine sciences cannot be replicated and repeated at will: "Sometimes truth flashes out to us so that we think it is day, and then matter and habit in their various forms conceal it so that we find ourselves again in an obscure night, almost as we were at first" (7). According to Maimonides, proper understanding in abstract metaphysical matters depends on liberation from matter and habit; consequently, the ability to remain in this state depends on man's degree of perfection. The writing or teaching of metaphysical matters is actually the attempt to reconstruct a particular state of consciousness in order to transmit it to someone else. Because of the elusive nature of truth, however, the writer cannot successfully duplicate the state of consciousness entirely, so that he must resort to parable in order to point to and hint at it.

Unlike this approach, which focuses on restrictions arising from the existential nature of man as a bodily creature, in his doctrine of negative attributes Maimonides focuses on the limitations of language itself as a suitable vehicle of expression. The predicative structure of propositions in human language cannot provide a suitable characterization of divine unity, which has neither subject nor object. Similarly, the understanding of attributes like "existing" or "wise" depends on there being a shared characteristic of a common group of objects or persons which bear those attributes. Otherwise, these attributes would become proper names. The assignment of attributes to God bridges between Him and other objects in the world. Thus, the use of language to refer to God not only blemishes the purity of the concept of unity, but also the complete otherness of God from the world. These two limitations of religious language are defined by Maimonides in the following way: "Know that when you make an affirmation ascribing another thing to Him, you become more remote from Him in two respects: one of them is that everything you affirm is a perfection only with reference to us, and the other is that He does not possess a thing other than His essence, which, as we have made clear, is identical with His perfections" (*Guide* I:59, p. 139). As language is limited by its very nature, any verbal expression attempting to describe God is necessarily blemished. Consequently, the instructed one does not employ symbols or hints but instead obliges himself to remain silent: "For of whatever we say intending to magnify and exalt, on the one hand we find that it can have some application to Him, may He be exalted, and on the other we perceive in it some deficiency. Accordingly, silence and limiting oneself to the apprehensions of the intellects are more appropriate—just as the perfect ones have enjoined when they said: 'Commune with your own heart upon your bed, and be still. Selah'" (I:59, pp. 139–140).

The question as to what the secret of *Guide of the Perplexed* is, which has troubled generations of exegetes and scholars of Maimonides,[11] is not central to our discussion. We seek to clarify what justifications esotericism provided for itself and how the boundaries of esotericism are defined. We cannot, however, separate the two questions entirely. If the secret of Maimonides in *Guide of the Perplexed* is, as some of his present and past readers claim, that the world is eternal and not created, and, consequently, that the concepts of providence, miracle, prophecy, revelation, and the World to Come must be reinterpreted, than the main focus of the esotericism issue is political.[12] According to this understanding of the secret of *Guide of the Perplexed*, esotericism is motivated by the need to protect society from the philosophical view of the eternal existence of the world, which denies that God has a will through whose power he created the world at a particular point in time. The concept of eternity denies God any component of personality. Without this, the essential beliefs on providence and divine reward and punishment crumble, and consequently the authority of the law as the expression of the sovereign will of God.

In contrast to political esotericism and its inner connection to the concept of eternity, the concept of essential esotericism leads to an alternate understanding of the secret of *Guide of the Perplexed*, one advocated by

Shlomo Pines in one of his later articles.[13] In this conception, the structural limitations of language at the root of essential esotericism lead to a skeptical position with respect to the possibilities of cognition of God, and this is the true secret of *Guide of the Perplexed*. The secret is, one might say, that there is no secret. The secret which may not be diffused is that human cognition does not have the capacity to formulate truths about God, and, consequently, that there is no immortality of the soul, since immortality of the soul, in the Aristotelian tradition, depends on the level of metaphysical cognition it has attained. In the Middle Ages, this position is attributed to al-Farabi. If this motif of esotericism is indeed to be found in the writings of Maimonides, than al-Farabi and Maimonides raised early on an idea that manifests deep presence in modern literature—in Kafka and Borges, for example. This is, then, once-removed esotericism, whose meaning is not the protection of certain secret contents, but rather the fact that in reality such contents do not exist. Esotericism is thus a barrier against demystification, since the very existence of the esoteric idea is important and must be defended. The esotericists know that the domain of the esoteric is the null and void.

The Breaching of the Limits of the Esoteric: Concealment and Disclosure in Maimonidean Esotericism

MAIMONIDES INVESTED significant efforts not only in expounding the secrets of the Torah, but also in order to explain, from various angles, why the category of concealment was necessary. Among all the medieval scholars who dealt with the secrets of the Torah, Maimonides dealt most systematically with the esoteric idea, as well as with the method of writing his own esoteric teachings. Maimonides' extensive attempt in clarifying why esotericism was needed was an integral part of his exegetical strategy. He explained to the perplexed person that the Scriptures contain a concealed layer of meaning that can resolve his perplexity; in doing so, he must explain to his reader the reasons for the existence of such a level. Without a sufficient and satisfying explanation for the need for esotericism, especially as it pertains to certain matters that Maimonides defines as the secrets of the Torah, his exegetical method loses its credibility. In his broad development of the need for esotericism, he prepares the hearts of the perplexed to accept the claim that the true meaning of Jewish tradition must be sought beyond the revealed and inflexible layer of the Holy Scriptures. The various explanations for the existence of esoteric Jewish teachings were derived, as we have seen, from the Greco-Arabic philosophical tradition. Thus, Maimonides employs a path of double integration: not only did he integrate metaphysical contents and theological conceptions of the cultural milieu around him through the medium of esoteric teaching, but the very concept of esotericism was borrowed from the philosophical culture and incorporated into Jewish tradition. Maimonides' ability to interpret the limitations of esotericism in the talmudic tradition in philosophical terms enabled him to interpret the very contents of esotericism as linked to philosophical concepts. On the other hand, the assumption that the secrets of the Torah were linked to the philosophical tradition lent greater force to the idea that esotericism is dependent on considerations raised by the philosophical tradition. Thus we have a closed, perfect circle of content and framework arguments, which mutually support one another.

Maimonides' conscious and extensive discussion of the esoteric and its justifications testifies to a certain loosening of the limits of secrecy.

The esotericist who reveals the existence of a secret and speaks of the justifications for its concealment treads the line between disclosure and concealment, for the total protection of the esoteric is rendered impossible by the very mention of its existence. For a dissident in a totalitarian regime writing a play that is a concealed allegory of the horror of the repressive regime, it would have been an act of political suicide to introduce the work by claiming that he was forced to write in a coded fashion. The harsh attention of the censor would have been drawn to his work even more if, following the practice of Maimonides, he had also explained at length the need for such concealment and the literary techniques that he was employing in the process. It is clear that Maimonides was interested in revealing that he is hiding no less than in concealing.

At this point, it is important to shift the focus of our discussion from the research dealing primarily with esotericism and its justifications to the question of the testing of the boundaries of the esoteric. How did Maimonides tread the thin line between concealment and disclosure, and how did he relate to his own position in the history of esotericism?

Maimonides was aware that his book *Guide of the Perplexed* was unprecedented in the history of Jewish esoteric teaching. From his point of view, before his day no composition had ever been addressed to esotericists alone. While the Bible and the agaddah undoubtedly contain an esoteric layer, they are addressed to two different communities at the same time. *Guide of the Perplexed*, on the other hand, is addressed to a single community alone—the reader who can, of his own understanding, fathom the secrets of the Torah. Consequently, as Maimonides himself proclaimed, *Guide of the Perplexed* fundamentally changed the nature of esoteric writing. If the esoteric writing of the Bible and the Midrash were characterized by parables and equivocal words, Maimonides eschewed the use of parables for the transmission of concealed messages. If the purpose of *Guide of the Perplexed* was the explanation of the secrets of the Torah, the addition of parable upon parable would be counterproductive. Maimonides describes a previous attempt of his in esoteric writing, an attempt that remained incomplete:

We had already promised in the commentary on the Mishna that we would explain [strange subjects in the *Book of Prophecy* and in the *Book of Correspondence*—the latter being a book in which we promised to explain] all the difficult passages in the Midrashim where the external sense manifestly contradicts the truth and departs from the intelligible. They are all parables. However, when, many years ago, we began these books and composed a part of them, our beginning to explain matters in this way did not commend itself to us. For we saw that if we should adhere to parables and to concealment of what ought to be concealed, we would not be deviating from the primary purpose. We would, as it were, have replaced one individual by another of the same species. (Introduction to *Guide*, p. 9)

Maimonides abandoned the strategy of employing parables in esoteric writing, as he chose not to address his words to two communities simultaneously. *Guide of the Perplexed* is addressed to those who can understand the inner content of the parable without harm. In his words, "My speech in the present Treatise is directed, as I have mentioned, to one who has philosophized and has knowledge of the true sciences" (Introduction to *Guide*, p. 10). He switches from the use of parallels to an alternative technique of esoteric writing, that of chapter headings. Thus, in *Guide of the Perplexed*, the secrets of the Torah are transmitted a bit here and a bit there, scattered among other teachings. The instructed one knows how to connect them and develop them into a unified system:

Hence you should not ask of me here anything beyond the chapter headings. And even those are not set down in order or arranged in coherent fashion in this Treatise, but rather are scattered and entangled with other subjects that are to be clarified. For my purpose is that the truths be glimpsed and then again be concealed, so as not to oppose that divine purpose which one cannot possibly oppose and which has concealed from the vulgar among the people those truths especially requisite for His apprehension. As He has said: "The secret of the Lord is with them that fear Him." (Introduction to *Guide*, pp. 6–7)

This esoteric style is based on a talmudic source that states that to one who is a sage and understands of his own knowledge one may transmit chapter headings alone. But although Maimonides, in his writing, bases himself on a traditional esoteric technique, he made a substantial breach in its boundaries. The transmission of chapter headings is a technique of oral transmission to individuals. Writing, on the other hand, even if it is limited to chapter headings, is by nature not restricted to the sage who understands of his own knowledge. This breaking of the esoteric code was of concern to Maimonides as well:

They have already made it clear how secret the account of the chariot was and how foreign to the mind of the multitude. And it has been made clear that even that portion of it that becomes clear to him who has been given access to the understanding of it, is subject to a legal prohibition against its being taught and explained except orally to one man having certain stated qualities, and even to that one only the chapter headings may be mentioned. This is the reason why the knowledge of the matter has ceased to exist in the entire religious community, so that nothing great or small remains of it. And it had to happen like this, for this knowledge was only transmitted from one chief to another and has never been set down in writing. If this is so, what stratagem can I use to draw attention toward that which may have appeared to me as indubitably clear, manifest, and evident in my opinion, according to what I have understood in these matters? (*Guide*, Introduction to Part 3, p. 415)

Maimonides thus clearly identifies two different techniques of transmission of esoteric knowledge. The first is the simultaneous address to two separate publics by means of parables and equivocal words. This is a technique of esoteric writing, as he describes explicitly: "Know that with regard to natural matters as well, it is impossible to give a clear exposition when teaching some of their principles as they are. For you know the saying of [the Sages], may their memory be blessed: 'The Account of the Beginning ought not to be taught in the presence of two men.' Now if someone explained all those matters in a book, he in effect would be teaching them to thousands of men. Hence these matters too occur in parables in the books of prophecy" (Introduction to *Guide*, p. 7). The other technique—transmission of chapter headings to one who understands of his own knowledge—is exclusively a method of oral transmission. Maimonides breaches the barriers of secrecy by eschewing the use of parables and by committing chapter headings to writing. The parable is a more guarded degree of esoteric writing, for it does not reveal, even in part, esoteric contents, and especially because it does not claim to be esoteric. The proclamation of esotericism is the first step toward its disclosure, as the history of *Guide of the Perplexed* proves. Beginning with the second half of the thirteenth century, its secrets were the subject of widespread commentary. The writing of a composition that declares itself to be an esoteric composition on the secrets of the Torah, even if only through chapter headings, is a quantum leap in the treatment of esoteric matters.[1]

Consequently, Maimonides attempted to narrow the breach by means of a literary device identified by Strauss.[2] The "narrative frame" that Maimonides supplies for the writing of *Guide of the Perplexed* describes its genesis as a collection of letters, sent chapter by chapter to a student who departed for a faraway land. A letter is the form of writing closest to oral transmission, as it is destined to one sole addressee. In the case of *Guide of the Perplexed*, the letter is intended for all those addressees who possess qualities similar to the original recipient of the letter, that is, those who are sages and understand of their own knowledge. By employing the literary device of the letter, Maimonides attempted to create a genre of writing that would be extremely close to direct restricted transmission. In addition, Maimonides adjures the understanding reader not to reveal the secrets of *Guide of the Perplexed* to others. *Guide of the Perplexed* remains, however, an open public letter; thus, all these devices did not succeed in calming Maimonides' own conscience over the breaching of the barriers of esotericism.

Maimonides' hesitations and his justifications for violating the traditions of esotericism are evident in his words in the introduction to *Guide of the Perplexed* and in the introduction to the third part of the composition. Maimonides provides a justification for the disclosure of secrets by authoring a sophisticated reconstruction for the history of esotericism, and by defining his own unique place in that tradition. In his opinion, the esoteric tradition in Israel died out because (among other reasons) the restrictions on esotericism were strictly enforced:

> They have already made it clear how secret the Account of the Chariot was and how foreign to the mind of the multitude. And it has been made clear that even that portion of it that becomes clear to him who has been given access to the understanding of it, is subject to a legal prohibition against its being taught and explained except orally to one man having certain stated qualities, and even to that one only the chapter headings may be mentioned. This is the reason why the knowledge of the matter has ceased to exist in the entire religious community, so that nothing great or small remains of it. And it had to happen like this, for this knowledge was only transmitted from one chief to another and has never been set down in writing. (*Guide*, Introduction to Part III, p. 415)[3]

The continuity of the esoteric tradition as strictly regulated oral transmission depends on territorial and institutional continuity, which is impossible given the situation of Israel in exile. Moreover, the influence of Christian philosophy and the Kalam on Jewish thinkers resulted in the corruption of the correct scientific tradition that was employed by the sages before the period of exile: "Know that the many sciences devoted to establishing the truth regarding these matters that have existed in our religious community have perished because of the length of time that has passed, because of our being dominated by the pagan nations, and because, as we have made clear, it is not permitted to divulge these matters to all people. For the only thing it is permitted to divulge to all people are the texts of the books" (*Guide* I:71, p. 175). According to Maimonides, the internal and deep meaning of Jewish tradition was lost; he believes that he too possesses no esoteric tradition: "Nor did I receive what I believe in this matter from a teacher" (*Guide*, Introduction to Part III, p. 416). This claim is of utmost importance, if we compare it to some of the kabbalistic conceptions, which present Torah secrets as traditions dating from time immemorial.[4]

The esoteric world that was forgotten and lost was reconstructed by Maimonides, as he writes, through his own intellect. In the continuation of his introduction to Part III of *Guide of the Perplexed*, he presents the crisis situation as the reason for its commission to writing: "On the other hand, if I had omitted setting down something of that which has appeared to me as clear, so that knowledge will perish when I perish, as is inevitable, I should have considered that conduct as extremely cowardly with regard to you and everyone who is perplexed. It would have been, as it were, robbing one who deserves the truth of the truth, or begrudging an heir his inheritance" (*Guide*, Introduction to Part III, pp. 415–416). Maimonides described himself as a sudden manifestation of a Jewish esoteric doctrine that has no continuous past and which will have no continuation once he leaves this world. His life was a moment of grace which, in the future, may be hidden and vanished, becoming part of the history of an extinct tradition. The survival of the internal meaning of the Jewish tradition thus depends on Maimonides' readiness to break the bounds of willful silence, and disseminate esoteric teachings. The historical picture of the genealogy of Jewish esoteric doctrine, as painted by Maimonides, as well as the singular, incomparable status enjoyed by Maimonides within this picture (based on his own self-consciousness), legitimize the breaching of esoteric boundaries in *Guide of the Perplexed*.

Moreover, the defining of the addressee of esotericism as perplexed intensifies the crisis that serves as justification for the weakening of esoteric restrictions. This perplexed person is described as one faithful to the religion of Israel, bearing a scientific and philosophical education, and as one unaware of the esoteric layer of Scripture. He is troubled in his relationship to the revealed layer of religion:

> Hence he would remain in a state of perplexity and confusion as to whether he should follow his intellect, renounce what he knew concerning the terms in question, and consequently consider that he has renounced the foundations of the Law. Or he should hold fast to his understanding of these terms and not let himself be drawn on together with his intellect, rather turning his back on it and moving away from it, while at the same time perceiving that he had brought loss to himself and harm to his religion. He would be left with those imaginary beliefs to which he owes his fear and difficulty and would not cease to suffer from heartache and great perplexity. (Introduction to *Guide*, pp. 5–6)

Consequently, the disclosure of secrets through hints and through writing is a necessary means of preserving the instructed Jewish elite from the crisis it is undergoing. Maimonides writes this explicitly as part of his

testament at the opening of *Guide of the Perplexed*, after describing his
hesitations over the writing of the secrets of the Torah:

> God (may He be exalted) knows that I have never ceased to be exceed-
> ingly apprehensive about setting down the things that I wish to set
> down in this Treatise. . . . However, I relied on two premises, the one
> being [the Sages] saying in a similar case, "It is time to do something
> for the Lord [they may violate Your Law]" and so on; the second being
> their saying, "Let all thy acts be for the sake of Heaven." Upon these
> two premises have I relied when setting down what I have composed in
> some of the chapters of this Treatise.
>
> To sum up: I am the man who when the concern pressed him and his
> way was straitened and he could find no other device by which to teach
> demonstrated truth other than by giving satisfaction to a single virtu-
> ous man while displeasing ten thousand ignoramuses—I am he who
> prefers to address that single man by himself, and I do not heed the
> blame of many creatures. For I claim to liberate that virtuous man
> from that into which he has sunk, and I shall guide him in his perplex-
> ity until he becomes perfect and he finds rest. (Introduction to *Guide*,
> pp. 16–17)

The breach of esoteric barriers, which is akin to the violation of the
Law, is done for the sake of Heaven, for the spiritual state of the Jewish
elite is endangered. The characterization of the esoteric community as
perplexed and the description of its distress magnify the sense of crisis,
which serves as the justification for writing. In addition to the description
that the secrets of the Torah were forgotten and have disappeared, and
that *Guide of the Perplexed* presents the only possibility for reconstruct-
ing them, Maimonides presents an additional claim: that the loss of the
esoteric tradition results in confusion and crisis among the elite. Maimonides thus preferred to consecrate his efforts to saving the elite, while
paying the social and political price that resulted from the emergence of
philosophy from underground.[5] The fate of the instructed Jewish elite
depends on the breaching of the barriers of secrecy; in his own self-
consciousness, Maimonides was convinced that his teaching was the sole
and final opportunity to save this group.

The claim that a severe crisis was taking place in the esoteric tradition,
as justification for the breaching of the boundaries of esotericism from
the inside, that is, on the part of those who declare their faithfulness to
that tradition, is a standard device in esoteric literature. We have already
discussed the consciousness of crisis as justification for the disclosure of
secrets in the Hekhalot literature, and this claim will continue to surface
in various contexts. But Maimonides lent this form a unique tinge. The
particular crisis designated by Maimonides, that is, the perplexity of the

instructed persons, is tied to the particular function of the esoteric idea in medieval philosophical tradition. In his description of the perplexed one and his confusion, Maimonides clearly delineated the function of esoteric doctrine, as we described earlier. The esoteric realm enables the integration of two apparently contradictory worlds—the plain meaning of Scripture and the philosophical and scientific context in which the perplexed person is immersed. This contradiction is resolved through a systematic understanding of the hidden layer of the text, which integrates philosophical and scientific matters.

Leo Strauss claimed that Maimonidean esotericism was linked to the tension between truth and society as well as to the survival of philosophy as an unrestricted occupation. In his opinion, Maimonides belonged to a movement that saw philosophy as an esoteric occupation, and treated it esoterically in his own writings. While those elements are indeed present in Maimonides' thought, it would seem that the esoteric idea has an additional, more central role in his conception. Maimonides details his struggle with the need for secrecy; he frequently repeats his claim for the existence of Torah secrets, while focusing explicitly and consciously on the nature of his own writings and the fact that they breach the boundaries of secrecy. These factors demonstrate that more important than Maimonides' interest in preserving secrecy was his interest in utilizing the esoteric idea. Moreover, the presence of apparently esoteric philosophical ideas in Maimonides' public halakhic writings, in his *Commentary on the Mishna*, and in his *Mishneh Torah*, as demonstrated by David Hartman,[6] blurs the distinction between the revealed and the concealed as a distinction between halakha and philosophy. If Leo Strauss were correct in his understanding of the meaning of esotericism in the writings of Maimonides, then Maimonides' systematic preoccupation with the existence of the esoteric, with the need for secrecy, and with esoteric writing would be out of place, as one who wishes to preserve secrecy should avoid mention of secrets. Thus, Maimonides is not a direct successor to the esoteric philosophical tradition; rather, he added an additional claim to it. The nature of his claim is that once the philosophers have determined that philosophy is an esoteric science, and once Maimonides had identified physics and metaphysics with the work of creation and the vision of the chariot, and thus linked the esoteric philosophical tradition to the talmudic one, he could now convince the instructed person that an esoteric level existed in Scripture itself, and that the recognition of the existence of this level could redeem him from his confusion.

Strauss remarked that the reading of *Guide of the Perplexed* drew his attention to the sociology of philosophy and to its esoteric side, and from *Guide of the Perplexed* he turned to an analysis of the more ancient sources of this phenomenon. But *Guide of the Perplexed* enables us to identify clearly the place of the esoteric phenomenon in the history of philosophy, specifically because Maimonides deviated from previous practice, while claiming for himself a unique and separate place in the history of the esoteric tradition.[7] This deviation is already explicit, as we have shown, in the conscious and reflexive discussion of the phenomenon of esotericism, and is linked to the fact that Maimonides employed the esoteric idea for the purpose of effecting a revolutionary integration between apparently contradictory cultural traditions. To the traditional position with respect to the esoteric conception of Maimonides, which claims that secrecy is a way of protecting philosophy's position as a separate autonomous realm, we must add the conception that esotericism is a means of incorporating philosophy into the interior of the tradition. These opposing poles define the fragile tension between concealment and disclosure in the new molds created by Maimonides in his transmission of the esoteric.

CHAPTER 9

From Transmission to Writing: Hinting, Leaking, and Orthodoxy in Early Kabbalah

IN THE TWELFTH AND THIRTEENTH centuries, while Ibn Ezra's and Maimonides' esoteric projects were flourishing, a parallel yet strikingly different esoteric option emerged through the various traditions of the Kabbalah. This form of Jewish mysticism, quite distinct from its earlier tradition of the Hekhalot, constructed divinity as a living organism emanating from the depth of God's infinite essence into his revealed and complex dimensions—the *sefirot*. The first text that testified to this form of esoteric knowledge was the book of *Bahir*, which surfaced in Provence in the middle of the twelfth century. The earlier kabbalistic centers known to us in Provence and subsequently at the beginning of the thirteenth century in Gerona perceived the Torah as a forest of symbols for God's inner life, mirroring the complex and fragile balance between the *sefirot*. These esoteric traditions were geared toward postulating the role of humans as maintaining the proper harmony and flow of God's inner being through the practice of the commandments. The specific content of the various esoteric doctrines developed in the early Kabbalah will not concern us here. Rather, I wish to focus on the concept of esotericism itself, on its justifications, and its social and cultural functions, as well as the varied and contradictory ways in which kabbalists and kabbalistic streams throughout the twelfth and thirteenth centuries tested the boundaries of esotericism and the means of its transmission. This period opens with *Sefer Habahir* in the second half of the twelfth century and ends about a hundred years later with the composition of the *Zohar*. The kabbalistic literature created during this period includes the traditions and writings of the kabbalists of Provence, the writings of the kabbalists of Gerona, the Kabbalah of Naḥmanides, the *Ḥug Ha'iyun* (Circle of Contemplation), and the writings of the Cohen brothers and those of Meir Ibn Sahula and Moses of Burgos. Notwithstanding the tremendous differences between the thought of Ibn Ezra and Maimonides and that of the early kabbalists, they do share an important common feature: their consciousness of explaining the hidden layer of the sacred scriptures and the encoding of their own explanations in one form or another. This is a thought-provoking fact. Why did esotericism flourish specifically during this period, in which every one of the major streams of Jewish thought presented their teachings as esoteric explanations of esoteric layers? Did esotericism serve similar functions in widely differing contexts? After discussing in detail the conceptions of esotericism and its limits in the early Kabbalah, we will focus our attention on the significance of the simultaneous flourishing of this wide variety of esoteric traditions.

Beyond the astounding structural parallels among the different esoteric traditions, the means of transmission of esoteric teachings and the testing of the limits of esotericism are constantly nourished by the mutual relations among the various movements. As we will see, the guarding of esotericism fosters the coexistence of radically differing worldviews. In the esoteric situation, the revealed level is the common unifying platform, while differing and contradictory positions develop beneath the surface; these differing positions may coexist only as long as they remain secret. Once, however, the boundaries of secrecy in any one movement are burst, this fragile coexistence is destabilized; this in turn sets off a kind of chain reaction, which results in significant changes in the definition of the boundaries of esotericism of the other movements and in its means of transmission and writing.[1] Before we investigate this dynamic in detail, we should examine the different ways in which esotericism was formulated in the writings of the early kabbalists.

The earliest discussion of esotericism and the paths of transmission of kabbalistic knowledge is found in a letter of Rabbi Isaac the Blind to Nahmanides and Rabbi Yonah Gerondi. Isaac the Blind, the first known author of a kabbalistic text, wrote a highly esoteric commentary on *Sefer Yetzira*. A descendent of the aristocracy of Jewish learning and scholarship in Provence—his father was Ravad (Avraham ben David), the great talmudist from Posquières, and his grandfather was Avraham ben Yitzhak, author of *Sefer Ha'eshkol*—Isaac the Blind became the dominant figure of the kabbalistic center in Provence and attributed his kabbalistic traditions to his great aristocratic ancestry. He was called "Hehasid" (the pious one) by his revering students, two of whom, Ezra and Azriel, carried his teaching from Provence to Catalonia and established a kabbalistic school in Gerona. Given the decisive role of Isaac the Blind in the emergence of Kabbalah, such a letter, which was published and discussed by Gershom Scholem, is a precious document that reveals the shape of the esoteric tradition and its inner logic. The letter raises the issue of the internal tensions relating to esotericism in the early Kabbalah, and describes essential changes in the patterns of esotericism in kabbalistic knowledge that occurred during the initial decades of the thirteenth century. Rabbi Isaac the Blind rails against the dissemination of the Kabbalah, and contrasts its dissemination with the deeds of his forefathers:

And I come neither in rebellion nor in betrayal, and until now I have not spoken; I do so now only out of my great fear and trepidation; for

I have seen the sage and wise and pious who wagged their tongues and stretched out their hands to write of great and awesome things in their books and letters. But what is written abides in no cabinet; for often, it may be lost or its owner may die, and the books thus come into the hands of fools and mockers, and consequently, the Name of Heaven is desecrated. And so it happened through them. While I was with them, I warned them in person many times. But once I departed from them, a mishap occurred at their hands. For I was not accustomed to this, for my fathers were the nobles of the land and disseminators of the Torah among many, and no such thing ever departed from their lips. For they would act toward others as if they were not versed in wisdom, and I observed them and took heed. I have also heard from the lands around you and from the people of the city of Burgos that they speak openly in marketplaces and in the streets as agitated and confused people, and from their words it is clear that their hearts have turned away from the divine and they have cut down the shoots. For the matters are united as a flame to its blazing coal, for there is but one Lord and there is none other beside Him.[2]

Rabbi Isaac the Blind describes his father and grandfather, early kabbalists who lived in the second half of the twelfth century, as strict esotericists. Not only did they not commit hinted disclosures of Torah secrets to writing, but they even presented themselves to their surroundings as if they were completely unaware of esoteric knowledge. This esoteric mold was soon broken by none other than Rabbi Isaac the Blind himself, who wrote an enigmatic commentary on *Sefer Yetzira*,[3] and especially by his disciples, Rabbi Ezra and Rabbi Azriel. As Gershom Scholem surmised, the main thrust of Rabbi Isaac the Blind's criticism is directed toward them. Rabbi Isaac the Blind briefly presents the conditions leading to this dissemination: "And once I departed from them, a mishap occurred at their hands." The unraveling of the organic ties of transmission, controlled by the transmitter, and the need of his students to establish their own center created the conditions in which the barriers of esotericism were breached. Rabbi Isaac the Blind publicly opposes the writing of Torah secrets because such literature may fall into the hands of those who do not understand it correctly, or into the hands of those who seek to mock it; thus its dissemination results in a desecration of the name of God. Scholem advanced the hypothesis that these words were written in response to the polemic letter of Rabbi Meir ben Shimon against the Kabbalah, in which he argued that the Kabbalah is a heresy which undermines the unity of God. Aside from its sharp criticism, the letter describes the destruction of books of Kabbalah, which were carried out around the fourth decade of the thirteenth century, with the approval of Rabbi

Meir's uncle, Rabbi Meshulam ben Moshe, the author of the *Hashlamah*. According to Scholem, Rabbi Isaac the Blind accused his disciples of a lack of discretion leading to desecration of the name of God.

Isaac the Blind showed esteem toward the kabbalists of Gerona, calling them "sage and wise and pious, by whose hands a mishap occurred." His attitude toward the kabbalists of Burgos was totally hostile. Whereas the former erred in diffusing their knowledge though their Kabbalah was true, the kabbalists of Burgos, in his estimation, spread heresy: "They speak openly in marketplaces and in the streets as agitated and confused people, and from their words it is clear that their hearts have turned away from the divine and they have cut down the shoots. For the matters are united as a flame to its blazing coal." Whatever the exact circumstances surrounding the writing of the letter may be, it indicates that the concealment of the kabbalistic conception stems from the fact that the doctrine of the *sefirot* creates a theosophy that treads the thin and dangerous line between the unity and the plurality of the godhead. The exposure of this position may influence fools to believe in a plurality of gods, as a result of their erroneous understanding of the authoritative sources of esoteric doctrine. In the less harmful case, this dissemination can provide the kabbalists' opponents with ammunition for their accusations of heresy. Esoteric doctrine lies on the border of heresy; thus it must be restricted to the elite. The esotericists must therefore see to the initiation of individuals who are able to walk at the edge of the yawning abyss of plurality without stumbling, and to distinguish the fine, fine line between faith and heresy.

Echoes of the letter rebuking the disseminators of esotericism may be heard in the writings of Asher ben David, the nephew of Isaac the Blind. In his letter, Rabbi Isaac stated that Asher ben David is his faithful spokesman. In Asher ben David's writings, however, we find a dramatic change that pushes the frontiers of esotericism a step further. The writings of Asher ben David reveal far more than what was breached by Rabbi Ezra and Rabbi Azriel; in their explicit, didactic nature, they are quite distant from the strict esotericism of the kabbalists of Provence, among them the Ravad, the grandfather of Rabbi Asher ben David. At the conclusion of *Sefer Hayihud*, which repeatedly and extensively emphasize the nature and unity of the *sefirot*, Rabbi Asher addresses himself and clarifies his orientation toward the question of esotericism:

> And in all these matters I have wrote and rewrote again and again, and mentioned each and every time the reason for the matter. . . . Thus, I came to speak at length in several areas where I should have been more brief; I would not have done so, if not for those who speak boastfully, with haughtiness and mockery; they opened wide their mouths and wagged their tongues and spoke things untrue of the agreeable and

delightful disciples, who received their teachings from the instructed of Israel, seekers of the Lord, pious of the Most High, who cry out to Him and are answered, who take pain in all the troubles of their fellows, and seek the visage of their Creator on their behalf and receive His response. Their prayers are accepted and several miracles have been performed by them, both for individuals and for the public. For against the students who studied before them and received the tradition from their mouths, the slanderers have spoken evil, things that were not so, and they nearly stretched their hands out against their teachers!" (*Sefer Hayiḥud*, p. 120)

As heresy and denial of God was wrongly imputed to the kabbalists, both to the disciples and to their masters, Rabbi Asher ben David saw a need to set things straight, even at the cost of violating the restrictions of secrecy. His words were apparently written in defense of Rabbi Isaac the Blind, whose great piety is described in the passage, as well as his students Rabbi Ezra and Rabbi Azriel. In spite of this, Rabbi Asher does not spare the rod from Rabbi Ezra and Rabbi Azriel. He describes the chain reaction in which he finds himself, which pushes, in an almost uncontrolled manner, toward publication of the esoteric:

For it may be that they brought this upon themselves, by not being sufficiently discreet before all persons in their language, whether in writing or in speech. Even if their intentions were good, their lips stammered and their wisdom was shunned; for they have not the ability to speak or write in a way that satiates the instructed, while satisfying the needs of the fool, so that one not mislead the other with words that have two faces, by making their words obscure in places where they should not have, or by explaining too much in places where they would do better to conceal their secrets. He who read their books or heard their words did not fathom their meaning and stumbled in their purposes, and imagined in their hearts that they believed in two divine realms, and they became in their eyes apostates of the true religion, that they corporealize the Primum Mobile through skillful stratagems, and they plotted against them and spoke against them and said that they place hornets (intermediaries)[4] between themselves and their Creator. (*Sefer Hayiḥud*, p. 120)

The criticism of the kabbalists was engendered by disciples who scattered kabbalistic hints before everyone, both orally and in writing. These intimations, which were supposed to filter the reading public faced with esotericism—to draw those with understanding closer while repelling the fools—created erroneous understandings and confusion. They were insufficient to dispel the doubts of the instructed, or to teach the uninstructed what the subject matter was, and they were better left entirely unsaid. At this point, Rabbi Asher ben David raised a profound argument concerning the essential nature of the medium of hinting. This medium, by nature, suffers from an internal problematic: if the hint is too transparent, it betrays its function as a medium of concealment. On the other hand, if it is too opaque, it does not add to the knowledge of the instructed one, or else it leads to erroneous understandings and false explanations. The hint seems to be fundamentally invalid, and it was better not to hint in writing at all. This incisive short passage points to the inherent self-defeating attempt at proper calibration of the hint as a medium of esotericism, a feature that will haunt the esoteric project as a whole. Once matters have been made public, however, Rabbi Asher had no choice but to unveil the entire picture and to shatter the barriers of writing entirely: "Thus, I allowed my tongue to wag, and my lips to speak, to make the knowledge of our masters known to the many, for they taught us the paths of life, the ways of God, so that I may be innocent in the eyes of God and man" (*Sefer Hayihud*, p. 120).

A deeper look at the letter of Rabbi Isaac the Blind and the words of his nephew Asher ben David reveals the marked and decisive change that took place in the kabbalistic corpus over a period of only several decades—from the end of the twelfth century to the thirties of the thirteenth century, from the severe esotericism of the Ravad, who concealed the very fact of his being an esotericist, to the systematic and exoteric exposition of esoteric doctrine by his grandson, Rabbi Asher. Between these two poles, the turning point that effected this amazing change was the failed attempt at writing esoteric intimations by the disciples of Isaac the Blind. Although earlier, Rabbi Abraham ben Yitzhak, the author of *Sefer Ha'eshkol*, was credited with kabbalistic writing, there we find only a listing of names of symbolic significance, which may be interpreted only by one who is privy to the secrets of the kabbalists.[5] To the outside observer, this work seems meaningless, a sort of agglomeration of meaningless names. Hinting, as opposed to this type of writing, is explicable; thus it is an unsuitable medium, since intimations, by their very nature, may be falsely interpreted, and a false interpretation on matters related to the esoteric is always heretical. Following the hinting, there had to be further clarification, and consequently the barriers of secrecy were ruptured completely.

Besides Rabbi Asher's criticism of the worthy disciples who spoke and wrote improperly, and thus were misunderstood, Rabbi Asher, like his uncle Isaac the Blind, also mentioned another group of Kabbalah scholars who committed the sin of heresy:

And although those disciples served their masters properly, they caused this (mishap) by their own superfluity. For they were not reticent in their words and expounded publicly. But some did not serve their masters properly, and did not fill their bellies (with the revealed Torah) sufficiently; thus, they knew not God and did not discern His handiwork. They hastened and sought to quickly climb the ladder to the upper stories, yet they did not even attain the lower rungs of the ladder, and many opened their mouths against them and mocked them. (*Sefer Hayihud*, p. 120)

This argument raises another dimension of the dynamics of disclosure: the attempt to establish, through open dissemination, a kind of canonical text, which attempts to expulse from the camp deviations which may arise as a result of the cloak of secrecy. The faithfulness of the esotericists to the limitations of esotericism leaves the public arena open to those whom the kabbalists consider as charlatans, pretenders, and heretics. While the kabbalists are bound by the fetters of secrecy, those others speak in the name of the revealed mystery. As such phenomena appear primarily in relatively peripheral areas such as Burgos, the aristocracy of esotericists—in this case, a member of the family of the Ravad—must crush such phenomena by publishing a transparent, authoritative text of esoteric doctrine that would fix its legitimate contents. Such a composition is meant to create an orthodox corpus of the movement, which could serve as an external, public standard for distinguishing between truth and heresy. The lack of such a work, as a consequence of the tight guarding of esotericism, facilitated the development of less restricted positions that dared to speak in the name of esotericism and adopted the esotericists' authority. This resulted in slanders against the kabbalists. It is this tight guard around the esoteric that created a sharp change from complete silence to total exposure; consequently, over the course of two generations, the nature of kabbalistic transmission changed completely.

Although Rabbi Asher emphasizes the revealed nature of his composition,[6] he immediately retreats within a cloak of secrecy, in the fear that some may attribute other meanings to his work:

For I beg and implore all the sages of the exile of Ariel, those instructed with wisdom, that if they see in my book an error and misdoing . . . that they will point out to me my errors, and if I can, I shall fix them or support my words, or else erase them from my book. And if, God forbid, their hearts be haughty so that they do not inform me and they open their mouths to accuse me, perhaps their limited understanding led them astray and they failed to discern their meaning in my words. . . . For the noble shepherds have warned us, saying that there are things that may be transmitted orally which one may not commit to writing, as no man is permitted to explain all of them, or even some of them entirely; even if he devote his heart to explain and write, he will not be able to write them accurately or plumb the depths of their concealed secrets. (*Sefer Hayiḥud*, p. 120)

This passage ends with a proclamation returning us to the level of hinting. Rabbi Asher's sudden return to secrecy is provoked by the fear that his disclosure and explication may be misunderstood, and is not a result of an intentional desire to conceal. After all, Rabbi Asher ben David was of the opinion that the attempt at hinting and concealment in writing was at the root of all the troubles. The esoteric cannot be completely revealed, even by those who desire to expose it; thus speech about it, even if transparent and direct, always bears the danger of misinterpretation. In his words: "Even if they devote their hearts to explain and write, they are not able to write precisely and to plumb the depths of their concealed secrets and not reveal them." The ineffable, inexplicable nature of the mystery casts doubts on the attempt to expose it and guard it from all error. As we know, additional explication also opens new possibilities for the generation of errors, especially when dealing with an area whose essence cannot be spoken of. The ambivalence that resulted from the fear of revealing the secrets led Rabbi Asher to cast doubts upon the role he attributed to his very own text.

Open Knowledge and Closed Knowledge: The Kabbalists of Gerona—Rabbi Azriel and Rabbi Ya'akov bar Sheshet

THE WORKS OF the kabbalists of Gerona, all of them active at the first half of the thirteenth century—Rabbi Ezra, Rabbi Azriel, and, subsequently, Rabbi Ya'akov bar Sheshet—induced the dramatic change in the means of transmission of kabbalistic knowledge, as we discussed above. Rabbi Asher ben David explained the change effected by these kabbalists as the product of an uncontrollable desire for publicity. A closer look at their words and their styles of writing, however, discloses their underlying positions with respect to the nature of kabbalistic knowledge, which resulted in these changes in the means of its transmission. A detailed examination of the ways in which Rabbi Azriel and Rabbi Ya'akov bar Sheshet tested the boundaries of esotericism exposes important patterns in the history of esotericism.

One of the most exoteric writings of this circle is the *Perush Eser Sefirot* (Explanation of the Ten Sefirot) of Rabbi Azriel.[1] This composition deviates entirely from the norm in kabbalistic writing, as it contains no exegetical elements; rather, it is a systematic exposition, clearly philosophically Neoplatonic, of the nature of the *sefirot*. The lack of any exegetical element in the work is not merely a question of style of presentation; it is an expression of a fundamental position. According to Rabbi Azriel, the *sefirot* may be deduced by reason alone, without reference to the sacred scriptures. At the outset of his work, the *sefirot* are presented as something that may be deduced by reason. Only subsequently does the discussion turn to the examination of the evidence for this doctrine in the Bible and in talmudic literature: "And if the inquirer continue to ask even after I have demonstrated to him by reasoning that these things are true and clear, if I have any evidence from Scripture or from the words of our Sages of blessed memory . . ." (*Perush Eser Sefirot*, p. 4). The doctrine of the *sefirot* is not presented as a secret tradition transmitted from Sinai or as the symbolic dictionary of the sacred scriptures. In this short composition, it is derived from introspection into the complex relations between the infinite and the finite. In general, the exegetical nature of kabbalistic texts, even the exoteric ones, hide and conceal the gap between contents and language, as the kabbalist constantly employs the forest of symbols offered him by sacred scripture. In the *Perush Eser Sefirot* of Rabbi Azriel, the translation of a system of symbols into conceptual language creates a rare and clear transparency. The act of disclosure is thus linked to the transition from a symbolic language to a conceptual one; this transition stems from the strictly Neoplatonic tendencies of Rabbi Azriel.

The breaching of the restrictions of secrecy in Rabbi Azriel was effected, among other means, through a new explanation of the traditional limits of esotericism; this explanation would later be repeated in other kabbalistic texts that sought to breach the barriers of secrecy. According to Rabbi Azriel, the normative limits of secrecy in talmudic literature relate to the essential hidden dimension in the godhead itself. That is, whatever was forbidden to reveal became the realm that is impossible to reveal. The traditional categories of the esoteric are no longer understood as rules limiting what is permissible to say, but as rules reflecting the limits of what can be said in words. In Rabbi Azriel's understanding, there is an intimate relation between the limits of thought and the limits of speech:

> Know that the infinite cannot be contained in thought, much less in speech. For even if it is intimated in (the words) that there is nothing outside of Him, that is, that there is no sign or name or writing or thing that may limit Him. . . . Thus it is written "unto you silence [is praise]," and our Sages explained that "the cure for all is silence," and they said that "the fence of wisdom is silence," and they said, "Do not expound what is concealed from you and do not investigate what is hidden from you." For it is written, "Is anything conveyed to Him when I speak? Can a man say anything that be not swallowed up?" which means that if what has no end is contained in speech and narrative, even if he "swallows" it, by including one thing in another and one saying in another, can he capture it in words? (*Perush Eser Sefirot*, p. 4)

The secrecy restrictions in Scripture and in talmudic literature are taken in this passage to refer to the impossibility of conceptualizing and expressing the infinite. According to Rabbi Azriel, these limitations do not refer to the realm that may not be spoken of, but the realm that *cannot* be spoken of; thus he is free of all prohibitions of disclosure. Whatever can be said may be said, and whatever may neither be spoken of nor thought about may, in any case, be only referred to in intimations.[2]

The diversion of the limits of secrecy to the ineffable dimension, in order to free oneself from the obligation of concealment, is a model frequently suggested in exoteric writing on hidden matters. This conception appears in the writings of one of the kabbalists of the Gerona circle, Rabbi Ya'akov bar Sheshet. If, however, the context of disclosure in the writings of Rabbi Azriel was the conceptual translation of kabbalistic teaching into Neoplatonic terms, in the writings of Rabbi Ya'akov bar Sheshet, the background for his disclosure is the concept that kabbalistic knowledge is knowledge open to all, subject to the same forms of innovation and argumentation as we might find in talmudic dialectics. The composition parallel to Rabbi Azriel's work in the writings of Rabbi Ya'akov bar Sheshet is the book *Sha'ar Hashamayim* (Gate to Heaven), an explanation of the Ten *sefirot*, one by one. Although the nature of this work is far less abstract and systematic than that of Rabbi Azriel, it too serves as a kind of introduction to the Kabbalah. The aim of disseminating kabbalistic matters beyond the circle of esotericists is mentioned at the beginning of the composition:

> For the secret of the ten utterances shall be explained forever in truth and uprightness. I shall explain each matter according to my ability, and what I received, what I acquired through effort and reasoning, I added to and expanded; I shall not let the words of holiness be cut off from their hearers, so that the last generation of children that be born may know and tell it to their children, and I shall bring evidence from the Law of Moses and from the words of our rabbis that I know, and of that of the nations there be none with me. I shall not remove my words from a mistaken person or a foolish one. And I shall include several other matters as you shall see, in conjunction with similar matters. And I shall explain some of the commandments and their principles, and I shall repair their torn fences, and I shall render accessible some of the sweet matters of truth, and rebuild its ruins, so that there my words may enlighten those to whom I leave it. I shall open doors and break the locks and the gates shall no (longer) be closed. (*Sha'ar Hashamayim*, pp. 154–155)

This passage, which precedes the detailed explanation of the system of *sefirot*, is laden with metaphors and verbs of disclosure and opening. The realm that Rabbi Ya'akov seeks to expose he describes as follows: "What I received, what I acquired through effort and reasoning, I added to and expanded." In his understanding, Kabbalah consists of two dimensions of knowledge—that transmitted through the tradition of esotericism and that which the kabbalist innovates through his deductions. Kabbalistic teaching is an open teaching, which may be added to and supports innovation. Later in his composition, Rabbi Ya'akov presents his words as knowledge of an open nature, which the reader may expand through analogies and reasoning, just as Torah scholars do with revealed matters: "I shall provide for each and every utterance some of the things that resemble it, and that adjoin it. And the matters that are omitted will be available to all those who desire them, so that they may understand and deduce from what there is to what there is not. Let your wellsprings flow forth!" (*Sha'ar Hashamayim*, p. 155). The study of the Kabbalah is not a process of strict transmission of sealed, closed knowledge, but rather a process of discovery and innovation. The expanding nature of kabbalistic knowledge, which results from his learning process and gives rise to creativity and innovation, also influences the extent of its dissemination. The relation between his conception of learning and the breadth of its dissemination, which is based upon the ambiguity of the concept of disclosure itself, is especially marked in Rabbi Ya'akov's words: "May your wellsprings flow forth."[3] By means of this verse, Rabbi Ya'akov encourages his reader to expand his kabbalistic knowledge through innovative, creative learning while at the same time diffusing that knowledge.[4]

Rabbi Ya'akov bar Sheshet's approach to kabbalistic knowledge as open knowledge is manifested in various places throughout his writings, and, as we stated, it profoundly influenced the question of esotericism. In his book *Ha'emunah vehabitahon* (Faith and Trust), he wrote as follows: "Know that the words of our Sages of blessed memory are the words of the living God and may not be contradicted, but it is a commandment for every person to innovate in the Torah according to his ability" (*Kitvei HaRamban* 2:264). In the same composition he writes: "Let this not be difficult in your eyes, for had I not innovated this of my own heart, I would have said that it was a law given to Moses on Mount Sinai" (*Kitvei HaRamban* 2:310). One of the most interesting expressions of this conception is that Rabbi Ya'akov bar Sheshet grants kabbalistic knowledge the qualities of variety and plurality, by translating the concept of disputation from the field of halakha to the theosophical questions of esoteric teaching. Since some of the matters of the Kabbalah are dependent on the opinions of those who innovate them, they are open to the same process of give and take that is widely accepted in questions of legal reasoning.[5] Similarly, since kabbalistic knowledge is being updated and expanded all the time, and is not sealed in the secret traditions of those who transmit what they have heard, the disputations that arise in such matters are not necessarily the result of mishaps in transmission or the expression of different traditions; rather, they are differences that arise from the natural process of creation and the exegetical development of the Kabbalah. These differences of opinion may be accounted for by the same understanding of plurality that accounts for differences in halakhic matters. In the words of Rabbi Ya'akov:

Even if there be differences between explanations, neither should be rejected. Perhaps one of them was chosen by Heaven, and we cannot know which is correct, whether it be this one or that one, or if both are correct, for there are seventy facets to the Law. For they said explicitly: "Lest one say, because these prohibit and those permit, because these invalidate and those accept, because these render impure and those render pure, how then should I learn the Law?" Thus: all were given by a single shepherd, both these and those are the words of the living God, all were uttered by one God. (*Kitvei HaRamban* 2:445)[6]

The presentation of kabbalistic knowledge as open knowledge to which innovative interpretations of the Law are being added all the time, and which is characterized by disputations that depend on judgment and exegetical techniques, undermines the esoteric conception in the eyes of theosophists. Esotericists seal the realm of knowledge they study, in part in conscious opposition to the way that revealed open knowledge circulates. Disclosure and dissemination necessarily engender plurality, differences of opinion, and incessant addition of traits to the revealed core. Esotericists seek to isolate a closed, guarded realm of Torah from this chaos, a realm immune to the disorder of widespread knowledge. The innovative analogy that Rabbi Ya'akov bar Sheshet draws between the two realms—the theosophical and the halakhic—in fact undermines the basic motivation of esotericism. Kabbalah, like other revealed halakhic matters, is open knowledge, subject to innovation, plurality, and variety. The esoteric is not a realm that must be guarded, but one that must be revealed and exposed, with the awareness of the ever-increasing plurality of the secret contents that are revealed.[7]

The decisive turning point in the means of transmission of kabbalistic knowledge, which took place in the first half of the thirteenth century, was described by Rabbi Asher ben David as an unwanted chain reaction to a series of leaks, intimations, and forgeries that obliged the aristocracy of esotericists to create a canonical and revealed orthodoxy of the esoteric. By contrast, in the writings of Rabbi Azriel and Rabbi Ya'akov bar Sheshet, the first creators of the written kabbalistic corpus, we find a new conception of the essence and nature of kabbalistic knowledge, and the question of disclosure is formulated in a far broader context. Rabbi Azriel translates the concepts of the doctrine of the *sefirot* into the Neoplatonic world, whereas Rabbi Ya'akov bar Sheshet understands kabbalistic knowledge as knowledge of an open nature, paralleling that found in the Oral Law in general.[8] Moshe Idel has argued that Naḥmanides was opposed to the exoteric tendency of Rabbi Azriel and Rabbi Ya'akov bar Sheshet.[9] This view of Naḥmanides, the greatest talmudic scholar of the thirteenth century and one of its most important kabbalists, as a counterweight to the kabbalists of Gerona enables us to examine the question of esotericism as a particular conception of the essence of knowledge. Indeed, Naḥmanides' attitude toward the esoteric posture of kabbalists deserves special attention. Unlike Ezra and Azriel, who were known only for their contributions to Kabbalah, Naḥmanides' authority and breadth of achievements are of a far deeper and broader scope. Naḥmanides (1195–1270) would still be considered the greatest Jewish scholar of the thirteenth century even if he had not dealt with Kabbalah at all. His widely read commentary on the Torah is path-breaking in its originality and subtlety. His teachings led to a flourishing talmudic school in Catalonia and inspired a generation of scholars. His halakhic stature was central to the reception of Kabbalah as an authentic Jewish esoteric tradition, providing the shield of institutional rabbinic endorsement. By dispersing dozens of short esoteric kabbalistic hints in his popular commentary on the Torah, he lent authority and prestige to the Kabbalah even for the vast majority of his readers who could not decipher a word of these coded hints. Thus any conception of Naḥmanides as representing an opposing view on esotericism must take into consideration his central role in the history of Kabbalah.

Tradition, Closed Knowledge, and the Esoteric: Secrecy and Hinting in Naḥmanides' Kabbalah

IN THE INTRODUCTION to his commentary on the Penateuch, Naḥmanides specifies his position with respect to the question of the esoteric nature of the Kabbalah:

> Now behold I bring into a faithful covenant and give proper counsel to all who look into this book not to reason or entertain any thought concerning any of the hints which I write regarding the hidden matters of the Torah, for I do hereby firmly make known to him [the reader] that my words will not be comprehended nor known at all by any reasoning or contemplation, excepting from the mouth of a wise Kabbalist speaking into the ear of an understanding recipient. Reasoning about them is foolishness; any unrelated thought brings much damage and withholds the benefit. "Let him not trust in vanity, deceiving himself," for these reasonings will bring him nothing but evil as if they spoke falsely against God, which cannot be forgiven, as it is said, "The man that strayeth out of understanding shall rest in the congregation of the shades." . . . Let them take moral instruction from the mouths of our holy Rabbis: "Into that which is beyond you, do not seek; into that which is more powerful than you, do not inquire; about that which is concealed from you, do not desire to know; about that which is hidden from you, do not ask. Contemplate that which is permitted to you, and engage not yourself in hidden things." (Chavel 1:15–16)

Unlike Rabbi Ya'akov bar Sheshet's conception of the nature of the Kabbalah, Naḥmanides presents the Kabbalah as a realm of closed knowledge. Whereas Rabbi Ya'akov bar Sheshet encourages the learner to deduce one thing from another and to expand and innovate in the knowledge of Kabbalah, Naḥmanides warns him not to make any attempt at deduction or commentary based on the power of reasoning. For him, the creation of kabbalistic teaching without the sanction of tradition leads to the irreparable danger of heresy. In Naḥmanides' introduction, he repeatedly emphasizes the nature of Kabbalah as tradition. The mysteries of the Torah were revealed to Moses on Mount Sinai: "God informed Moses first of the manner of the creation of heaven and earth and all their hosts, that is, the creation of all things, high and low. Likewise, [He informed him of] everything that had been said by prophecy concerning the secrets of the divine Chariot [in the vision of Ezekiel] and the process of Creation, and what has been transmitted about them to the Sages" (Chavel 1:9). Further on in his introduction, Naḥmanides describes the possibility of a different reading of the Torah based on another division of the sequence of letters, which will result in a continuous series of names of God. Of such a radical reading of the sacred scriptures, he says that it was given unto Moses: "It was given to Moses our teacher using the division of words which express the commandment, and orally it was transmitted to him in the rendition which consists of the Divine Names" (Chavel 1:15).[1]

The concept of the Kabbalah as an esoteric tradition transmitted from generation to generation is in tension with another motif in Naḥmanides' introduction to the Torah: the totalistic nature of the biblical text, a text that contains everything and whose revealed level is only one interpretive possibility, the tip of the iceberg of the entire text. In his words, "all of it was written in the Torah, explicitly or by implication" (Chavel 1:9). Further on, he writes: "[All] was written in the Torah explicitly or by implication in words, in the numerical value of the letters or in the form of the letters, that is, whether written normally or with some change in form such as bent or crooked letters and other deviations, or in the tips of the letters and their crownlets" (Chavel 1:10). The concept of the complete semantic fullness of the Torah seemingly enables an approach to the esoteric which depends not on tradition, but on the use of an exegetical technique. Naḥmanides, however, blocks the infinite exegetical breadth which would result from his exegetical approach by determining that not only is the knowledge transmitted from generation to generation, but the exegetical hints are part of that tradition: "For these hints cannot be understood except from mouth to mouth [through an oral tradition which can be traced] to Moses, who received it on Sinai" (Chavel 1:11).[2]

Naḥmanides is one of the important halakhic scholars who consciously formulated his conception of halakha as open knowledge, in which innovations arise through the power of reasoning. He was apparently the first to call his work of halakhic exegesis *ḥidushim* (innovations).[3] Moreover, his approach to Torah innovations accords with his position with respect to the fundamental variety of halakhic knowledge and his understanding of disputation as the multifaceted nature of the text, whose meaning is determined by the Sages. This understanding of Naḥmanides is opposed to other concepts in the history of halakha, from the schools of the *geonim* and Maimonides, in its emphasis on the understanding of halakhah as open knowledge.[4] The well-formulated concept of Naḥmanides on the nature of talmudic disputations sharpens the contrast he created between exoteric and esoteric knowledge. According to Naḥmanides, unlike the approach of Rabbi Ya'akov bar Sheshet, the esoteric limitations placed on the secrets of the Torah are linked organically to its nature as the closed realm.[5] The distinction between tradition and reasoning dictated by Naḥmanides also reflects a fundamental position invalidating the reliance on reason in all that concerns theosophy; it is also in sharp contrast to the way that Rabbi Azriel presented the esoteric realm. The secrets of the godhead can only be known through tradition, and any attempt to discuss them through reasoning will result in heresy and destruction. Thus, Naḥmanides does not apply the esoteric instructions in talmudic literature with which he closes his introduction to the realm of the ineffable, as the kabbalists of Gerona did. Instead, Naḥmanides applies these instructions toward the free study of guarded knowledge that is transmitted through tradition. Let no man reveal the hints of Naḥmanides, neither to himself and certainly not to others, if he does not possess a tradition orally transmitted from one Sage to another.

The conception of the Kabbalah as a fixed tradition, into which no innovations may be introduced, serves Naḥmanides himself in situations in which he objects to alternative kabbalistic interpretations which are opposed to his own traditions, as well as in places where he chooses to remain silent, since he has no traditions from his rabbis to enlighten him in the matter.[6] The concept of kabbalistic knowledge as closed knowledge determines Naḥmanides' strategy in writing hints. He writes of the secrets of the Torah in hints, in order to make it difficult for the reader to make inductions or even find an initial thread that would enable him to expand the idea further. To the short, hermetic notes on esoteric matters in Naḥmanides, it is difficult to assign any interpretation whatsoever, even a misguided one. When viewed against the background of his attitude toward the Kabbalah, Naḥmanides' consistent stance as an esotericist, as opposed to the tendency of his predecessors in Gerona, raises the following question: If knowledge of the Kabbalah is entirely dependent on oral transmission from rabbi to disciple, and may not be derived from hints, why should it be written down? Why does Naḥmanides scatter so many enigmatic hints to esoteric doctrines in his commentaries on the Pentateuch? In other words, why did Naḥmanides not employ a more severe strategy, like that of the Ravad or Naḥmanides' relative, Rabbi Yonah Girondi, who concealed the very fact that they possessed secrets, that is, that they were possessors of kabbalistic doctrine? After all, in spite of Naḥmanides' warnings not to systematically expand his words, or perhaps because of them, not a few writings were consecrated to the deciphering of the secrets of Naḥmanides. Any thinker who announces the existence of a secret and hints at its content, notwithstanding the enigmatic nature of his sayings and the severe warnings he issues, inevitably tests the limits of secrecy. He wants to tell and not tell at the same time, even if he formulates his esoteric position in opposition to more blatant attempts at disclosure of secrets. What were the limits of secrecy of the greatest esotericist of the thirteenth century?

At the beginning of his commentary on the Pentateuch, Naḥmanides deals with the famous question quoted by Rashi: Why did the Torah begin with Genesis and not with the first commandment given to the Israelites, "This month shall be unto you"? Naḥmanides applies this question to the need for the inclusion of the creation narrative in the Pentateuch. For Naḥmanides, it is clear that this question cannot be directed toward the very mention of the principle of creation in the Pentateuch, for without this principle the whole idea of revelation is undermined. Thus, Naḥmanides is of the opinion that Rabbi Yitzḥak's question concerned the specification of the detailed account of creation in the Torah. He writes:

> The process of creation is a deep mystery not to be understood from the verses, and it cannot truly be known except through the tradition going back to Moses our teacher who received it from the mouth of the Almighty, and those who know it are obliged to conceal it. It is for this reason that Rabbi Yitzḥak said that it was not necessary for the Torah to begin with the chapter of "In the beginning God created" and the narration of what was created on the first day, what was done on the second and other days, as well as a prolonged account of the creation of Adam and Eve, their sin and punishment, and the story of the Garden of Eden and the expulsion of Adam from it. (Genesis 1:1; Chavel 1:18)

Naḥmanides repeats his concept that the Kabbalah is closed knowledge, and claims that this position was meant to prevent the writing down, even in hints, of anything relating to Torah secrets. This dictum, however, is especially applicable to the hints about Torah secrets in Naḥmanides' own commentary.

A preliminary answer to the question of the limits of esotericism was provided by Naḥmanides in his transgressions of his self-determined limits. The urge to reveal secrets in those cases is grounded in his dispute with other esoteric traditions—those of Maimonides and especially Ibn Ezra. Ibn Ezra was the first to integrate esoteric matters into a popular commentary on the Pentateuch; in doing so, he sought to demarcate the esoteric realm and define the body of the instructed (*maskilim*). Throughout his commentary, Naḥmanides conducts a complex and ambivalent dialogue with Ibn Ezra; consequently, he must propose an alternative from the esoteric realm, employing the same medium as Ibn Ezra—namely, a commentary on the Pentateuch.[7] Beyond the many exegetical questions in which Naḥmanides takes issue with Ibn Ezra, he also disputes Ibn Ezra's positions on the dissemination of Torah secrets, on the intricacies of the Torah, and on the definition of the composition and nature of the religious aristocracy. This dispute is expressed, among other ways, through Naḥmanides' somewhat ironic employment of Ibn Ezra's common formula "and the instructed (*maskil*) shall understand." The instructed person referred to by Naḥmanides is not one versed in the hermetic-astrological cultural milieu, but one familiar with the kabbalistic traditions that Naḥmanides transmits from his rabbis.

The processes of disclosure related to the struggle over publication of Torah secrets became most evident in two places that also deal with the relation of the instructed one (*maskil*) to the writings of the Sages. Ibn Ezra mockingly criticized Rashi's tendency to integrate midrashic teachings in his commentary, especially if Ibn Ezra saw them as teachings of a homlietic didactic nature and devoid of exegetical intentions: "For this is the way of the Sages in the lands of the Greeks and the Edomites [Christians], that they do not sufficiently weigh up matters, but trust in the way of the midrash as good instruction and illumination. But since these midrashim are to be found in the ancient books, why should the later scholars fatigue us by writing them over?" (introduction to the Pentateuch; Weiser 1:7). Ibn Ezra brings an example from the midrashim quoted by Rashi on the first word of the Torah, *Bereshit* (In the beginning), as referring to the Torah, the fear of God, the first fruits, and more. After quoting Rashi's words, Naḥmanides refers to this group of midrashim:

> Rashi wrote: "This verse calls aloud for elucidation, as our Rabbis have explained it: 'For the sake of the Torah which is called *reshit*, as it is said, "The Eternal made me as *reshit* (the beginning) of His way," and for the sake of Israel who is called *reshit*, as it is said, "Israel is the Eternal's hallowed portion, the *reshit* (first fruits) of His increase." This Midrash of our Rabbis is very hidden and secret, for there are many things the Rabbis found that are called *reshit* and concerning which they give midrashic interpretations, and those wanting in faith count their multitude. (Genesis 1:1; Chavel 1:20–21)

As part of his dispute with Ibn Ezra, who Naḥmanides refers to as "wanting in faith," he turns to an exegesis of the esoteric dimension in the explication of the word *bereshit*: "Their intent in the above texts is as follows: the word *bereshit* alludes to the creation of the world by Ten *Sefirot*, and hints in particular to the emanation called Wisdom, in which is the foundation of everything" (Genesis 1:1; Chavel 1:21). In a relatively long passage on esoteric matters, Naḥmanides continues to explain the symbolic meaning of these teachings, some of which are directed toward the emanation of *Ḥokhmah* (wisdom) and others toward the last of the *sefirot*, *Shekhina*. Both of them are of the dimension of *reshit* (beginning)— *Ḥokhmah* as the beginning of the world of the *sefirot* and the *Shekhina* as the beginning of the universe. Naḥmanides concludes the passage with the following words: "Now it is impossible to discuss this explanation at length in writing, and even a hint is dangerous since people might have thoughts concerning it which are untrue. But I have mentioned this in order to close the mouths of those wanting in faith and of little wisdom, who scoff at the words of our Rabbis" (Genesis 1:1; Chavel 1:22). Naḥmanides is forced to explain Torah secrets, he tells us, as a result of his dispute with Ibn Ezra.[8] The disclosure of a single Torah secret, even by hinting, forces even strict esotericists of the opposing camp to reveal more than they would care to.

Naḥmanides' apology for the traversing of the boundaries of secrecy as a result of this dispute brings the problematic nature of his position as an esotericist into sharp relief. Naḥmanides is of the opinion that the secrets of the Torah cannot be deduced by reason, but must be received by tradition. Thus, he is of the opinion that the transmission of hints is a completely invalid form of transmission: "Great is the damage of the hint, for many will deduce ideas from them which are devoid of truth." The essential purpose of the hint is to invite the wise reader to arrive at conclusions by his deductive capacities, relying on his faith in them. Consequently, an esotericist who understands the secrets of the Torah as closed knowledge must choose between two possibilities. Either he may transmit the secrets of the Torah in their entirety, without resorting to hints (but the writing of such secrets in explicit form is undoubtedly forbidden); or else he may remain completely silent. Providing oral hints is another possibility, as the teacher may follow the process and see what conclusions are deduced by the disciple. But the writing of hints is problematic in either case. Had Naḥmanides shared the opinion of Rabbi Ya'akov bar Sheshet, that the student should be encouraged to complete the teaching through his own learning and innovate, he would undoubtedly agree that hinting was the proper medium for the transmission of knowledge. This, however, was not his way. Naḥmanides maintained that whoever knew of Torah secrets from an instructed rabbi had no need of hints, whereas for those who did not receive such a tradition, such hints were of no use, and perhaps even damaging, since they invited the reader to deduce one thing from another. In his composition dedicated to matters of reward and punishment, *Sha'ar Hagemul* (The Gate of Retribution), Naḥmanides claims that the resolution of the problem of evil is related to the secret of intercalation, of which he says: "But this is one of the secrets of the Torah which is hidden from all but those who are worthy of receiving them through the Kabbalah; it is prohibited to explain them in writing, and hints are useless" (*Kitvei HaRamban* 2:279). Since the hint is an invalid means of transmission of secrets, Naḥmanides presents the reader with two possibilities: "But this doubt [the sufferings of the righteous] . . . [may be resolved] through the secret mentioned in the mystery of intercalation, if God be favorable toward him so that he may know from the true Kabbalah, after taking guard from all stumbling blocks and errors, for there be not many wise. But if he has not heard of it, let him entrust the matter to those who know" (*Kitvei HaRamban* 2:281). The reader is presented with two options: either he has heard the secret through a trustworthy oral tradition or else he should rely upon those who know it. Hinting, as an intermediate option, is ruled out in principle. Naḥmanides is not only forced to reveal what should not be revealed, he must also use a means of transmission of Torah secrets that is opposed to his own principles: hinting.

Naḥmanides does not deny that the technique of hinting is based on the instructed one's (*maskil's*) ability to supply the missing information from his own knowledge. In his commentary on the Pentateuch, he directs the instructed to derive certain conclusions by means of repeated formulae, such as "But if you will merit and understand the secret of the word *bereshit* and why Scripture does not begin by saying, 'God created in the beginning,' you will know that, in the way of truth, Scripture tells about the lower creations and alludes to the higher ones" (Genesis 1:3; Chavel 1:27). Elsewhere, he writes: "The truth is that the blessing on the Sabbath day is the fountain of blessings and constitutes the foundation of the world. 'And He sanctified it' that it draw its sanctity from the Sanctuary on high. If you will understand this comment of mine you will grasp what the Rabbis have said in Bereshit Rabbah concerning the Sabbath: '[Why did He bless the Sabbath? It is] because it has no partner' and that which they have further related [that God said to the Sabbath]: 'The congregation of Israel will be thy partner.' And then you will comprehend that on the Sabbath there is truly an extra soul" (Genesis 2:3; Chavel 1:60). In his explanation on the sabbatical year and the jubilee, Naḥmanides says: "Now here [in the Torat Kohanim mentioned above, the Rabbis] have roused our attention to one of the great secrets of the Torah. . . . Bend now your ear to understand that which I am permitted to inform you about it in the words that I will cause you to hear, and if you will be worthy you will contemplate them and understand them" (Leviticus 25:2; Chavel 4:415–416). Such guiding formulas are intended only for one who understands his own knowledge. They appear in many places in which Naḥmanides mentions Torah secrets.[9] Although Naḥmanides was obliged to write down his hints, he encouraged the instructed one to complete the hint through his own wisdom and reasoning, even in areas where reasoning is useless or even dangerous.

Naḥmanides minimizes the internal difficulty inherent in the act of hinting through his particular use of the medium of hinting. While the hint is designed to increase the knowledge of the instructed, Naḥmanides formulates his hints in a manner so enigmatic that it requires an exceptionally wide common background and knowledge. This, in turn, assures that any deductions made will be based on this common background. For someone not completely familiar with these assumptions, the hint will remain completely opaque, obviating any deduction whatsoever, even mistaken ones. Indeed, without the voluminous literature explaining the secrets of Nahmanides, composed by the school of the students of Rashba, which was based on oral traditions handed down from Nahmanides to his students, it would be difficult to decipher Nahmanides' hints. The hint is formulated in a way that enables its understanding only on the basis of a wide background and previous knowledge, which ensures that the deduction will be made in the appropriate direction. But beyond the enigmatic formulation of the hint, which filters out those who approach the text in order to understand it of their own knowledge, the unique use of hints by Nahmanides enabled him to determine the direction of future deductions from it.

In order to clarify the issue, we should distinguish between two directions of hints, the horizontal and the vertical. The vertical hint designates hidden contents, which refer to the godhead itself. In this case, the secret of the verse is the reflection of the divine life, the relations between the *sefirot*, the order of their emanation and the complex, intricate balance between them. From Scripture, man can learn what is in front and what is behind, what is below and what is above. The horizontal hint, on the other hand, refers to the network of symbols themselves. The function of the hint is to thicken the significance of the symbol and to join distant expressions or similar expressions from apparently different contexts into a single unity. Nahmanides' hints are usually of the horizontal sort, linking together an entire network of expressions and symbols and giving them a kabbalistic significance. A typical example of horizontal hinting may be found in Nahmanides' commentary on the verse "and God blessed Abraham in all (*bakol*)" (Genesis 24:1). Nahmanides explains the relation between the word *kol* and the *Shekhina* and then says: "And if you understand what I wrote, know that the saying of the cursed women who said 'since we ceased to offer incense to the queen of heaven we are lacking all (*kol*)' and why the word was written without the letter *aleph* and you will understand many enigmatic matters in the Pentateuch and the Scriptures" (Genesis 24:1). Nahmanides directs the instructed one's attention to an additional explanation of *kol* in Scripture, which is relevant to the symbolic meaning of the expression *kol* in the blessing of Abraham. The hint, in the words of Nahmanides, directs attention to "the enigmatic matters in the Pentateuch and the Scriptures." We may say that the function of the system of *sefirot* in Nahmanides' exegetical framework is to explain the links between biblical meanings and not the other way around. The hint directs the instructed one to delve into the depths of additional scriptural verses and midrashim, and thus to understand each through the other.

The horizontal nature of the majority of Naḥmanides' hints demonstrates that the main thrust of his hinting is not theosophical but exegetical.

Of course, Naḥmanides was also aware of the vertical aspect of esotericism, or, as he says elsewhere, the *tziyur* and the *mashal* (both terms synonymous with parables of symbols). A clear example of this appears in his description of the Garden of Eden and the Tabernacle. In Naḥmanides' opinion, both reality in general and humans in particular have an isomorphic structure, which reflects the system of *sefirot* and the secret of the godhead. The Garden of Eden and the Tabernacle are, in his opinion, spaces whose isomorphic-symbolic nature is more transparently clear, so that investigation of them enables a clearer and sharper view of the system of the godhead itself:

> For the Garden of Eden and the four rivers, the tree of life and the tree of wisdom which God planted there . . . all of these should be understood in their literal meaning, the words are faithful and true, and yet they are a concealed secret, for they are like designs which enable us to understand a deep secret through a parable . . . for so is the sacred design of the Tabernacle . . . and everything related to each and every position of the vessels and the form of the cherubim, they all enable us to understand secrets of matters in the world above and in the intermediate and lower worlds and all the hints referring to the chariot are there. (*Kitvei HaRamban* 2:296)[10]

Naḥmanides himself, however, never reveals or directs his hints and secrets to the vertical dimension. Such references remain opaque and obscure: "for their secret is deep and reserved for those who receive the transmitted faith" (*Kitvei HaRamban* 2:297). Naḥmanides does not provide, even through hints, the map for the understanding of the system of *sefirot* and the isomorphic structure of reality, as we find, for example, in Rabbi Ya'akov bar Sheshet's composition *Sha'ar Hashamayim*. According to Naḥmanides, such secrets are to be transmitted orally. The horizontal-exegetical nature of the hint in Naḥmanides' writings restricts the range of possible error. The instructed person who errs through improper use of reason may risk falsely attributing kabbalistic significance to a difficult scriptural passage. He may, for example, interpret an instance of the word *kol* in Scripture as part of the symbolic system of the *Shekhina*, even though, in that context, the word is void of any esoteric significance. By contrast, a mistake on the vertical level, which relates to the nature and qualities of the system of *sefirot*, is a flaw in the conception of the divinity, and has elements of denial and heresy. The enigmatic and horizontal nature of the hint is the way Naḥmanides chose to deal with the difficulties of esoteric hints, as part of his worldview that the Kabbalah is closed knowledge.[11]

In his writings, Naḥmanides shaped his esoteric conception and the means of its transmission of secrets in reaction to two different challenges, which pull his esoteric molds in opposing directions. The first challenge, posed by the exoteric kabbalists of Gerona, resulted in the reestablishment of the limits of secrecy. Naḥmanides' position was an attempt to stand in the breach and essentially refute the previous positions, which viewed Kabbalah as open knowledge. In opposition to them, Naḥmanides presented an entirely different approach, based on the conception of the Kabbalah as closed knowledge. On this front, Naḥmanides sought to restore the barriers of esotericism that had been breached, as Naḥmanides recognized only one appropriate medium for the transmission of the Kabbalah—oral transmission from a knowledgeable rabbi to an understanding disciple. On the other front, Naḥmanides struggled with Ibn Ezra, who, in his commentary on the Pentateuch, defined the realm of esotericism and the class of the instructed as a function of the cultural relation to hermetic and astrological traditions. Naḥmanides saw his commentary on the Pentateuch as a means of establishing a broad alternative to the world of Ibn Ezra, with which he was in constant dialogue. This alternative related, among other things, to the question of which esoteric trend represents the hidden meaning of Torah, and how the religious elite is defined. Ibn Ezra's hints forced Naḥmanides to reveal, even if only through hints, things he would rather not have exposed. As a result of the tension between these two struggles, Naḥmanides created his unique form of hinting.

From Tradition to Literature: Shem Tov Ibn Gaon and the Critique of Kabbalistic Literature

THE ATTEMPTS OF Naḥmanides to restore the limits of secrecy, and sub-sequently the attempts of the Rashba (Shlomo ibn Adret), Namanides' great student and his heir as the main talmudic authority of Spanish Jewry, and the Rashba's own students, do not reflect the state of esotericism in the thirteenth century. The conception of the Kabbalah as a tradition given to Moses on Mount Sinai, which Naḥmanides attempted to marshal in order to grant his kabbalistic position absolute authority, disintegrated when faced with alternative formulations of kabbalistic knowledge. The writings of the kabbalists of Castile, who were active in the mid-thirteenth century, are in part of a markedly exoteric nature. Isaac the Blind described the situation in Castile in extremely acerbic language: "For I have heard of the lands around you and of the people of the town of Burgos that they speak openly in the marketplaces and streets as frightened and confused people." It may be that his words were directed against the kabbalists of the *Ḥug Ha'iyun*, the most exoteric circle in the early Kabbalah.[1] This circle has bequeathed us a large number of creative and daring pseudepi-graphic works, which neither display any unity of thought nor rely on any clear and recognized line of transmission. This obscure circle did not attempt to preserve a relation of familial tradition or careful transmission from teacher to disciple; rather, these writings derive their authority from a mythical figure in whose name they speak and through which they attempt to break through the closed circle of tradition.

Meir Ibn Sahula, a Castilean kabbalist of the thirteenth century, described his kabbalistic learning as acquired from books rather than authors.[2] According to his testimony, he was already in possession of a sort of kabbalistic library of writings from Provence and Gerona, and his knowledge was not based on a continuous oral transmission but on crit-ical synthesis of differing textual traditions. In his commentary on *Sefer Yetzira*, he writes:

> For several years already, I have been studying these things relating to all secrets, starting with the *Sefer Habahir*, which explains some mat-ters, and the writings of Rabbi Asher, who wrote the *Perush Shlosh Esreh Middot* and the *Perush Hashevu'ah*, and Rabbi Ezra, Rabbi

Azariel, and Rabbi Moshe ben Naḥman, all of blessed memory. Also, I studied those chapters. And I acquired some of the commentary on *Sefer Yetzira* attributed to Rabbi Moshe bar Naḥman of blessed memory, but I was unable to acquire all of it. (MS Rome Angelika 1/145, p. 2b)

The existence of a kabbalistic library, whose items are enumerated by Ibn Sahula, and which serve as the basis for his kabbalistic knowledge, teaches us about the rapid shift from oral tradition to an independent literary corpus. Along with his understanding of the Kabbalah as a literary corpus, Rabbi Meir promotes the value of independent inquiry, as he writes at the opening of his commentary: "We must investigate the words according to our understanding, and walk in them in the paths walked by the prophets in their generation and in the generations before us, during the two hundred years of kabbalists to date, and they call the wisdom of the ten *sefirot* and some of the reasons for the commandments Kabbalah" (*Sefer Yetzira*, p. 2b). Rabbi Meir relies on the historical traditions he possesses relating to the kabbalistic tradition. Unlike Naḥmanides, Rabbi Meir grounds the roots of this tradition not in Sinai, but in the previous two hundred years of Kabbalah. The restriction of the scope of the tradition empowers the investigative position and his reliance on reasoning.[3] Furthermore, later in his composition he undermines the conception of authority that Naḥmanides claimed for his own kabbalistic position: "At each point, I shall mention the position of Naḥmanides of blessed memory, in his own name, and then try as best I can to contradict or support it." Ibn Sahula also presents an attitude toward esoteric questions different from that of Naḥmanides. In the context of an exegetical argument with Naḥmanides over the issue of *keter* and *en sof*, he raises an argument reminiscent of the words of Rabbi Asher against the writing of hints: "It seems to me that he should not have revealed it here in this way but through more expansive language and a lengthier introduction, that he build a more sturdy fence so that others may not stumble over it, as it is written, 'What is amazing to you, do not expound'" (*Sefer Yetzira*, p. 108b).

The transformation of the Kabbalah into a literary corpus intensified in the last third of the thirteenth century through the writings of Yosef Gikatila, Moshe de Leon, and others. These kabbalists created a voluminous kabbalistic literature, whose epitome was the *Zohar*. The *Zohar* presents a perfect alternative to the concept that the Kabbalah is closed knowledge. The esoteric conception of the *Zohar* is a broad issue, which goes beyond the frame of this work. Based on the works of Yehuda Liebes and Elliot Wolfson, however, we may dwell on several points of this matter.[4] First, the *Zohar* describes itself as an exegetical mystical work, which embodies in its essence a process of disclosure and innovation.[5] Furthermore, not only do the boundaries of esotericism change in the *Zohar*, but the very concept of esotericism acquires new meaning. In the *Zohar*, esotericism applies not only to a body of knowledge which may not be transmitted, but to a hidden dimension of the godhead—the *sefira* of *yesod*, which is depicted as opposed to the revealed side of the godhead, the *Shekhina*. The *sefira* of *yesod*, which is described in the *Zohar* through phallic images, is a being that must remain hidden, and its disclosure is compared to exposure of nakedness. In the words of the *Zohar* (1:236b): "And what is the highest secret of the Law? We should say, it is the sign of the holy covenant [circumcision], which is called 'the secret of the Lord, the holy covenant.'" The erotic analogy between the disclosure of the secret and the exposure of nakedness conceptualizes the esoteric as a realm which ought to remain hidden, not because disclosure can lead to severe mishaps, but because the very disclosure of those secrets is an act of desecration. The norms of concealment are linked to concepts of shame and intimacy. The link between secrecy and eros created by the *Zohar* encompasses as well the urge to reveal, for the tension between concealment and disclosure is contained within the godhead's essential nature, as an overflowing and blessing entity. Disclosure and concealment are two aspects of courtship and modesty, impulse and shame. As in sexuality, the person, the time, and the gesture make the difference between pleasurable desire and terrible violation.[6]

The link created by the *Zohar* between the disclosure of secrets and the exposure of nakedness makes esotericism a non-instrumental internal restriction. The instrumental esoteric conception prohibits disclosure, because it may engender unwanted results, like heresy resulting from improper understanding, or harm befalling the esotericists. By contrast, the *Zohar's* approach to the question of disclosure of secrets returns to the most fundamental conception of concealment, which sees the very fact of disclosure as an act of harm and desecration. A similar non-instrumental conception exists in the Hekhalot literature in which the very act of disclosure entails desecration. In the Hekhalot literature, however, the consciousness of desecration inherent in divulgence of secrets is expressed through a political analogy. In this analogy, with its complicated bureaucratic structure, inaccessibility and secrecy establish the conception of sublimity; thus inappropriate vision is an offense against the sovereign and his power. The *Zohar* evokes another background as its non-instrumental model for concealment—the erotic analogy. What these two concepts have in common is that the esoteric is not the ineffable or knowledge that may not be diffused. In both cases, esotericism reflects a fundamental intuition linking exposure to desecration. This distinction between internal and instrumental arguments for esotericism will be central to the phenomenological analysis as we proceed. For the time being it is important to draw the attention to the particular form of esoteric argument presented in the *Zohar* and the Hekhalot literature. The positing of creativity as an essential element of the hermeneutic and mystical experience and the reinterpretation of the concept of esotericism with internal tension arising between concealment and disclosure are a defiant challenge to the concept of Kabbalah as a closed corpus of knowledge.

A critical, sharp, and perspicacious look at the process of transformation of the Kabbalah into a literary corpus in the thirteenth century, as well as one of the richest discussions of the question of esotericism I know, may be found in the work *Badei Ha'aron* of Shem Tov Ibn Gaon. Shem Tov Ibn Gaon, one of the students of the Rashba and a distinguished follower of Naḥmanides' Kabbalah in the early fourteenth century,[7] sought to revive the concept of the Kabbalah as a primarily oral tradition and counter the widespread transgressions of the limits of secrecy of the second half of the thirteenth century. As a member of this circle, and as a proponent of the closed nature of kabbalistic knowledge, he attempted to found the authority and power of Naḥmanides' Kabbalah on a continuous tradition whose sources were at Sinai:

> For no sage can know of them through his own sagacity, and no wise man may understand through his own wisdom, and no researcher through his research, and no expositor through his exposition; only the kabbalist may know based on the Kabbalah that he received, passed down orally from one man to another, going back to the chain of the greats of the renowned generation, who received it form their masters, and the fathers of their fathers, going back to Moses, may peace be upon him, who received it as Law from Sinai. And they are listed in my *Keter Shem Tov*, just as I received them from my masters, the great Rabbi Shlomo ben Rabbi Avraham ben Aderet, of blessed memory, and Rabbi Yitzḥak ben Rabbi Todros, may his soul rest, who received it from the mouth of Rabbi Moshe ben Rabbi Naḥman (Naḥmanides) of blessed memory, and the pious Rabbi Isaac the Blind of blessed memory, son of the great master, Rabbi Avraham ben Rabbi David, the righteous one of blessed memory, whose wisdom was known and whose nature was exemplary. (*Badei Ha'aron*, p. 27)

At the beginning of the fourteenth century, this tradition was in conflict with the concept of the Kabbalah as literature. Shem Tov begins his discourse with the following warning:

> For I have found something of which every man whom the spirit of God is within must take heed. This is the saying of our Sages, " 'from the mouths of authors and not from books"; lest he find books written

with this wisdom, for perhaps the whole of what he received is but chapter headings; then he may come to study such books and fall in the deep pit as a result of the sweet words he finds there; for he may rejoice in them, or desire their secrets or the sweetness of the lofty language he finds there. Bur perhaps their author has not received the Kabbalah properly, passed down orally from one to another; he may only have been intelligent or skilled in poetry or and rhetoric . . . and have left the true path, as our Sages of blessed memory warned, "in the measure of his sharpness, so is his error." Perhaps he also came across other books that the instructed kabbalists referred to merely in passing, and he does not know why or in what measure. (*Badei Ha'aron*, pp. 25–26)

Shem Tov Ibn Gaon is aware that kabbalistic knowledge has become literature and is no longer an oral tradition. Consequently, he emphasizes one of the essential distinctions between the transmission of closed knowledge and the rise of literature. The controlled transmission of chapter headings avoids the use of rhetorical literary devices, because the tradition derives its reliability from its spare and precise formulation. The creative and rhetorical nature of kabbalistic literature, on the other hand, has an anti-traditional dimension. A text of poetic character is not merely a conduit for the transmission of traditions. Such a text establishes itself as an object worthy of regard in its poetic dimensions, which are not strictly means for transmission of knowledge. Consequently, from the point of view of the kabbalist, who sees the Kabbalah as closed knowledge, reliability and art are contradictory. It may very well be that Shem Tov Ibn Gaon was warning his readers against the *Zohar*, which is the epitome of the development of the Kabbalah as literature, as its marvelous literary qualities are powerfully seductive. Indeed, the tremendous difference between the Kabbalah as literature and the Kabbalah as tradition may be witnessed in the gap between the *Zohar* and Naḥmanides' writings. Naḥmanides' writings are devoid of any literary quality. They have no narrative frames or mythic characters, nor do they display complex weaves of midrashim and explanations, whereas in the *Zohar* we find these elements in abundance. The seductive appeal of the literary kabbalistic works threaten its status as a precise tradition handed down by Moses on Mount Sinai; it is this threat that Shem Tov struggled with.

Another element undermining the structure of closed knowledge is the pseudepigraphical nature of this literature. Shem Tov relates to this dimension later on in his writings: "God forbid, for the earlier instructed ones and the bearers of tradition have already proclaimed against this, saying that the wise man should not read any book unless he knows the name of its author. And this is just, for when he knows who its author is, he will understand its path and intention, [transmitted] from one man to another until the members of his generation. Thus, he may know if its author was a legitimate authority, and from whom he received it and whether his wisdom is renowned" (*Badei Ha'aron*, p. 26). The pseudepigraphic literature, like the writings of the *Ḥug Ha'iyun*, which was attributed to the enigmatic image of Rabbi Ḥamai, claimed for itself the status of independent canonical literature. The nature of its author, his place in the kabbalistic tradition, and his reliability as a transmitter of oral tradition all vanish in this type of literature. Consequently, Shem Tov Ibn Gaon warns his readers against such literature. Later on in his writings, Shem Tov contrasts the ways of his masters with those of the pseudepigraphic literature: "For all of them [Shem Tov's masters] were careful not to compose unattributed literature, writing only in their own names. Furthermore, they never explained anything based on their own knowledge, unless they made public to all readers how they arrived at such knowledge through their own reasoning. They publicized their names in their works so that all who come after them may know what guarded measure and in which paths light may be found" (*Badei Ha'aron*, p. 29). The transmission of tradition entails the keeping of genealogies. The name of the author and his place in the authoritative line of transmission is the source of his strength and the authority of his knowledge. Similarly, whoever writes down the secrets of the Torah transmitted from Mount Sinai must carefully distinguish between what was transmitted to him and what he says of his own knowledge, as practiced by Shem Tov's masters, according to his testimony.

As a consequence of his approach to the oral nature of Kabbalah, Shem Tov Ibn Gaon came to see even the canonical works of the Kabbalah—*Sefer Yetzira, Sefer Habahir*, and *Sefer Shi'ur Komah*—as a function of oral transmission:

> And now I shall return to the warnings and reminders that I mentioned and say that in our day there are no well-known works of Kabbalah that rest on firm foundation except for those I mentioned. In any case, if a person receive from the mouth of a well-known kabbalist the transmission of the *Sefer Yetzira, Sefer Habahir*, or the chapter of *Shi'ur Komah* . . . these may serve as supplementary knowledge for him, and it is worthy for the instructed one to cleave unto them, to memorize the principles until the words and chapters he received from his master be etched upon the tablet of his heart with a pen of iron and lead, so that he may not need any book, when he reads it in a chant or repeats it in tune. (*Badei Ha'aron*, p. 32)

The preceding canonical kabbalistic works, which risked becoming literature, derive their authority, according to Shem Tov, from the framework of oral tansmission: "if he receive them from the mouth of a

well-known kabbalist." Even after these works have been transmitted to
the disciple, Shem Tov places restrictions on their function as written literature. The student must repeat the chapters and sayings and learn them
by heart, through chanting and song.

Aside from the essential distinctions that Shem Tov Ibn Gaon makes
between the secrets of the Torah as tradition and as closed knowledge and
the secrets of the Torah as literature, he also describes the kinds of writing
and esoteric transmission practiced in the esoteric tradition of Naḥmanides.
This testimony, written down in order to revive Naḥmanides' concept of
kabbalistic knowledge and restore its authority, is of exceptional quality.
In one passage the Ravad and the Rashba are described as the strictest of
kabbalists in esoteric matters:

> My master, the Rashba of blessed memory, also composed a special
> prayer for himself, in which he hinted at the correct chapter headings,
> and composed a commentary based on some of the sayings of the
> Talmud, which may be understood on an explicit level, and may serve
> to refute the claims of heretics; but he inserted in hints one or two
> words which reveal some of the secrets to the ear of the kabbalist. Yet
> he did not explain all of them, nor did he hint at all of them, as the
> pious sages Rabbi Ezra and Rabbi Azariel of Gerona, of blessed mem-
> ory, had already done so earlier, in their compositions explaining the
> haggadot. (Badei Ha'aron, p. 28)

In the Rashba's commentary on the haggadot, unlike those of Rabbi
Ezra and Rabbi Azriel, except for rare places, there are no esoteric hints.
Thus, the reader of the extant commentary on the haggadot of the
Rashba will find difficulty identifying him as an esotericist. The Rashba's
style of writing contains a concealed criticism of the exegetical path chosen
by Rabbi Ezra and Rabbi Azriel in their commentaries on the haggadot.
Those commentaries were designed to explain the esoteric level of the aggadah. The Rashba advocated restricting, rather than expanding those
commentaries. Shem Tov describes the path taken by the Ravad in terms
close to the strict approach of the Rashba: "And the Ravad, of blessed
memory, provided hints only at places where he saw it absolutely necessary and no more, and he had enough in what his son the master [Isaac
the Blind] revealed, as he was known for this wisdom which he received
from [the Ravad's] mouth" (Badei Ha'aron, p. 28). In contrast to the
Ravad and the Rashba, the path of Naḥmanides was seen as more generous and methodical in its providing of enigmatic hints:

> The great master Rabbi Moses ben Naḥman of blessed memory also
> wrote his book and his commentary on Job, and in each and every
> place hinted at hidden things, in order to properly awaken the reader,

based on what he had received. Nevertheless, he made his words very enigmatic, for it is written, "Honey and milk are under your tongue," etc. . . . . He also commented only on the first chapter of *Sefer Yetzira*, for he received no more from other kabbalists. But the great pious Rabbi Isaac the Blind of blessed memory explained it in its entirety, as he received it. (*Badei Ha'aron*, p. 29)

Naḥmanides hinted everywhere at what he received, but his words are enigmatic and his commentary on *Sefer Yetzira* covers only the section for which he had received an esoteric tradition.

In his description of a no longer extant kabbalistic text—which, according to Shem Tov, was composed by Rabbi Avraham ben Yitzḥak, the Ravad's father-in-law—Shem Tov describes a style of writing different from the enigmatic hints of Naḥmanides or the almost total silence of the Rashba and the Ravad: "For Rabbi Avraham, Head of the Court, of blessed memory, wrote down chapter headings alone. And I saw them publicizing wonderful words to awaken all kabbalists; wherever they may find a word of them in Scripture, it may awaken them" (*Badei Ha'aron*, p. 29). This minimalistic text, which Shem Tov viewed as the pole diametrically opposed to kabbalistic "literature," is made up of a mere list of words and lacks all rhetoric or poetic dimension. This list contains no hint, reference, or instruction, and is nothing more than a set of reminders, in Shem Tov's words "mere chapter headings." This may be the primary and pure form of the transmission of chapter headings—a list of key words. In the esoteric tradition described by Shem Tov, we find a complex variety of approaches to the hidden. But what all the works to which Shem Tov is faithful have in common is the assumption that writing in hints is a conduit for transmission of secret traditions, and not an attempt at creating a kabbalistic literature.

In addition to the description of the different levels of esoteric writing, Shem Tov also documented the process of oral transmission, as it took place in the academies of his masters, the Rashba and Rabbi Yitzḥak ben Todros:

And I saw some of the students who received some of the esoteric matters and began with the chapter headings, received from the mouths of our masters, may their souls repose. But they were not diligent in their studies as befit their capacities, and left the eternal life to repose in the ways of the world, so that my masters regretted what they had transmitted to them, and did not add to their teaching. When they transmitted [this knowledge] to me, they did so on condition that I not transmit it to others except under three conditions that must be fulfilled by anyone who comes to receive matters of the initiates: the first is that he be a talmudic scholar, the second that he be forty years old or more, and the third that he be pious and humble in spirit. (*Badei Ha'aron*, p. 30)

The expression "to receive the matters of *ḥaverut* (membership)" is a technical term for initiation. In the passage above, one such process of initiation is described. A great deal can be learned from this passage, specifically because it describes a case in which the process failed. According to this rare description, oral transmission is not the organized, systematic transmission of Torah secrets. As in written transmission, it was also done through hints and a little at a time. The student received the chapter headings and his masters examined how he developed and understood them on his own; only when he was found worthy did they expand the range of hints and transmit additional chapter headings and so on. This method of transmission provides the masters with long-term control over the learning process, and enables the process to be halted at various points. Furthermore, this method attempts to put into practice the conditions prescribed in the Mishna for entry into esotericism, namely, that the student must be wise and understand his own knowledge. According to this condition, one who is worthy of secrets already knows them on his own—that is, the previous knowledge of the Torah secrets transmitted to the student is what prepares him to be worthy of receiving them.

The paradoxical sense of this mishnaic condition is further reinforced by the text of the more reliable Mishna manuscripts. In the Kaufmann and Parma manuscripts the text reads *ḥakham vehevin mida'ato* ("wise and understood of his own knowledge"). The reading *mevin mida'ato* ("wise and understands of his own knowledge") refers to the student's capabilities, whereas the reading *vehevin mida'ato* is a statement of fact. One may only transmit to one who knows the secret on his own, who already understood of his own knowledge. The transmission of the secret thus becomes a problem, for if the student fulfilled the conditions for initiation and understood of his own knowledge there is no need to instruct him, whereas if he does not understand of his own knowledge, he is unworthy of receiving the secret. The transmission through hinting, which is gradually amplified in accordance with the student's own progress, reflects the circular nature of the condition. Consequently, even teaching to selected individuals through oral transmission must be based on hints, by means of which the student can prove that he knows the matters of his own knowledge and capacities. The circular conditions of entry are the profoundest expression of the elitism of the esoteric. One may not join the esoteric circle, as it is based on a tautology—whoever knows the secret is worthy of receiving it. Esotericism thus entails a strong sense of privacy: only those who already understand me can understand me.

It is striking how prevalent such a circularity of initiation exists in a variety of esoteric modes; among other texts this condition is mentioned in the primary philosophical credo of esotericism, Plato's *Seventh Letter*.

I found such an esoteric declaration in a text much later than the Mishna, namely, Wittgenstein's *Tractatus*. In the first sentence of the introduction of this elusive, esoteric, and intriguing text, Wittgenstein states: "Perhaps this book will be understood only by someone who has himself already had the thoughts that are expressed in it, or at least similar thoughts; so it is not a text book its purpose will be achieved if it gave pleasure to one person who read and understood it." If having Wittgenstein's thoughts is a condition for understanding him, what is the point of writing? Those who do not have his thoughts will not understand him in any event, and those who have them through their own reasoning do not need Wittgenstein to enlighten them. (And how would someone know that he had the right thoughts, if the text does not independently direct the reader to them?) Wittgenstein comes up with an interesting answer to the problem of writing within this circular condition. He wrote his book for the sake of the pleasure of the one initiate, who will be redeemed out of his solitude by meeting another member of the elect group, a philosophical soul mate. Such a mode of esotericism is echoed as well in people with an extreme sense of privacy. When it comes to self-disclosure they claim that only those who already understand me are worthy of my revelation, or in a more extreme fashion only those who already know are capable of knowing what I think or feel. And yet if they already understand, there is no need for me to tell them. Since the person who is worthy of the secret is the one who already understood it, hinting is a way of identifying the one who is already a member of the elect group, rather than a form of indirect disclosure. Under the strict circular condition for entry to the esoteric circle the procedure of initiation blurs the distinction between teaching and identifying.

There is something else we may learn from Shem Tov's testimony on the initiation proceedings. The hinted and gradual transmission of knowledge was accompanied by a commitment on the part of the student to accept the restrictions on further transmission of that knowledge.[8] Shem Tov describes this commitment as an integral part of the process of transmission: "When they transmitted [this knowledge] to me, they did so on condition that I not transmit it to others except under three conditions, to anyone who comes to receive the matters of the initiates: the first is that he be a talmudic scholar, the second that he be forty years old or more, and the third that he be pious and humble in spirit" (*Badei Ha'aron*, p. 30). This passage is one of the first mentions of the restriction of transmission to those under forty; if indeed this was practiced in the school of the Rashba, it designates a severely restrictive tendency in instruction.[9]

An additional restriction mentioned by Shem Tov, "that he be a talmudic scholar," was designed to create a situation in which the realm of closed knowledge would remain the sole property of the Torah scholars.

This restriction had institutional and social significance that far surpassed the question of the student's aptitude for receiving Torah secrets. Esoteric teachings might pose a threat to authority structures and halakhic frameworks, because they present themselves as the inner meaning of religion. The attempt to restrict the Kabbalah to traditions transmitted amongst Torah scholars is a means of preventing its becoming a body of knowledge and authority that could compete with the halakhic world. This restriction creates an identity between the esotericists and the Torah scholars, so that the threatening force of esotericism might be harnessed to increase the power of the Torah sages. Esotericism thus draws its authority from its transmission through the institutional frameworks of the halakhic masters and receives legitimacy, as an integral part of the tradition, because the halakhic masters take it under their auspices. Undoubtedly, strict esoteric concepts of the Kabbalah were common among halakhic masters, as claimed by Moshe Idel.[10] The personalities whose esoteric practices were described by Shem Tov were outstanding halakhic scholars: Rabbi Avraham, head of the Rabbinical Court, the Ravad, Naḥmanides, the Rashba, Rabbi Yitzḥak ben Todros; to this list we may add Rabbi Yonah Girondi. By contrast, Rabbi Ezra, Rabbi Azriel, and the kabbalists of Castile, who slackened the reins of esotericism, did not belong to the rabbinical elite.

Shem Tov's composition touches directly on the relation between the halakhic scholars and esotericism. Shem Tov usually avoids mentioning the names of the kabbalists and compositions that are the targets of his criticism. Aside from the kabbalists of Provence and Gerona, on whom Shem Tov bases what he considers the proper tradition, the only ones mentioned among the kabbalists of Castile are the Cohen brothers and Rabbi Moshe of Burgos:

> For I have heard it said, two seeds at the summit of a tall tree, that they made themselves stronger than rock and emery, to receive from the mouths of holy ones, the heads of the academies, and the seed of great men; they moved their legs and toiled all their days and nights to fastidiously study their chapters. Verily, they are the sages, the pious brothers Rabbi Yitzḥak and Rabbi Ya'akov Cohen, the sons of Rabbi Ya'akov Hacohen of blessed memory, whose birthplace is the town of Suraya, which is also my birthplace, for their family is related to mine. They died without leaving male issue, and they left their riches and the greatness of their wisdom in the hands of their student the sage Rabbi Moshe of blessed memory, the son of Shim'on from the town of Burgos. But because they were not of my time, and I did not walk in their path, I avoided speaking of them; I only knew their aforementioned student, whom I met in the days of my youth, and I saw that it was a

straight and suitable way that he chose for himself, for he was pious and humble and decent in all his ways. But as I did not test his wisdom, I have remained silent and avoided following his way as one who shelters me in his tent. I only know that they were not great teachers of the Talmud, which is the pillar of learning of what is above and below and for the four winds of the world in its length and breadth, for the truth shall be taught through its ways. (*Badei Ha'aron*, p. 33)

Although the Cohen brothers and Rabbi Moshe of Burgos are not linked directly to the chain of tradition of the Kabbalah of Naḥmanides, as constructed by Shem Tov, his evaluation of their trustworthiness is quite restrained. The Cohen brothers are described as bearers of tradition that they learned from holy ones, while their disciple, Rabbi Moshe of Burgos, with whom he was well acquainted in his youth, is described as a man of stature. The Kabbalah of the Cohen brothers and Rabbi Moshe of Burgos is indeed of an esoteric character in comparison with the *Hug Ha'iyun* and the kabbalists of Castile who followed them. In the writings of the Cohen brothers, and especially in the case of Rabbi Moshe of Burgos, who transmit traditions from the school of Naḥmanides, the Kabbalah is perceived as closed knowledge.[11] In spite of this, Shem Tov refused to include them in the kabbalistic canon he created because they were not halakhic scholars: "I only know this, that they were not great teachers of the Talmud."[12] The esotericists of Naḥmanides' circle derive their credibility and authority from their being talmudic scholars. The rabbinical elite attempts to keep the esoteric tradition within its own domain, so that it not becomes a competing institution of authority and inspiration.[13] Shem Tov Ibn Gaon presents us with a polemical picture, full and rare, of an esoteric tradition that has lost its power. He describes the features of this tradition, drawing a profound distinction between tradition and literature, by providing a sharp and vivid description of the esoteric practices of writing and of oral transmission.

"The Widening of the Apertures of the Showpiece": Shmuel Ibn Tibon and the End of the Era of Esotericism

THE TENSION BETWEEN concealment and disclosure in the kabbalistic tradition of the thirteenth century, the process of erosion of the boundaries of secrecy and the attempt to re-erect them later on in that century, find a parallel in a similar process within the Maimonidean tradition in that century. The height of this process is the dispute over the teaching of philosophy in the early fourteenth century, in which the question of the status of philosophy as an esoteric realm of knowledge broke forth in full force. The great change in the molds of esoteric writing in the philosophical tradition took place at the beginning of the thirteenth century, in the writings of Shmuel Ibn Tibon. Shmuel Ibn Tibon, born in Lunel in the middle of the twelfth century, belonged to a great family of translators and philosophers who emigrated from Andalusia and settled in Provence. This line of translators and scholars, which started with Shmuel's father, Yehuda ibn Tibon, had an immense role in spreading Arabic philosophy and science to the west and in transmitting Jewish Arabic culture to the Jewish communities across the Pyrenees. As an agent of cultural transformation and change, Shmuel is known to us mainly as the first translator of *Guide of the Perplexed* from Arabic to Hebrew. His fragile and complex status as a descendent of Andalusian culture planted in a foreign milieu in Provence, as well as his daring in promoting the Andalusian ethos in the most exoteric fashion, situated him in the middle of the culture clash between the philosophers and their opponents in the thirteenth century. Among other concerns, his position on esotericism was a major component in his influential role in medieval Jewish culture. He played a central role in the history of the esoteric idea, in philosophy and in Kabbalah, both through the way that he tested the boundaries of the esoteric, as well as through his immediate influence on the writing of the secret. In his two compositions, *Perush Lekohelet* (Commentary on Ecclesiastes) and *Ma'amar Yikavu Hamayim* (Treatise on the Gathering of the Waters), esoteric matters are revealed at length and with a clarity that is unprecedented. Ibn Tibon himself was aware that he was initiating a revolution in the history of esotericism; thus, he consecrated the last chapter of

Ma'amar Yikavu Hamayim to "apologize for having revealed too much of the matters which our sages, of blessed memory, commanded be concealed" (173). His commentary on Ecclesiastes contains many matters dealing with Torah secrets. It is also written in overt and clear language. This commentary contains, among other things, introductions to Aristotelian epistemology and to the question of the immortality of the soul in Arabic philosophy. If the way of the esotericists was to abridge matters and to disperse their hints in chapter headings, Shmuel Ibn Tibon said of himself, than he tended to expound at length:

> For the reason why each commentator attempts to abridge his words in his commentary—that is, so that the teacher or the student shall not lose too much time from his reading because of the lengthiness of his words—does not apply to my commentary here. For I did not write it to interest students or instructors of children, but only for those who previously have learned and known the great treatise, the treatise of *Guide of the Perplexed*, and has scented some of the wisdoms and desires to know the words of the parables of the prophets and the sages and their riddles. . . . Similarly, if one wishes to know the matter of a particular verse in this book, he will undoubtedly rejoice if he finds in it an extensive explanation, and his spirit will not become impatient at its length; perhaps in several places of [the commentary], he will say, if only the explanations were still longer and broader than this! (*Perush Lekohelet* 11b)

Ibn Tibon's exoteric tendencies in his philosophical works are, obviously, inseparable from his central role as translator of the Judeo-Arabic corpus into Hebrew. The language barrier is the first and most blatant obstacle in approaching a text, so that translation is an act of enlargement and exposure. Ibn Tibon's translations to *Guide of the Perplexed* and various parts of the Arabic commentary to Aristotle are part of a wider cultural move, in which Andalusian Jewish culture was transferred to Christian Spain, especially to Provence. Like Maimonides, Shmuel Ibn Tibon justified the revolution he initiated in the disclosure of Torah secrets by sketching the history of esotericism in Jewish tradition. But, while Maimonides places himself at a crisis, a breaking point in history, Ibn Tibon paints the history of disclosure of Torah secrets in Jewish tradition as a continuous process of revelation of mysteries, which reached its pinnacle in his day and age. This continuous process, which finally emptied the concept of esotericism of all its content, is described in *Ma'amar Yikavu Hamayim*, and at greater length in his commentary on the book of Ecclesiastes. I examine in detail a passage in his commentary on Ecclesiastes, which is based on the exegesis of the verses "The fruit of the righteous is a tree of life" (Proverbs 11:30) and "The labor of righteous man makes for life" (Proverbs 10:16). Ibn Tibon explains that the word "fruit" refers to oral transmission, whereas the word "labor" (*peulot*) refers to writing.

In this section, which deals with the history of secrecy, Ibn Tibon opens with an interesting distinction between oral tradition and writing, which serves as part of the backdrop for the claim that the origin of esoteric transmission is oral teaching:

> For the great benefit that derives from them [the Sages] is in his tongue [and not in his books]; this was especially true in those days and in our nation. For this wisdom, which, it is hinted, is life, no one of our nation was allowed to expound in public; rather, he would transmit chapter headings to those who understood and were worthy of receiving it in a way that would enable them to understand the entire matter based on the first hints. This may be done in person, face to face, mouth to mouth. There the wise teacher may employ many ruses and tricks and permutations of words, in order that the right students understand their intention, even if he does not explain and make it explicit—which cannot be done through writing in a book. It is like a man who tells his fellow that he did well when he did a particular thing, and yet the hearer may understand that indeed the speaker thought badly of it, for he discerns this not from the thing said in itself, for what was meant was the opposite of what was said to him. But the listener may understand the meaning from other occurrences that accompany those words, whether it be through the facial appearance of the speaker, whose face may redden or turn green as one angered, or perhaps through his voice, that is, that it may not have been said pleasantly, as a man speaks when he means exactly what he says. . . . All this is extremely difficult to do in a book, as some of the meanings transmitted through the facial appearance and the qualities of voice are obscured. (*Perush Lekohelet* 9a)

Already in the introduction, which formulates the restrictions on public exposition in the past tense, certain questions are raised: "No man in our nation was permitted to expound it"; that is, in Ibn Tibon's time, the reins were slackened. At that stage, however, Ibn Tibon does not yet reveal the significance of his use of the past tense in referring to the restrictions of secrecy. He determines that oral transmission is preferable to writing, for in conversation the significance of what is said is understood in accordance with gestures and vocal inflections, which accompany the spoken words. Writing is a kind of freezing of the spoken word. The word loses the subtleties of meaning of ironic or bitter speech, because it is bereft of the living link of gesture or tonal expression.

Later on in the passage, Ibn Tibon repeats Maimonides' argument, that the paucity of writing on matters of wisdom is related to another advantage of oral transmission over writing. According to Maimonides, the written text may be interpreted in different directions and enshrines a situation of dispute, in contrast to the oral tradition, which is preserved in a state of purity. In spite of all this, Ibn Tibon determines: "Nevertheless, all those who felt empowered to do so did not hesitate to transmit chapter headings in writing without revealing secrets to write and compile in matters of wisdom what the wise would understand from their reading" (*Perush Lekohelet* 9a).

At this point, Ibn Tibon begins to describe the history of hinting:

> Our master Moses, may peace be upon him, was the founder of what we have found. For he employed the two channels we mentioned [speech and writing]. For all his predecessors among the prophets and sages, and Shem and Ever, [among them] we never find that they composed a book. Rather, they would teach and expound face to face until the master of prophets came and composed, by the will of God, a book, and explained in it what ought to be explained and transmitted in chapter headings whatever was not fit to be revealed before all. . . . Thus he taught to his people, by the command of God and by speaking mouth to mouth, the commandments, ordinances and laws, and wisdom and deep sciences" (*Perush Lekohelet* 9a).

Moses was not the first source of wisdom, for it existed as oral tradition among the sages of old, like Shem and Ever. Moses was, however, the first to write down chapter headings of the secrets of the Torah, alongside the oral tradition that he continued to transmit. Following Moses, Ibn Tibon mentions David, who further developed the hints of Moses in the Psalms; Solomon, whose books the Song of Songs, Proverbs, and Ecclesiastes deal with the secrets of the Torah; Isaiah, who describes the chariot; Ezekiel, who expands the description of the chariot mentioned in Isaiah; the Sages of the Mishna and the Talmud, who scattered hints of the secrets of the Torah in their midrashim. At the end of the chain of esotericism, Ibn Tibon places Maimonides, describing him in terms of a dramatic revelation in the history of esotericism.

In this construction of the history of esotericism, Ibn Tibon skips over the entire tradition of thought and mysticism from the Talmud until Maimonides. This lapse accords with Maimonides' self-understanding, who saw his project as a unique moment in the history of esotericism, which had no immediate precedent. The corpus that Maimonides related to is not the Jewish philosophy that preceded it, but rather to the canonical texts of Jewish tradition—Scripture, the Mishna, and the Talmud. Ibn Tibon characterized Maimonides' project in writing secrets with the following metaphor: "He widened the apertures of the showpiece." This metaphor is based in the verse that Maimonides, in his introduction to *Guide of the Perplexed*, sees as the embodiment of the teaching through parables: "Like golden apples in silver showpieces is a phrase well turned" (Proverbs 25:11). The inner, hidden kernel of the parable is the golden apple, which is kept in a lattice of silver. This lattice represents both the revealed meaning of the proverb, which has intrinsic value, and the fact that through its narrow apertures one may recognize the inner content of the secret. According to Ibn Tibon, each and every historical stage of the esoteric is an additional widening of the apertures of the lattice:

> And I would like to say that [Maimonides] provided an explanation through hints and his ordering of things and separation of items, so that he widened the apertures of the showpiece that enclosed the hidden things that Moses, may peace be upon him, wrote about such matters, in addition to what Solomon, may peace be upon him, and the Sages already widened, so that one who was not aware of them might now recognize them thanks to those additions. . . . Thus [Maimonides] followed the path in which the wise Solomon trod through his proverbs and the other things found in his books, for he continued to provide explanations for the secrets he found in the Torah and in its concealed parts, for he saw that those who understood had diminished. . . . And that wise man of blessed memory, when he saw that the widening of the apertures of the showpiece enclosing the secrets of the Torah by Solomon, of blessed memory, was insufficient, and the widening of the Sages, of blessed memory, was insufficient for the limited wisdom and insufficient effort in attainment of wisdom of the people of our generation, he added explanation upon explanation and widened them further. (*Perush Lekohelet* 10b)[1]

Ibn Tibon, in his commentary on Ecclesiastes and in *Ma'amar Yikavu Hamayim*, applied the exegetical principle that the parables and hints in the biblical text become progressively more transparent. The words of Solomon in Ecclesiastes facilitate a clearer understanding of the words of Moses, and the Psalms dealing with creation are the key to understanding the creation narrative in Genesis, as described in *Ma'amar Yikavu Hamayim*. Ibn Tibon describes Solomon's project relating to Torah secrets as follows: "Thus [Solomon] did in the deepest matters: he applied them to other simpler matters, so that they could be understood by those who could not understand [those other matters]. Thus, all Solomon's efforts were directed to widening the apertures of the showpiece covering the golden apple until the wise man could see what was inside it" (*Perush Lekohelet* 151b). Ibn Tibon, who focused on the Psalms and Ecclesiastes as the key to the narrative of creation, wove an intricate network of hints and parables, which explain earlier, more opaque hints and parables. In doing so, Shmuel Ibn Tibon employed the formula of

"widening the apertures of the showpiece" several times—that is, that esoteric Pentateuchal expressions become clearer in Psalms and Ecclesiastes.[2]

In his comments on the verse "a time for silence and a time for speaking" (Ecclesiastes 3:7), Ibn Tibon explains the factor that facilitates the
gradual process of the "widening the apertures of the showpiece," even
contrary to the way of the Torah and the prohibitions of the Sages. He
places his conception in the mouth of Solomon, who apologizes for revealing the secrets of the Torah pertaining to the act of creation. In the
creation narrative in the Torah, God alone is mentioned as involved in
the creation. In the opinion of Ibn Tibon, Solomon revealed that creation
was not entirely a direct, willed act of God, but that intermediate powers
were involved in it from the very first day on, namely the separate intelli-
gences and spheres:

> You may explain this pair [a time for silence and a time for speaking]
> as an apology on the part of Solomon, for his disclosure the matter of
> the times. For Moses hid it profoundly and did not mention it in the
> narrative of creation of all beings except for the word *elohim*, and He
> is known there as the primal cause. . . . But he intended to hide it so
> that no man would know about the times, that is, so that the masses
> will not become aware of any intermediary powers. . . . And [Solomon]
> offered apologies for this, in that he expanded the explanation of the
> secrets of the Torah at a time when he, may peace be upon him, should
> have remained silent—that is to say, as Moses, may peace be upon him,
> remained silent. But there is also a time for him, may peace be upon
> him, to speak as well. That is to say, the speech of Solomon, but he said
> no more. But what he meant to say in that place is that Moses, may
> peace be upon him gave the Torah, which was destined for the entire
> world, including the Sabean nation, who did not believe in the exis-
> tence of anything except for those things that could be apprehended by
> the senses. . . . Thus, he wished to uproot the disease from the start
> and he mentioned God's creation of the main things in the world, with-
> out mentioning the intermediary powers, in order to teach that those
> actions should not be attributed to them at all. . . . But in the time of
> Solomon, may peace be upon him, the existence of God and His angels
> had become accepted in the world . . . so that the need for concealing
> this was no longer present. Thus, Solomon did not avoid mentioning
> the existence of intermediary powers by way of a hint. . . . And he
> spoke of the matter of the times, that Moses, may peace be upon him,
> made great efforts to hide it completely from consciousness, for the
> hint he hinted at was extremely obscure. It is not that Solomon, may
> peace be upon him, made it up or that he stood against the Torah
> and disagreed, for truly it was hinted at in many places; one of them is

the mention of *elohim*, which is in the plural form. (*Perush Lekohelet* 69b–70a)

As Aviezer Ravitzky pointed out, according to Ibn Tibon, the gradual process of disclosure depends on the advancement of scientific metaphysical knowledge in the world.[3] Since, in Moses' time, the belief in the power of the heavenly bodies without a transcendental God was prevalent, Scripture explicitly denied the function of the heavenly bodies in creation. Solomon wrote his books at a time when the belief in God and His angels was prevalent; thus he did not hesitate to hint at the participation of the heavenly bodies in the process of creation. Solomon did not come up with the idea on his own. He explained a hint well concealed within the Torah itself. Moses already hinted at the participation of intermediary forces in creation, since the name of the godhead that appears in the description of creation, *elohim*, is common to God, angels, and powers, unlike the Tetragrammaton.[4] The progression of successively clearer hints in sacred scripture—from the spare and enigmatic hint of Moses to the more transparent ones of Solomon—is linked to the historical progress of metaphysical knowledge in the surrounding environment of the hinter.

Ibn Tibon employs the same concept that he uses in explaining internal Scriptural changes from Moses to Solomon—of the progress of human knowledge—with respect to his own works—the widening of the apertures of the showpiece:

> I furthermore wish to apologize for having revealed more than I should have on matters that our Sages of blessed memory ordered be hidden. For I bring heaven and earth as witnesses that I did so only for the sake of Heaven, for "in a time to do for the Lord [they violated Your Law]"—for I saw that the secrets that were hidden then by our prophets and the sages of our Torah, are today all well known among the nations of the world, and the secrets of the Torah and in the words of the prophets and those who speak by the Holy Spirit in many places are interpreted according to those truths. For our nation has become more foolish than them to the point that we have become a mockery in their eyes because of our foolishness. . . . So I said that at the time when the greatest of the prophets hid what he hid, these true matters were not known or widespread among the nations, based on what was known to them, through their unfounded beliefs. (*Ma'amar Yikavu Hamayim*, p. 173)

After he repeats his account of the historical process of the disclosure of secrets from Moses to Maimonides, he writes:

> And I, the youth who came after him [Maimonides] saw that the number of those who understood his [Maimonides'] hints had declined

greatly, how much more so those who understood the hints in Scripture. For I saw that true wisdom had become extremely widespread among the nations under whose rule and in whose land I live, far more than it had been in the lands of the Ishmaelites. Thus, I saw the great need to enlighten the eyes of the instructed with what God, may His name be exalted, enabled me by His grace to understand in His word and how he widened the apertures of the showpiece covering the apples of the parables of the prophets and those who speak by the Holy Spirit and the Sages of blessed memory. . . . Consequently, I revealed what I have revealed in this composition and in my commentary on Ecclesiastes, things that other men would not have revealed previously, so that we do not become a disgrace to our neighbors, a mockery and a derision in our surroundings. (*Ma'amar Yikavu Hamayim*, pp. 174–175)

The transfer of the Muslim philosophical culture to Christian Europe took place openly and with great vigor in the early thirteenth century. According to Shmuel Ibn Tibon, science and wisdom were more widespread in his time in the Christian world than in the Muslim world. The progress in knowledge had reached a level such that Torah secrets had been exposed in any case, including the exegesis of Scripture according to a philosophical glossary, which began to develop in the Christian world. Based on this new historical reality, Ibn Tibon derived the permissibility of unprecedented disclosure of Torah secrets. This argument, however, did not suffice for Ibn Tibon, even if it was a sufficient explanation for the changes in disclosure of secrets in the course of their transmission from Moses to David and Solomon. Ibn Tibon employed an additional argument in relation to his own writings, which increased the sense of urgency in breaking the frameworks of secrecy. He claimed that the number of those who understood wisdom among the Jews had diminished, and their sages had become an object of mockery and derision to their surrounding, while the sciences proliferated in the Christian world. The oppressive asymmetry between the expansion of the sciences among the nations of the world and the decrease of wisdom in Israel created the consciousness of a crisis. In such a situation, disclosure of secrets became justified even at the expense of breaking the law: "In the time to do for the Lord [they violated your Torah]." These words of Ibn Tibon are the epitome of the process of the transformation of the esoteric into a tool of cultural integration. Not only had the esoteric realm become the means that enabled the absorption of Aristotelian culture into the heart of Judaism, but now the esoteric must be revealed for two reasons: first of all, because it had been revealed anyway, and second, in order to withstand the pressures brought to bear on Judaism by that very culture. The esoteric golden apple was now exposed before all, without any showpiece whatsoever.

The relationship created by Ibn Tibon between his exoteric policy and the dissemination of philosophical knowledge in Christian Europe was not accidental. Unlike Muslim culture, in which esotericism was legitimate and common, medieval Christianity saw esotericism as a realm suspect of heresy. The doctrinal centralization of the church created a situation in which a thinker or movement that announced the existence of a secret thus testified that he had something to hide, and was automatically suspect of deviance and endangerment.[5] The entry of Aristotelianism into Christian theology was open and public, and did not take place through the medium of esoteric doctrine, as in the Muslim and Christian worlds. The lack of a centralized church in the Jewish world enabled, of course, the freer development of esoteric tendencies. The transfer of the Jewish philosophical tradition from the Muslim surroundings to the Christian one changed, among other things, Ibn Tibon's esoteric molds. We may surmise that it was not only the dissemination of knowledge in the Christian world that influenced the disclosure, but also the influence of the opposition to concealment in principle, which lent a different mold to philosophical writing.

In his book *Meshiv Devarim Nekhonim*, Ya'akov bar Sheshet sharply criticized Ibn Tibon's book and his conception of esotericism. It would seem that the abandonment of the limits of esotericism by Ibn Tibon served to provoke the kabbalists of Gerona to reveal their opposing secret. They saw themselves obligated to present their alternative understanding of the inner meaning of Jewish tradition, once Ibn Tibon had adopted that tradition as a kind of *crown* to be displayed in public. Small wonder, then, that Ya'akov bar Sheshet's composition, *Sha'ar Hashamayim*, which is a kind of introduction to the Kabbalah and the system of *sefirot*, concluded with a fierce attack on philosophical positions.

Esotericism, Sermons, and Curricula: Ya'akov Anatoli and the Dissemination of the Secret

THE PROCESS OF the transformation of philosophy into an exoteric culture in the thirteenth century, which was vigorously launched in the writings of Shmuel Ibn Tibon, continued on two levels: the first, the development of a literature of philosophical homilies, and the other, an attempt at anchoring the philosophical educational program as the central element of the Jewish curriculum. The process of expansion and dissemination of philosophical Torah secrets took place mainly in Provence, where Maimonidean culture gained the upper hand. This process, however, did not come about without struggle, a struggle that also touched upon the determination of the boundaries of secrecy. The tension between the secret and the revealed that marked thirteenth century esotericism reached a seething point in the dispute over philosophical sermons and the teaching of philosophy in the early fourteenth century. In this dispute, the esoteric problem became a political-communitarian problem of the first order, as it expanded beyond the question of the forms of writing and hinting and engaged far deeper and more fundamental questions, such as the canon of study and the public exposure of esoteric doctrines through the genre of philosophical sermons. An investigation of this process and the disputes it engendered bring to light profound aspects of the esoteric problem.

One of the key figures in this process was Ya'akov Anatoli, the son-in-law of Shmuel Ibn Tibon. In line with the cultural mission of his family, Anatoli (1194–1256) contributed as well to the translation and dissemination of Arabic learning in the West. His peculiar and fascinating place in this process is manifested in his work in Naples under the royal invitation and patronage of Frederick II in association with Michael Scot. Ya'akov Anatoli wrote *Malmad Hatalmidim*, the first book of philosophical sermons arranged according to the order of the weekly liturgical readings. The author of this book viewed it as a tool for public dissemination of philosophical ideas, and used it in order to increase public sympathy for the philosophical ethos. Ya'akov Anatoli himself is witness to the tension engendered by the appearance of this literary genre:

> As this book [*Guide of the Perplexed*] removed some of the blinds from my eyes, I devoted my heart to study and investigate some of the

writings of the Torah and the other holy books, and when I would study them I would sometimes expound on them at weddings. But as a result of my preoccupation with the vanities of this world that I acquired, I did not write even a single line of all the new insights that came to me through expounding those verses. And as I became accustomed to the matter, I agreed to expound publicly, a bit at a time, every Shabbat. But I left that path, as it met with the disapproval of some of my friends. (Introduction to *Malmad Hatalmidim*)

The book began as a series of public sermons at weddings and in synagogues, and Anatoli testifies that the criticism of this custom led him to change his custom of preaching philosophical sermons in public. The exoteric writing employed by Shmuel Ibn Tibon was intended, he says, for Torah scholars. Anatoly's turning to a wider audience, through the medium of public sermons, was another step in philosophy's departure from the esoteric realm. Ya'akov Anatoli uses the same reasoning as Shmuel Ibn Tibon in justifying the transgression of the boundaries of esotericism, but adds an interesting comment later in the introduction:

For we have reached the point where we have become a mockery among the nations because of our wisdom and the commandments of the Torah, for we no longer devote ourselves to learning how to respond to the heretic, as our masters warned us. For the heretics slander us and say that we eat the peelings, while they consume the fruit. For they make efforts to study and expound the Torah according to their faith, and preach it publicly at all times, to the point where falsehood has long overcome truth, and we have almost abandoned the path of truth transmitted us by God.

To Shmuel Ibn Tibon's words on the dissemination of wisdom in Christian lands, Ya'akov Anatoli adds that the public sermons of the Christians—"for they preach on matters of wisdom"—serves as preparation for the renewed exoteric level he creates. According to Ya'akov Anatoli, the development of philosophical sermons among the nations of the world calls forth, in response, a wider exposure of the philosophical exegesis of Scripture, through sermons in synagogues and at marriage ceremonies.

In addition to the development of a genre of public philosophical sermons, Ya'akov Anatoli also vehemently expressed his stand on the question of curriculum. He supported the making of the narrative of creation and the vision of the chariot into a central element of the education of the elite, while displacing the talmudic give-and-take from the core of the curriculum. Indeed, the esoteric realm is a threat to the talmudic curriculum, whose ideal type is, first and foremost, the Talmud sage and teacher. As we have seen, this dilemma was solved in the schools of Naḥmanides and the Rashba through a restrictive concept of esotericism that confined esoteric teachings to the Torah scholars alone. Ya'akov Anatoli formulated an opposing view, in which physics and metaphysics replace the Talmud in the traditional curriculum. Thus, the question of the limits of secrecy has ramifications for the formation of the cultural elite of the congregation. In his introduction to *Malmad Hatalmidim*, Ya'akov Anatoli outlines his position on the question of the place of the Talmud in the canon of learning:

> For we find explicitly that our rabbis were accustomed to study wisdom, for they said that the smallest among Hillel's eighty students left not a single type of wisdom unlearned, they praised him and said that he left neither small not great thing unlearned. For they of blessed memory explained that the vision of the chariot is the very great thing, and all wisdoms are directed toward it and are aids to it, for it alone has the great and perfect purpose, for with it man may approach the King. The doings of Abbaye and Rava [talmudic dialectics], on the other hand, they called a small thing, for the Mishnayot and other set legal compendia are sufficient material for those who seek wisdom. This is the opinion of our Rabbis of blessed memory. But today, the great thing in the eyes of the teachers of the Talmud is the preoccupation with the talmudic passages, not only with the legal decisions deriving from them but with the business of questions and answers. Whereas the small thing has become the vision of the chariot, which is the divine wisdom.

In this dispute, we may discern four assumptions:

1. The value of talmudic study lies strictly in clarifying the halakha, and not "the business of questions and answers." That is, the new insights, which arise in the course of the discussion and in its subsequent development.
2. The study of halakha is a means of achieving the highest wisdom, that is, the divine wisdom, metaphysics.
3. The Talmud scholars of his generation commit a great spiritual error in placing talmudic learning (the doings of Abbaye and Rava) at the heart of the curriculum.
4. Since the clarification of the halakha is the heart and purpose of the talmudic discussion, this work has already been accomplished through the major halakhic compendia of the Rif and Maimonides, so that there is no longer any need to deal with the world of talmudic dialectics, "for the Mishnayot and other set legal decisions are sufficient material for those who study wisdom."

Anatoli vehemently disputed the rabbinic position with respect to the spiritual importance of intensive talmudic study. If physics and metaphysics are the subjects that enable man to fulfill his spiritual destiny and actualize his potential perfection, the value of investigation of talmudic discussions is marginal. According to him, this activity serves only for clarification of the halakhah. Furthermore, Anatoli claims that even for knowledge of the halakhah itself, one need not study the talmudic passages directly, as we possess purely halakhic writings such as Maimonides' code. The learner should concentrate on the Mishna and other halakhic compendia, which are legal texts without give-and-take, and focus on the vision of the chariot, which is knowledge of nature—physics—and what is beyond nature—metaphysics. In the opinion of Ya'akov Anatoli, the Talmud is undoubtedly an authoritative text, for the binding norms of halakha are derived from it. But as a result of Maimonides' codification of the *Mishneh Torah*, combined with the concept that only intensive study of wisdom has intrinsic value, the Talmud becomes a marginal text in the curriculum. The esoteric mechanism, which was designed to base traditional education on its talmudic ideals, may lose its force entirely once the distinction between the secret and the revealed is blurred, and the narrative of creation and the vision of the chariot become defined as broad realms of knowledge which make up the canon of learning.

This position, as formulated by Anatoli, typified the non-talmudical branch of Jewish intellectual elite. Rabbi Shem Tov Falkeria adopts a similar position, both with respect to the value of Talmud study, as well as with respect to the central position of the *Mishneh Torah* as a replacement for the prevailing halakhic curriculum:

> In the beginning, he should study the Written Law, and afterward the Oral Law which is its explanation. At that time, it is sufficient that he read the laws of Rav Alfasi of blessed memory, and that he read the books of Rabbi Moshe [Maimonides] of blessed memory, which are called the *Mishneh Torah*, for they are true words. His commentary on the Mishna is also a very useful book, and for whoever would learn legal decisions, this is sufficient. And if he desires, it is good that he study Mishnayot and the Talmud, which is the commentary to them, in order to exercise his mind and sharpen it, for this is necessary in study, for the effort in it will make knowledge and understanding easier, and will aid in remembering these matters. But I will tell you something: It is unfitting to spend all one's days in questions and responses as many do, for they tire themselves all night in the reading of halakhah and in the morning, if someone asks of one of its matters, they have no answer. (*Sefer Hamevakesh* [Warsaw, 1884], p. 102)

According to Falkeria, the study of legal decisions is the main thing, while the study of the Talmud becomes marginal, and its purpose is merely the sharpening of the mind. Like Ya'akov Anatoli, he saw the compendia of halakhic decisions—the Rif and the *Mishneh Torah*—as replacements for the talmudic curriculum.

A similar, and even more extreme position, is found in the writings of Rabbi Yosef Ibn Kaspi. In his *Sefer Hamusar*, which is his testament to his son, he describes the Torah curriculum: "For today you are twelve years old. Thus, study the Torah and Scripture and the Talmud for two more years." After two years of study of mathematics, geometry, astronomy, and ethics, the Torah curriculum changes: "Fix times for study of the Torah and Scripture and the books of Rav Alfasi and Rabbi Moshe of Coucy and the *Mishneh Torah* of the perfect master" (*Sefer Hamusar*, p. 66).

The curriculum that Kaspi does recommend consists of logic, science, and metaphysics, and in it Talmud study ceases at age fourteen and is replaced by halakhic texts and *Sefer Mitzvot Gadol* of Rabbi Moshe of Coucy. Later on he describes a certain event, adopting a sarcastic and critical tone toward the devoted students and rabbis:

> One day. . . . I set my table and called to my beloved to eat and drink with me, for I had a family offering to bring; but the cursed maidservant went and put a milkmaid's spoon into the pot and the law escaped me. . . . So I went in a foul, angry mood to one of the respected rabbis among the people. . . . and he taught me and told me that the law was such and such. So I returned to my home and the guests and the poor were sitting and waiting for me, and I told them the entire story, for I am not embarrassed to say that I am unfamiliar with a certain halakahah or a certain trade, but I am familiar with another trade. For why should a legal decision or a teaching on the knowledge of the Creator or His great unity not be as important as the spoon of a little milkmaid? (*Sefer Hamusar*, p. 69)[1]

We should not be surprised that we do not find a single new insight into questions of talmudic give-and-take from these circles. These circles developed the study of wisdom in its broadest sense as the central element of Jewish education, and thus they defiantly opposed the tendency within esotericism that saw the talmudic sage as the superior esotericist.[2]

Philosophical culture created alternative understandings toward talmudic study and the role of Maimonides' *Mishneh Torah*. According to this position, it was, paradoxically, the codification of the Talmud, which was designed to increase its authority and normative canonicity, which made it a marginal text in the learned canon.[3] Philosophers like Ya'akov Anatoli were of the opinion that Maimonides attempted to introduce a major change in the Jewish curriculum through the *Mishneh Torah*, in order to remove the "small thing" from the way, and enable devotion to the "big thing." The traditional curriculum, as molded by Anatoli, created a separation between esotericists and Talmud scholars, as opposed to the attempt made by the school of the Rashba, to prevent the development of a competing elite. Thus, another important element of esotericism was eroded, that which attempted to keep the tradition of the secret within the circle of halakhic authorities.

The Ambivalence of Secrecy: The Dispute over Philosophy in the Early Fourteenth Century

AT THE CORE of the dispute over the study of philosophy that raged in Provence in the early fourteenth century was the rise of the philosophical sermons and the transformation of the curriculum, the two elements emphasized in Anatoli's writings, whose influence on the esoteric structure was far-reaching. This dispute deserves to be examined in detail, as it deals entirely with the problem of secrecy. Here, the tensions between disclosure and concealment, which developed in the thirteenth century, erupted into a fierce dispute transcending communal borders.[1] According to the testimony of the instigator of this dispute, Abba Mari, the event that set off the dispute was a public sermon in which the preacher compared Abraham and Sarah to matter and form, in accordance with the commonly accepted dictionary of philosophical allegory.[2] Abba Mari, who was at the time a rabbi in Montpelier, left a detailed and impressive account of the dispute in the text *Minḥat Kna'ot* (Offering of Zeal), which includes a handful of letters that were exchanged between the parties and their allies in the dispute. This collection of letters is an invaluable resource for the understanding of the politics of esotericism and its basic structures. In 1303, Abba Mari attempted to mobilize the Rashba to battle against the philosophical circles in Provence and against public philosophical sermons. In this request, which in fact was the opening salvo of the struggle, Abba Mari did not limit himself to the internal debate in Provence, but enlarged its boundaries by seeking support in Barcelona, among the greatest halakhic authorities of the generation. Shlomo ibn Adret, known as the Rashba, was the greatest of Naḥmanides' students. He continued the kabbalistic tradition of his teacher and became his heir as the leader of the Jewish community in Barcelona. His vast legal responsa, written to communities across Spain, serve as testimony to his widespread authority. Yet interfering with a cultural debate across the border in Provence was a completely different matter. It engaged Rashba in a drama that he at first hesitated to join. Abba Mari and the Rashba accused the allegorists of turning the historical forefathers of the nation into abstract concepts of Aristotelian physics.[3] According to the Rashba, the allegorical tendency of the preachers would quickly spread to the commandments themselves, turn the practical commandments to symbols of

Aristotelian typology, and even lead to their abolition.[4] Abba Mari and the Rashba also repeated the accusation that these circles uncritically accept the Aristotelian-Averroesean tradition, and as such, they deny the belief in *creation ex nihilo* and divine providence, which is a form of heresy threatening the very existence of the Jewish religion.

The Rashba fiercely attacked the philosophical tradition and allegorical sermonizing. He was aware that the Provencal elite would interpret his entry into the dispute as illegitimate, external meddling in internal cultural questions. Thus he was hesitant to get involved and urged Abba Mari and other Provencal figures to act on their own against the philosophical culture that was spreading in their region. After the Rashba failed to convince his supporters in Perpignan to do so, and after a failed attempt by Abba Mari and his faction to institute a ban in Montpelier, the Rashba consented. After lengthy negotiations, he accepted Abba Mari's suggestion that the Barcelona community place a ban on philosophy and, following the Barcelona precedent, which would bear the seal of the Rashba, the Provencal communities could then proclaim a ban of their own. On the ninth of Av in the year 5265 (1305),[5] the Barcelona congregation declared a ban on the study of the books of the non-Jewish philosophers dealing with physics and metaphysics for all those under the age of twenty-five. However, before Abba Mari and his supporters could declare a similar ban in Provence, his opponents hastened to declare a counter-ban contending that, since those who declared the ban in Barcelona did so unlawfully, they should be banned. Moreover, all who accepted the authority of the Barcelona ban and followed it would also come under this ban. Abba Mari attempted to marshal the support of as many halakhic masters as possible in order to annul the ban of his opponents, and pronounced a ban of his own on those who proclaimed the counter-ban. Bans and counter-bans did not lead to a solution. The entire struggle ceased as a result of the tragic circumstances of the expulsion of the Jews from France, including the Jews of Montpelier, among them Abba Mari, on the tenth of Av, 5266 (1306).

The complex structure of the ban, the alliances it created, and the confusion it generated are linked to a phenomenon that I would call the ambivalence of the esoteric. The attempt to reclaim a body of knowledge for the esoteric realm may be interpreted in two opposing ways. On the one hand, the renewed tightening of the restrictions of secrecy may be motivated by the desire to guard that knowledge as a preferred and valued realm, whose transmission must be strictly regulated. On the other hand, the restrictions on dissemination and teaching may be directed by the opposite desire to prevent the cumulative influence of such knowledge, as far as possible. Relegating a particular body of knowledge to the concealed is rooted in the traditional attempt to keep this body of knowledge privileged and precious. Yet concealment might serve to the contrary as a technique of repression and marginalization. The phenomenon of ambivalence with regard to esoteric doctrines was reflected in the alliance forged between Abba Mari and the Rashba, in spite of the profound differences between their worldviews. In order to appreciate these differences and their reflection in what I have called the ambivalence of the esoteric, I describe, at some length, the difference in their views.

The world of Abba Mari was shaped by the Maimonidean tradition. In his composition *Sefer Hayare'ah*, Abba Mari again confirmed the Maimonidean identification of physics and metaphysics with Jewish esoteric doctrines—the narration of creation and the vision of the chariot:

> It is known and evident to the sages that there are two kinds of wisdom, the first—the knowledge of nature, which is the wisdom of the work of creation, and the second, the knowledge of the Godhead, which is the vision of the chariot. . . . For there is great benefit to the sages who fear the Lord in each of the two purposes, for through them a person may discern the design of existence and may know and comprehend some of the wonders of God, may He be blessed. And he may proceed through those levels until he attains the two superior wisdoms, the work of creation and the vision of the chariot. Through them he may know and comprehend He who spoke and the world came into being. (*Minḥat Kna'ot*, pp. 648–649)[6]

According to Abba Mari, such wisdom was transmitted by an internal tradition among the sages of Israel, and preserved as an esoteric tradition: "It is evidently clear that those matters of wisdom were received from the pairs [of Sages mentioned in Tractate Avot 1 :1] and the pairs from the prophets." In exile, this wisdom was lost, and some of it was preserved in the Greek philosophical literature:

> Because our sins have increased, from the day we were exiled from our land, the wisdom of our sages was lost when the books written on hidden matters were lost, for they are the secrets of creation. But an extremely small portion of those words, which are like mountains hanging by a hair, were copied from them in the books of the nations, and were disseminated among the Gentiles, and they are the works of investigation written by the wise men of Greece, for there may be found there some of the honey that Solomon hinted at when he said, "For I have found honey, etc." And from there we may derive the complete proof of the existence of God, may he be blessed, and His unity and his noncorporeality. For this is the explanation of the first two of the Ten Commandments, "I am the Lord" and "Thou shalt have no other gods." . . . This is the honey and the incense and the good that is hidden in those

books. But what shall we do, and how shall we approach these things? It is like a jar of honey with a dragon entwined around it." (*Minḥat Kna'ot*, p. 653)

The source of Greek wisdom is thus to be found in Jewish esoteric teachings which have become lost and have found their way, in part, to the nations. In the opinion of Abba Mari, selective study of the philosophical literature enables one in practice to reconstitute the esoteric teachings of the work of creation and the vision of the chariot, and this literature, according to the Maimonidean tradition, has religious value. But into this corpus crept many errors pertaining to the eternity of the world and the denial of divine providence, which are dangerous for the believer.

As Abba Mari belonged to the rabbinic-Maimonidean world, an understanding of his struggle is quite complex. He argued that the spread of public philosophical sermons that employ an extreme allegorical approach to Scripture, like the allegory that Abraham and Sarah are matter and form, is what moved him to proclaim battle. Abba Mari truly believed that his efforts were aimed at reinstating the boundaries of esotericism that Maimonides himself fixed with respect to the study of philosophy and its dissemination. It is because philosophical wisdom is the Jewish esoteric teaching that its uncontrolled dissemination must be prohibited. He repeatedly explains that he is not out to attack the philosophical culture in Provence as a whole, but rather to reestablish it within the limits set by Maimonides. A programatic formulation of his point of view appears in the third chapter of *Sefer Hayare'ah*. In this chapter, he claims that such wisdom was part of the Jewish esoteric tradition, and it is clear to him that in earlier periods they were free of the dross of heresy that now adheres to it. Yet the Sages nevertheless regarded them as totally esoteric:

It is evidently clear that such knowledge was received in transmission from the pairs and the prophets. As that is so, we are certain that their study did not contain anything contradicting the foundations of the Torah or departure from the principles of religion. Nevertheless, our Sages of blessed memory said that one may not expound the vision of the chariot alone, nor the work of creation with fewer than two, unless he was a sage and understands of his own knowledge. Furthermore, they said that the secrets of the Torah may only be transmitted to the head of a rabbinic court, and then only if his heart fears within him. Moreover, it says that with respect to the learning of the forty-two-letter Name, a matter which is known through divine wisdom, as was written in the commentary of Rabbi Moses of blessed memory [Maimonides]. And, in general, those letters are an instruction and hint to that teaching. And [Maimonides] of blessed memory warned that it be taught only to humble individuals, as it is written, "and that only if he be humble and has lived out half his days." And the rabbi, the teacher of righteousness, wrote in *Sefer Hamada* that it is not fitting for a man to walk in the *pardes* until he has filled his belly with meat and wine, which is the interpretation of the Torah and the commandments. (*Minḥat Kna'ot*, pp. 650–651)

The restriction of the study of philosophy to those advanced in age is based, in his understanding, on the words of Maimonides himself, and accords with his Maimonidean worldview:

For this is what our rabbi, the teacher of righteousness, intended in his great book, *Guide of the Perplexed*, in Part 1, Chapter 34, and these are his words: "Consider how, by means of a text of a book, they laid down as conditions of the perfection of the individual, his being perfect in the varieties of political regimes as well as in the speculative sciences and withal his possessing natural perspicacity and understanding and the gift of finely expressing himself in communicating notions in hints. And yet, the mysteries of the Torah may not be transmitted to him" [*Guide*, p. 78, modified]. Until this point, these are the words of our great master, of blessed memory, and it is fitting that we take heed of them. (*Minḥat Kna'ot*, p. 652)

In order to support his claim, Abba Mari cites one of the outstanding representatives of the Maimonidean tradition, Rabbi David Kimḥi:

For I saw that the sage, Rabbi David Kimḥi of blessed memory, followed in the footsteps of our great master. For he wrote in his commentary on the verse "The beginning of wisdom [is the fear of the Lord]" as follows: "for if a person learn the wisdom of philosophy first, his spirit may falter, and he may become brazen and deny the great signs and wonders in the sacred scriptures. Thus, one must first study the Torah, which is the fear of the Lord. And he must place it in his heart to believe all that is written in it, from the creation *ex nihilo* of the world to the possibility of change in nature through signs and wonders. . . . Only then should he study the wisdom of philosophy, so that his mind not becomes confused through his learning of wisdom, thanks to the Torah that he learned previously. For he has planted his stake upon solid ground; thus he may use all his strength to draw the ways of wisdom closer to the Torah. (*Minḥat Kna'ot*, pp. 656–657)

Abba Mari thus concludes that one must reinstate the earlier restrictions on the study of wisdom:

Henceforth, we may not learn from their books not hear wisdom from their mouths, and even if they speak truth, we should not listen to them.

But for the great sages, the gate to the inner courts [of the sanctuary] is never locked, for they remove the coarse flour and take the fine meal. . . . But for other people, who have not perfected themselves in Torah and have not yet reached the requisite age for dealing with such wisdom, and do not know how to take heed, they should avoid this food, lest they choke on its shell. (*Minḥat Kna'ot*, pp. 659–660)[7]

By tightening the restrictions on esotericism, Abba Mari hopes to defend the moderate Maimonidean tradition against its more radical version. The postponement of study until a more advanced age, and its restriction to individuals, will prevent the questioning of faith in creation *ex nihilo* and providence. Consequently, these beliefs would be implanted as a solid basis preceding the student's exposure to philosophical texts. Furthermore, Abba Mari understands that the elite's continued preoccupation with talmudic dialectics, alongside the philosophical vision of the chariot, is largely dependent on postponing philosophical training until after the intensive study of Talmud. He expresses, in blatant language, his doubt in the success of the talmudic curriculum in successfully competing with the early study of philosophy: "Among them are those who choose to have their houses orphaned of all study of the books of the Talmud. And if one but approaches the books of *Debei Rav* [Talmud], it will seem as if a scorpion has bitten him. And to learn of the *On things Heard* (of Aristotle), he will hasten as an eagle to eat, but if they remove from him the book of *Sense and Sensibilia* (of Aristotle) it will seem as if a serpent has bitten him" (*Minḥat Kna'ot*, p. 652). He formulates his struggle as an internal Maimonidean struggle within the Provencal tradition, but this struggle reveals a violent outbreak of the tension between differing tendencies in the understanding of Maimonides' legacy. Abba Mari wrote to his internal opponents as follows: "For we have not come, God prevent us, to denounce wisdom. This never crossed our minds. But rather, to establish your words, and to fix a proper time for them, for they are no better than the vision of the chariot" (*Minḥat Kna'ot*, p. 447).

We may understand the change that takes place in this struggle by examining the motivations and intentions of the Rashba, Abba Mari's main ally; here, the ambivalence of the esoteric becomes evident. The Rashba was interested in setting limitations on the study of philosophy, but not because it dealt with the vision of the chariot, which demanded caution and esotericism. The Rashba, the prominent successor to the kabbalistic tradition of the school of Naḥmanides, maintained an entirely different position with respect to Jewish esoteric teachings. For him, the imposition of limits on the study of philosophy was a first step toward its eventual total eradication. In one of the first letters sent by the Rashba to

Abba Mari, the profound difference between the two allies is evident. The Rashba himself comments on this:

> For those incurable people whom you spoke of, who preach on the vision of the chariot before the multitudes in the synagogues, may heaven reveal their sin, for they preach foolish words and make public their madness. But in the matter of which you have accused them of revealing what the ancient One of the world has concealed, my heart tells me that they have revealed nothing of what is hidden. They are not guilty of the sin of disclosure, and their foolishness, and their lack of knowledge saves them from that sin. (*Minḥat Kna'ot*, p. 345)

Abba Mari accuses those who preach philosophical sermons of revealing the secrets of the vision of the chariot, whereas the Rashba, ironically, pardons them from this sin for, according to him, they revealed nothing of what was concealed.[8] From the point of view of the Rashba, those preachers preaching dangerous foolish words are not among those who entered *pardes* before their time, and consequently reveal secrets in public; rather they are among those who exchanged *pardes* for heresy.

In many of his letters, the Rashba attacked his opponents using the image of philosophy as the foreign woman who attempts to displace the Torah-queen in her own house. The comparison of the Torah to the childhood wife of Israel or to the woman betrothed to Israel is a well-known image in talmudic literature. Parallel to it, we find the image of Greek wisdom as the forbidden, alluring foreign woman. In one of the more blatant passages of the ban formulated by the Rashba and the notables of Barcelona, it is written:

> The voice of God calls to the city, the voice of God spews forth flames, the voice says "Read." Read in the ears of the people, who wreaked devastation in the land, who trampled the fence, who mock the discipline of the mother, and remove her from authority, who fornicated with the daughter of a foreign god and by every crossroads revealed her nakedness. (*Minḥat Kna'ot*, pp. 409–410)

The ban proposal was discussed in Montpelier and, of course, aroused tremendous opposition among the supporters of wisdom. Based on the words of the Rashba, they concluded that the struggle far surpassed the internal Maimonidean discussion, as Abba Mari sought to present it. For the supporters of wisdom, the ban was a direct attack on the entire Provencal culture. Their position was based, among other things, on the widespread reference to wisdom using metaphors of the daughter of a foreign god or as a foreign, forbidden woman. In order to refute their claims, Abba Mari asked for a clarification from the Rashba. This request reveals the yawning chasm between the two allies, as well as Abba Mari's approach, requesting that their differences be obscured, so that the struggle could be formulated as an internal Maimonidean dispute:

> In order to put into practice the validity of the epistle to seek the Lord without error, I the young one [Abba Mari] come and humbly supplicate before saint and angel [Rashba] that he lend me an ear. It is written in the epistle, "fornicated with the daughter of a foreign god and embracing a strange woman in his bosom." To our understanding, this speaks of those who deal in heresies, who preach false words which lead wisdom astray. For some people say that the letter intended to call the teachings of astronomy and the wisdom of philosophy "the daughter of a strange god." For the vision of their eyes was obscured, for the study of wisdom was prohibited only for those under thirty years old. For when the word of our master, well-explained, will arrive, those who understand your true words will be joyful and glad. (*Minḥat Kna'ot*, p. 444)

In this appeal, which was never answered, Abba Mari requests that the Rashba clarify his words on the daughter of the foreign god. Abba Mari quotes the Rashba's words and implores him to restrict them to the struggle against the denial of the belief in creation *ex nihilo* and the public sermons, and to clarify to his opponents that the metaphor of "the daughter of a foreign god" does not apply to the wisdom of nature and philosophy as a whole. As evidence for the interpretation he provides for the Rashba's words, Abba Mari states that the nature of the ban is unclear to his opponents: "For the vision of their eyes was obscured, for the study of wisdom was prohibited only for those under thirty years old." He claims that were the Rashba of the opinion that philosophy and the teachings of astronomy were daughters of a foreign god, and those who study it betray the wives of their youth, namely the Torah, why did the text of the ban permit the study of philosophy for those over thirty years of age? Abba Mari attempts to prove that, contrary to the interpretation given by his opponents to the initiative of the Rashba and the notables of Barcelona, the ban indeed accords with the internal limits that Maimonides himself would have set. He does not reject philosophy as something completely prohibited, but sees it as an esoteric realm, which must be studied cautiously, and only upon maturity. Similarly, the only study of wisdom that was prohibited by the ban were physics and metaphysics, but not logic, astronomy, and mathematics.

Among the figures who were enlisted to support the ban on philosophy was a great talmudic authority, Asher ben Yeḥiel, known as the Rosh. The Rosh resided at the time in Toledo, where he was the rabbi of the city, yet his origins were in Worms, Germany, where he had been the heir to Meir ben Barukh of Rothenburg. He was forced to move to Spain after the imprisonment of his teacher, and as a recognized rabbinic authority he was welcomed by the Rashba and his circles. Being educated in Ashkenaz he had no sympathy for the Jewish Arabic culture of Andalusia and its impact in Provence. In Toldeo he was engaged in a fierce struggle with the representative of the Andalusian cultures, who saw him as an alien figure who managed to marginalize the old Spanish Jewish elite. His reaction to the ban reveals a similar understanding to that of Abba Mari: he took exception to the ban for the same reasons that Abba Mari favored it. In his letter dealing with Abba Mari's attempt at acquiring the Rosh's support, he argues:

> For your honor knows that I signed your request against my better judgment and under duress. For how should I sign that one should not study [philosophy] before twenty-five years of age? It would result that I give permission [to study it] after twenty-five. In my opinion, it should be prohibited for his entire lifetime, but in order not to discourage others [from signing], I signed. (*Minḥat Kna'ot*, pp. 834–835)

If the ban were formulated to the Rosh's satisfaction, without the constraints of the Maimonidean-rabbinic movement in Provence, the study of philosophy would have been prohibited after the age of twenty-five as well! The Rosh testifies that he supported the ban under duress, and signed it only in order not to weaken the resolve of the other signatories.[9] Small wonder, then, that the request for clarification addressed to the Rashba by Abba Mari, in a tone that comes close to begging and displays a sense of urgency, was never answered. While the Rashba did formulate the ban in terms that were acceptable to the supporters of philosophy, he was not prepared to lend the ban the interpretation that Abba Mari lent it. The Rashba's rhetoric, in several of his letters, teaches us that he did not try to restrict the philosophical vision of the chariot to its desired boundaries as an esoteric doctrine, but rather saw the ban as a first step toward the expulsion of this daughter of the foreign god from the congregation of Israel.[10] The difference between Abba Mari and the Rashba in defining the purposes of the ban, on the one hand, and their cooperation, on the other, reveal a fundamental and essential tension within esotericism, which endows the entire esoteric idea with an ambivalent dimension: on the one hand, esotericism can preserve knowledge and lend it an exclusive status; on the other, esotericism is a means of making that very knowledge ineffectual and immaterial. Abba Mari sees esotericism as a safeguard, whereas the Rashba sees it as a means of suppression.

The ambivalent attitude toward the esoteric finds expression not only in the alliance between Abba Mari and the Rashba, but also in the shifting loyalties of another halakhic master who was involved in this dispute—Rabbi Menaḥem HaMeiri from Perpignan, the author of the great talmudic commentary *Beit Habeḥira* and a scholar with strong adherence to the Maimonidean philosophical culture. Abba Mari did not include HaMeiri's letter to him in his book *Minḥat Kna'ot*. This letter was preserved along with a critical comment of one of Abba Mari's students, Rabbi Shimon ben Yosef. Apparently, Abba Mari thought it best to suppress HaMeiri's response, because of his high status among Abba Mari's opponents.[11] HaMeiri's words and the response of Rabbi Shimon ben Yosef apparently deal with the relation between esotericism and autonomy.

According to the witness of HaMeiri himself, the mobilization of the Rashba, the kabbalist of Barcelona, in the struggle, completely reversed his position toward Abba Mari and his initiative. HaMeiri was opposed to the dissemination of Torah secrets, contrary to the position of Shmuel Ibn Tibon. He wrote Abba Mari that when he heard that he was declaring war on the public philosophical sermons, he identified with him completely and wanted to restrict the dissemination of Torah secrets:

> Before many days the rumor reached us, that you began to show your greatness and your mighty hand, and to cancel the matter of the sermons, both through agreements and through bans and oaths, to cancel them entirely, so that in the sermons they would speak only of the Torah, the Talmud, and the Midrash, and sometimes explain the verses through aggadot and wisdom, but in things that are not destructive and do not reveal secrets of the secrets of the Torah or of prophecy. We rejoiced over your sayings as one who finds a great treasure, we praised it and exalted it and we approved of it as we saw fit. We said that through your deed, God will grant us respite from our anger and our sadness. (*Ḥoshen Mishpat*, p. 150; Letter of Shimon ben Yosef, published by D. Kaufmann in *Jubelchrift zum neunzigsten Geburtstag des L. Zunz* [Berlin, 1884], Hebrew section, p. 147)

HaMeiri, however, completely reversed his position when Abba Mari turned to the Rashba, after his original failure, and asked him to join the struggle against the sermons: "For while we were still conversing, another came and said that when your advice was not immediately put in practice, you shook the earth, and before the master the Rabbi [Rashba] you sought to prove the well-foundedness of your case, thus casting wisdom before mockers and its students to perdition" (*Ḥoshen Mishpat*, p. 150). HaMeiri saw this appeal to the Rashba as a fundamental change in the struggle of Abba Mari. Once the Rashba became involved in the struggle, it was no longer, in his opinion, an internal philosophical struggle over the limits of dissemination of Torah secrets, but an all-out attack on philosophical culture. The dispute was transformed from an internal struggle within the camp of the masters of wisdom to a total struggle against wisdom. As HaMeiri writes: "Although our master the Rabbi is the father of us all and no one strays or opens his mouth to dispute the perfection of his greatness, you already know that in such matters, not all opinions are the same. They chose as their lot the wisdom of the Kabbalah, and most philosophical matters are for them devils and angels of destruction" (*Hoshen Mishpat*, pp. 150–151).

In his letter to Abba Mari, HaMeiri claimed that the Rashba was a kabbalist known for his opposition to philosophical wisdom, and through his involvement the dispute became an all-out clash between two cultures—Kabbalah and philosophy. HaMeiri deduces from the case of the Rashba to that of Abba Mari: "It is evident to me [HaMeiri] that many were awakened the spear of your [Abba Mari] wisdom, and mobilized your intention in conjunction with that of our master the rabbi [Rashba], to annul all matters of wisdom and to drive it out so that it has no inheritance in our land" (156). HaMeiri belongs to the camp of philosophical wisdom that fought an internal battle against philosophical sermons, so that his heart was with Abba Mari for as long as he waged an internal battle in Provence on the question of the exoteric nature of philosophy. Once the picture changed, and the Rashba joined the struggle, HaMeiri began to support the opponents of Abba Mari. The alliance between Abba Mari and the Rashba, which was constructed upon differing conceptions and an ambivalent approach to esotericism, resulted in HaMeiri's reversing his position completely.[12]

An interesting aspect of the exoteric question is revealed by one of the most interesting and sharpest criticisms levied by HaMeiri against the ban proclaimed in Barcelona. According to the text of the ban, it was prohibited for students under the age of twenty-five to learn the Greek books on nature and metaphysics, although they were permitted to study the books of the Jewish authors, including the writings of Maimonides. To this, HaMeiri poses the following question: If the ban had been designed to fight against the uncontrolled dissemination of philosophical ideas and philosophical sermons, it would have been preferable to fight the popular compositions and sermons of the Jewish authors, rather than prohibit Aristotelian metaphysics and physics—works that are difficult and esoteric by nature. In HaMeiri's opinion, the ban should have been formulated in an opposite way, as he writes Abba Mari:

And in this our decrees have been of no use, for the preacher does not preach on [the Aristotelian books] On Things Heard, On the Heavens, On the Universe, Meteorology, On Generation and Corruption, On Sense and Sensibilia, On the Soul, and Metaphsyics. Some of them have never read a page of these books, only whatever they read in the honorable book [Guide of the Perplexed], in Sefer Hamalmad and in the Commentary on Ecclesiastes, in Ma'amar Yikavu Hamayim, and in other books both old and new. For they see there certain allegories and they too work skillfully, they try their hand at all that their soul desires, for there is no height too lofty for them, and they conjoin one word to another. The result is that you our champion [Abba Mari] "blesses the main thing and exempts the negligible"; this is not the way to remove them from sin, and as a result it misses your desired, honorable and necessary intention. For the matter of the learning of [those Aristotelian] books, involve many difficulties. . . . Therefore, we ignore the corruption which is current and the evil that spreads each day among thousands of people. For now among the preachers a new sect springs up each day, and they recite their songs and go on their way. And instead we have latched on to the uncommon thing, in which corruption is rare. (Hoshen Mishpat, pp. 166–167)

Study of the philosophical books is possible only for individuals, because of the great difficulty in their comprehension. These compositions do not serve the preachers, who for the most part have no understanding whatsoever of the philosophical sources. Guide of the Perplexed, the books written by the Tibon family, and the work of Ya'akov Anatoli were the true sources of inspiration for the preachers. If the struggle of Abba Mari had focused on opposition of exotericism, a problem that also concerned HaMeiri, then he should have directed the ban against philosophical sermons and not against philosophy itself.

There was an additional dispute between HaMeiri and Abba Mari, which indicates differences of emphasis and sensitivity within the Maimonidean rabbinic movement, and which resulted in a deep cleavage within the group during the struggle over the ban. HaMeiri, as we have seen, was partner to the criticism of exotericism and philosophical sermons and even fought against them, "whether through agreement or through bans and oaths." He opposed, however, the additional and central element of the ban: age restrictions on the study of philosophical texts. From his point of view, such study is restricted to the elite anyway and does not constitute a breaking of the esoteric code. HaMeiri was prepared to take the risk inherent in early exposure to philosophical culture, the denial of creation ex nihilo and divine providence, for without such exposure, knowledge would die out: "For if one stumbles in his study once or twice, then he, by his sins, will be cut off and uprooted. But why then should wisdom die out? Were the gates of pardes locked when Elisha ben Abuya left them, breaching, deserting, and destroying?" (Hoshen Mishpat, p. 162). The termination of philosophical knowledge at an early age might result, in his opinion, in missing a rare opportunity to study wisdom:

> For you, our notable, know that man has chambers and different and unique dispositions one person tends toward this and one toward that. . . . Secondly, at this time the millstones are around our necks, and anything to which the gate has not been opened before is written on the sand, excepting those who deprive themselves of all other preoccupation and immerse himself in his study. . . . Third, one cannot merit learning from all, and those who know the secrets of wisdom are but the few among the few—one from a town and two from a family, and if there be no time restrictions, they will learn whatever they find. . . . And if there be time restrictions, when he reaches that time, a better time may have already passed. (*Ḥoshen Mishpat*, pp. 165–166)

The difficult circumstances of life and the scarcity of worthy teachers require that philosophy be studied whenever it can, even at an early age.

In spite of the accusation brought by opponents of the ban against Abba Mari and his circle, that they deviated from the Provencal rabbinic tradition, the members of the circle of Abba Mari saw themselves as the faithful successors to the Maimonidean esoteric conception.[13] Their self-understanding, which their struggle accorded with the terms of this tradition, is formulated most explicitly in Rabbi Shimon ben Yosef's response to the letter of HaMeiri. This response expresses the deep disappointment of Abba Mari and his circle from HaMeiri's response, since they, the followers of the rabbinic Maimonidean tradition in Provence, saw HaMeiri as a natural ally. They claimed that HaMeiri was incited by their opponents and distorted their intention.[14] The esoteric conception of Abba Mari and his circle is clearly emphasized in one of the most illuminating passages of Rabbi Shimon's response to HaMeiri's arguments against Abba Mari: "And before the master the Rabbi [Rashba] you sought to prove the well-foundedness of your case, thus casting wisdom before mockers and its students to perdition." He responded to this argument as follows:

> For our brother [Abba Mari] has a portion and inheritance with you in wisdom, and let your ears hear his love and compassion for her [wisdom]. Lest improper persons attack and reveal her nakedness he joined the opinion of the Rabbi [Rashba] and ordered the youths not to approach her until they grow up and see her glory and the glory of God, in whose service are peace and tranquility. They shall behave with her as is customary among ladies, to take her and betroth her. No cries of desperation shall be heard in her borders. Who then has cast wisdom to perdition and its learners to the mockers, if not the youth who learns

not, who makes his way in the Greek sea and sails unknown courses in stormy waters? Our brother [Abba Mari] did not shake the earth to annul wisdom, and did not trample its border. He did not think of rendering the pure impure or declaring the creeping thing pure. For among the heads of the people who had unnatural relations with her [wisdom], their sin and the guilt testify that she fabricated lies. . . . What shall we do for our sister on the day that one speaks of her? For they tell tales about her, both her servants and her hirelings? Blessed be those people who take pity upon her honor, and keep guard over her and do not allow the evil one to become privy to her secrets. Blessed be the man whose Torah study teaches him to close the gate behind her. (*Ḥoshen Mishpat*, p. 150)

The metaphor of wisdom as a woman in Rabbi Shimon's writing reflects another fascinating development. The Rashba, Abba Mari's ally, calls wisdom the daughter of a foreign god, whereas Rabbi Shimon turns wisdom into a lady, a princess whose glory is on the interior. In his words, Abba Mari does not cast out wisdom, but rather is her lover, contrary to HaMeiri's accusation. Through the prohibition of early and public study of philosophy, he protects her from those who would expose her before the eyes of all and thus defile her. In his words: "Those who have unnatural relations with her." The return to esotericism is not an attempt to marginalize philosophy, but rather to strengthen it by claiming that lady wisdom is worthy only of the king: "Her face shall not be seen except by he whose soul has been purified." The dissemination of wisdom is depicted in vivid colors as the violation and humiliation of the princess whom all may abuse.[15] The ability to turn the metaphor on its head—from daughter of a foreign god to princess—demonstrates the ambiguity inherent in esotericism. The ban on early study and uncontrolled exposure of philosophy might be seen as a first step in the expulsion of wisdom, or else as a desperate attempt to preserve her honor. The complex web of alliances, like that between the Rashba and Abba Mari, of shifting loyalties and accusations, of varying and sometimes contradictory interpretations given to those very alliances—this entire network is based on the double meaning inherent in the guarding and concealment of a body of knowledge.

The central figures active in the dispute over philosophy and esotericism were halakhic masters, and they confronted each other over the definition of the limits of the transmission and dissemination of philosophical knowledge. This phenomenon parallels the attempt of kabbalists who were halakhic scholars and rabbinic authorities to define the Kabbalah as an esoteric realm, among other reasons in order to keep it within their province, as an area that would not compete with the structure of study and the traditional principles of authority. The halakhic masters we discussed above attempted to hedge in and confine philosophical activity within differing strictures of esotericism: Abba Mari through his struggle against philosophical sermons and the philosophical curriculum, and HaMeiri by taking exception to philosophical sermons. The dispute over philosophy and esotericism were a political and communal expression of the tension between esotericism and exotericism. This tension increased steadily throughout the thirteenth century and reached a boiling point in the early fourteenth century.

CHAPTER 16

Esotericism, Discontent, and Co-Existence

ESOTERIC DOCTRINE, as we have seen, was the most unguarded area of the tradition, precisely because it was the most guarded and protected of all. Secrecy is the medium that enables integration of different cultural contexts into the tradition. Under the cloak of esotericism, radically conflicting positions were integrated into the heart of Judaism. Each of these positions granted totally different significance to the meaning of halakhah and the system of Jewish beliefs. But as long as each side guarded its Torah secrets in secret, the radical multiplicity of competing and conflicting positions could be tolerated. The open and revealed level enabled a co-existence based on mutual respect for secrecy. Within the same congregation and in the same synagogue, people who completely rejected each other's views might be found together; but this, on condition that the conflicting sides preserved their esoteric doctrines at a proper distance from the revealed side of their worldviews.

This imposed tolerance of the esoteric was made possible in part by its ambivalent structure. Esotericism supports two interpretations: on the one hand, the esoteric contents are accorded superior status, and thus must be protected; on the other hand, they seem to be foolishness or even heresy, so that if they cannot be uprooted from the world completely, at least they should remain closed and enigmatic. Thus, the Rashba was prepared to support philosophy, as long as it remained a hidden subject whose faithful would not try to disseminate it among the larger Jewish public. It would seem that this co-existence could be preserved, since the bearers of the philosophical tradition also agreed that this realm should be guarded in secret, although for entirely different reasons. This fragile structure of co-existence collapsed, however, once the esoteric tradition traversed the boundaries of secrecy and leaked out onto the surface. This leaking had several expressions: differing degrees of transparency in writing, public sermons, and the creation of a basic curriculum based on the principles of Torah secrets.

The history of Jewish culture in the thirteenth century and in the early fourteenth century manifests a strong link between disclosure and dispute. Great and violent struggles took place when the concealed traditions ceased guarding the esoteric code in one measure or another. When the esotericists turned outward, they set in motion a chain reaction that led to severe confrontation. The Rashba, who was a devout esotericist in kabbalistic matters, sought to establish co-existence by reversing the process of disclosure. But after a lengthy process of widening the apertures of the showpiece, as Ibn Tibon called it, the attempt to reestablish the borders of secrecy proved to be anachronistic. The devotees of philosophical culture were not prepared to compromise their accomplishments. They interpreted what was offered them, under the guise of guarding Torah secrets, as an attempt to marginalize their culture, and to relegate it to the status of a sectarian, marginal, and closed culture. The exact same process took place in the third and fourth decades of the thirteenth century, with the writing down of the kabbalistic tradition. This writing led to a severe struggle, culminating in the burning of kabbalistic manuscripts by Rabbi Meshulam ben Moshe and his nephew, Rabbi Meir ben Shimon. Isaac the Blind's attempt at restoring the crown to its previous glory, as well as the esoteric position of Naḥmanides and his disciples, could not close the breach. The bursting open of the boundaries of secrecy is fueled by an internal dynamic that brought the esotericists to almost total disclosure. Indeed, in Gerona and in Castile, an entirely different approach to the esoteric question transformed the tradition into literature.

Not only did the attempt to reinstate the previous boundaries of secrecy fail, but the attempt itself resulted in excessive dissemination of Torah secrets. This was one of the points raised by HaMeiri against Abba Mari's appeal to the Rashba. HaMeiri heard a rumor that Abba Mari had revealed to the Rashba hidden things from the manuscripts of one of the sages of Provence. In his opinion, had Abba Mari merely reported about the public philosophical sermons, which would have been bad enough. But Abba Mari compounded his sin by exposing the esoteric tradition of philosophy in Provence:

> It was told in our ears that you [Abba Mari] wrote in your letter to our master, the Rabbi [Rashba], that after the death of one of the sages, who is one of the best-known among us during his life in good deeds and piety and fear of sin, it was found among his books and the treasures of his writings that Abraham and Sarah are hints of matter and spirit, and that the tribes hint at the twelve signs of the zodiac. We heard as well that our master, the Rabbi [Rashba], publicized this in a letter he sent out. And you [Abba Mari], the man who is perched upon a lofty cedar of Lebanon, diverted from your goal and intention to inform our master, the Rabbi, of the content of the sermons, and instead had told him of the content of the books and hidden scrolls which may only be read by select individuals. And in your great intelligence you showed him what may be seen from the inside, rather than informing

him only what can be seen from the outside and may be heard by all whether wise or foolish. (*Ḥoshen Mishpat*, pp. 153–155)

The careful guarding of esotericism expresses preservation of cultural autonomy in the face of external criticism; according to HaMeiri, the revelation of secret scrolls damages the communal autonomy of Provence.

We may call the twelfth and thirteenth centuries "the centuries of concealment and revelation of Jewish creativity." The writings of the central thinkers of this period, Ibn Ezra, Maimonides, and Naḥmanides, which reflect the important movements in medieval Judaism, are all esoteric commentaries of the hidden layer of the Jewish canon. The expansion of the esoteric idea was accompanied by constant testing of its boundaries and by tension between the concealed and the revealed. In the midst of this tension, several fundamental problems arose within the various esoteric traditions: the nature of knowledge—is it open or closed? The manner of transmission of knowledge—from controlled oral transmission to hinting, to the creation of a literature and sermons; the depth of stratification of the learning public; the competition of esoteric circles with halakhic masters and the traditional curriculum; and, finally, the mutual relationships between the different secret traditions that co-existed alongside each other.

We may now return to the question we raised at the beginning of the book: Why did the esoteric idea become such an important phenomenon in the major trends of Jewish thought in the Middle Ages? Leo Strauss, who devoted his attention to the existence of the esoteric phenomenon, attempted to explain the esoteric phenomenon in terms of the tension between philosophy and society. The philosopher protects himself and the society by going underground. Certainly this is one of the elements of the medieval esoteric phenomenon, but it is a limited explanation of the phenomenon both in terms of its scope and in terms of its subtlety and complexity. Strauss, who began his investigation through the reading of *Guide of the Perplexed*, placed Maimonides within a tradition of philosophical esotericism, a tradition ushered in by Plato and continued until Spinoza and the unfortunate decline in modern philosophy. Yet the medieval esoteric project, of which Maimonides was a part, encompassed a variety of trends in which the philosophical pursuit of rational inquiry is just one among many. Naḥmanides and Ibn Ezra, representing Kabbalah and astrology, were also deeply immersed in the esoteric project. The esotericism of *Guide of the Perplexed* has to be examined as well through that prism of a major cultural and religious occupation with the hidden, which cut across various theological points of view. What they all share in developing and expanding the concealed realm, as I explain below, is a sense of acute crisis.

The focus on the self-preservation of the philosopher fails to address not only the scope of the phenomenon but its ambiguity and subtlety. Maimonides' constant preoccupation with his own esotericism, declaring that he conceals a hidden doctrine for his own protection and the protection of the masses, and his enumeration of the techniques of his concealment, is a rather suicidal policy if what motivates him is self-preservation. This problem is magnified when we discover his constant preoccupation with the limits of secrecy, which accompanies the esoteric idea itself. The incredible speed with which revealed esoteric traditions became the ethos of entire communities demands explanation. If the question of the protection of the freedom of knowledge was at the center of the esoteric realm, why then were the esotericists themselves so publicly preoccupied with the idea of concealment and its existence time and time again? Why did an entire literature arise in the thirteenth century around esoteric traditions that were to be transmitted orally or written down in fuzzy chapter headings? Furthermore, during the fourteenth century, dozens of compositions were written solely with the sole purpose of explaining the esoteric hints in the writings of Ibn Ezra, *Guide of the Perplexed*, and Naḥmanides' commentaries. It is true that it is difficult to keep secrets, but we must remember that this difficulty largely depends on the desire of the secret keeper to expose more than a small portion of it. Thus, the esoteric, which was to represent the internal meaning of the tradition, expanded steadily and expropriated more and more of the surface or revealed tradition. In the fourteenth century, only a thin shell remained of the revealed layer. The core of the secret doctrine in these centuries was not the survival of the esotericists by going underground, as Strauss supposed, but rather the use of the medium of secrecy in order to absorb and introduce new theologies into the heart of Judaism.

The rise of esoteric teachings is linked to a crisis, to discontent with the revealed layer of the Torah. Secrecy enables the absorption and integration of new elements, because its very existence expands the receptivity of authoritative texts to new meanings by an immeasurable quotient. Furthermore, as a result of what was called above the paradox of esotericism, it is precisely *because* the secret is guarded that one may attribute to it layers substantially different from the revealed layer of the tradition. The power of the esoteric as a medium of absorption is increased because an idea that penetrates the secret realm enjoys the privileged status of the internal foundation of religion. In spite of the tremendous differences between different conceptions of secrecy, all of them share a discontent with the worldview that medieval Jews inherited from the biblical and talmudic traditions. Astrology, philosophy, and Kabbalah all confronted biblical and talmudic anthropomorphism—in Ibn Ezra by emphasizing the hermetic and astrological elements of a causal nature; in Maimonides by establishing the Aristotelian concept of nature and creating a constant tension between wisdom and will; and in Kabbalah through the complex organic structure of the godhead, whose balance is causally dependent on man's theurgic actions. Each movement presented an entirely different concept of the causal mechanism, but all of them confront the concept of God as a personality, in one way or another, with a deep level of causality. Being, we might say, combats personality. The deeper we penetrate the esoteric layers, it becomes apparent that the search for casual explanation is at the heart of the esoteric project. The biblical and rabbinic understanding that history, law, and nature are expressions of the covenantal relationship between two personalities, God and Israel, became an inadequate picture for the medieval Jewish esoteric elites. The world of Athens, mediated through Arabic philosophy and science, which posited causality and being as the ultimate explanation, penetrated to the heart of Judaism. Despite all the deep differences between kabbalists and philosophers, they share a weighty cultural fact: the dominance given to nature as the central explanatory category. The religious activity in which this rapture is most manifested is the revolution in the understanding of prayer. In its essence, prayer is an act of appeasing and convincing, which in its details is based on the interpersonal relationship that exists between humans and God, like a slave appeasing his master or a child attempting to convince a parent. In the medieval period, the status of prayer as an expression of an interpersonal relationship begins to disappear. From an activity of convincing and appeasing it became a complex causal activation in the kabbalistic tradition, or a meditative contemplative exercise reflecting philosophical trends. Those medieval movements upon which the esoteric concept left no mark teach us much about the other movements. In the commentaries on Scripture of Rashi or the Rashbam, there is no esoteric level,[1] primarily because they were devoid of the consciousness of crisis and confusion when faced with the revealed layer of the text.[2] Rashi did have an esoteric tradition, which was restricted to the creation story and the chapters on the chariot in Ezekiel. In many ways, his esoteric conception was similar to the Hekhalot literature. But the idea of the esoteric as an accompanying level of meaning, which runs parallel to the surface of the text and which transforms the very meaning of tradition, is completely absent from Rashi's writings. Such an understanding of the esoteric project was limited to the medieval elites who were struggling with an urgent sense of crisis.

This composition dealt with the esoteric idea and its development until the early fourteenth century. The termination of the discussion at this point in time is not entirely arbitrary, since in the twelfth and thirteenth centuries the question of concealment and revelation was at the center of Jewish thought. A systematic consideration of this question in the fourteenth century and afterward is beyond the scope of the current discussion. It is, however, worthwhile to raise several general points, which have wider conceptual ramifications for the problem of esotericism, and which concern mainly the sixteenth and seventeenth centuries and the modern period.

The phenomenon that characterizes medieval Jewish thought—the preoccupation with Torah secrets and the use of the idea of the esoteric as a basic hermeneutic position—is completely absent from Jewish thought in the modern period. Moses Mendelssohn, Hermann Cohen, Martin Buber, Franz Rosenzweig, Abraham Joshua Heschel, Joseph Dov Soloveitchik, and others never claimed they were attempting to clarify Torah secrets, that the community they addressed was divided, or that they themselves employed techniques of concealment. While we may characterize the difference between medieval thought and modern thought in many ways, the discussion of esotericism focuses our attention on one essential difference: the absence of the idea of secrecy in modern Jewish thought, as opposed to its centrality in the Middle Ages. The absence of an element of secrecy from modern Jewish thought deprives this thought of a powerful hermeneutic tool, which endowed medieval thought with extraordinary flexibility. Medieval thought had a far more radical character than modern thought, since through the esoteric idea it transformed the astrological, Gnostic, Aristotelian, or Neoplatonic cultural contexts into the inner and deep meaning of Judaism. Furthermore, medieval thought presented a far larger variety of essentially conflicting positions in comparison with the modern period, as a result of what we have described as the paradox of esotericism, that is, the unguarded nature of the esoteric realm. The absence of the esoteric idea in the modern period thus has a restrictive effect, and we must raise the question: why did such a central element vanish in the modern period?

One answer is linked to the change in the dissemination of knowledge, which took place as a result of the invention of print, from the sixteenth century on. Print undermined the closed frameworks of teaching and initiation and the local nature of tradition. In the early fourteenth century, Shem Tov Ibn Gaon defined the esoteric ethic as involving teaching "from authors and not from books," even though this ethos had already been weakened during the second half of the thirteenth century. The reliance on oral initiation became almost meaningless in the age of print, in which the book became an item of mass production, so that from the sixteenth century on, the structure of transmission of knowledge in traditional Jewish society changed completely.[3]

Another answer goes beyond the revolutionary changes in the possibilities of dissemination of knowledge from the sixteenth century onward and is related to the Enlightenment movement of the modern period, which made the idea of transparency a central element of their worldview.

Knowledge was supposed to be based on solid foundations, clear to any knowledgeable person. This would enable the construction of a framework that would uproot ignorance and enlighten the furthest corners of society with the light of knowledge. In the modern ideology of the enlightenment, the very existence of the masses is seen as the essential problem, and not the guarding of knowledge from the masses. Even if not all the streams of modern Jewish thought are committed to the ideals of enlightenment, the absence of the esoteric as a legitimate philosophical category influenced Jewish thought. This category is not at the service of modern Jewish thinkers, as it was in the Middle Ages, and they cannot divide the community of their readers into an elite and the masses. The assumption of esotericism of the Middle Ages, which enabled the flourishing of the idea of secrecy, was that, under conditions of total transparency, society would disintegrate. This assumption is in fundamental contradiction with the idea of the enlightenment, and particularly in opposition to the political ethos of democratic societies which promote transparency. It is at this point of departure entering the modern condition that I wish to turn my gaze from the historical analysis to the conceptual and philosophical concerns.

CHAPTER 17

Taxonomy and Paradoxes of Esotericism: Conceptual Conclusion

I

The historical material examined thus far gives rise to three kinds of esotericism which will guide the taxonomy of the hidden and concealed—the *internal*, the *instrumental*, and the *essential*. The primary motivating force for the existence of an esoteric hidden domain is based on an internal non-instrumental motivation that establishes a connection between the transcendence and the hidden, or in reverse between exposure and violation. Unlike internal non-instrumental arguments, instrumental reasons for esotericism argue for the problematic consequences of revealing knowledge. The procedure of producing nuclear bombs, for example, should not be disclosed since it will fall in the hands of irresponsible, cruel leaders. The internal non-instrumental argument advances a more fundamental, stronger claim, asserting that the body of knowledge itself will be transformed and diminished by its disclosure. Two different motivations for protecting privacy shed light on this distinction. Privacy might be protected for instrumental reasons, when betrayal of trust will cause future harm to someone. It might as well be protected because exposure itself diminishes the value of the subject or the relationships at stake. There might be an essential difference for securing privacy in lawyer-client relationship, and securing privacy in the context of a therapist and a patient.

This internal motivation is attached to complex relations between the hidden and the surface that are expressed in the most fundamental structure of the self. In a situation of total transparency, without any concealment, it would be impossible to maintain a bounded self, since the self as a bounded entity exists because it is concealed. If a person's thoughts were written on his forehead, exposed before all, the distinction between interior and exterior would vanish, and with it also individuation. Privacy, expressed through the possibility of concealment, thus protects the very ability of a person to define himself as an individual. Furthermore, the self may create special relationships by displaying differential measures of exposure and intimacy. He moves through social space by allotting revelation and concealment and establishing differential measures of distance and closeness. Thus, the self defines himself and distinguishes between friends and others and between intimates and strangers, through the privileged position he has to his interiority.

Improper exposure, contrary to a person's will, results in shame, and every moment of shame, even the slightest, is a profound wound to one's consciousness of boundedness, a sort of death blow. The possibility of experiencing shame is a self-protective emotion in its most basic form. In this sense, it was pointed out that shame is to be differentiated from guilt. Guilt is expressed in the desire to clean a stain that sticks to a person, and expresses the need to reinstate the self that has been sullied. Shame, by contrast, colors the entire self. Shame does not stain, but defiles the entire surface. It arouses the desire to disappear and be effaced, because it results from an injury to the tissues that constitute the self and its boundaries.

Philosophers who have dealt with shame argue about the degree to which an outside perspective is constitutive of the emotion of shame. Some phenomenological accounts argue that such perspective is not constitutive to shame since it can be internalized by the agent, looking at himself as if from the outside. Yet there are cases which constitute the core of shame where the outside gaze is essential to the emotion of shame. A distinction between primary and secondary shame might shed light on this problem. Primary shame which has its roots in the experience of exposure concerns a state or an event that is not inherently wrong as such so long as it is not observed in the improper context. The covering of nakedness is the archetypal example of primary shame. There is nothing wrong with nakedness as such; rather, the emotion of shame is created by condition of improper exposure. Similarly, there is nothing wrong with singing aloud in the shower or posing before a mirror, although some might feel shame or embarrassment when they have been perceived doing either. Secondary shame is a case in which something is wrong in the act or the person as such, even when not being observed, and the exposure of such events or deficiencies causes that added pain of shame.

To further clarify the distinction, we can refer to Sartre's example of someone who peeks through a keyhole and thus transgresses the limits of privacy while at the same time someone else passes by and sees him committing this act.[1] Let us expand the story and imagine that the door suddenly opens and that the person inside, who had been naked, realizes that he had been watched. There are two people here who experience shame, the one in the room who was watched while naked, and the person who was observed watching. Each of them experiences a different kind of shame, which is manifested in the different role that the observer has in constituting the shame. The person who was observed peeking internalizes the observer's point of view concerning him. In such a case the outside eye does not play a constitutive role in shame; it is triggering a shift in self-perception, which the person who is watched is experiencing. He has been made to perceive himself watching. He was shaken from his immersion in the act into a position of realization that is caused by looking at himself from the outside. We can imagine that such person might be attacked by an emotion of shame, even without an outside observer, in a case in which he found himself observing his own actions as if from a distance. Such a change of self-perception might occur without the trigger of an outside eye.

In the case of the person who was naked inside the room the role of the outside eye is far more constitutive. In such a case of what I called primary shame, the observer is constitutive in a stronger sense, since he causes a transformation in the description of the thing exposed, which is not the case in secondary shame. Nudity becomes a concern when it is improperly observed; it is the contact with the eye that makes it shameful. The outside eye does not have the mere role triggering a transformation of self-perception; in such a case it is perception that counts rather than self-perception. In that respect, because of the constitutive role of the observer, shame and guilt are clearly distinguishable in cases of primary shame but not in secondary shame.

There could be delicate and nuanced shifts from primary shame to secondary and vice versa. In certain cultures nakedness might become a source for secondary shame, viewing the body itself as the source of sin. Augustine's reading of the passages in Genesis of the original sin and the fall is such an example. According to his interpretation, the fall caused the erotic drive to become independent of our will. While before the original sin Adam had erection at will in the same way that he could move his hand at will, after the fall the sexual drive became a force inhabiting the person independent of his direct will. The body therefore turned into a shameful object onto itself, reminding ourselves that we are at the mercy of a blind force that emerges regardless of our will. According to Augustine, the source of shame of nakedness lies in the fact that the erotic drive captures our mental field and controls our actions, a paradigm for our loss of control. This is the reason why humans cover their sexual organs and why humans have intercourse only in private. Augustine turns what seems to be a primary shame, in which nakedness is a source of shame only when perceived by an undesired eye, into a secondary shame in which nakedness, regardless of the observer, is shameful. In radical shame cultures, if they exist altogether, the opposite shift happens. Every secondary shame is a case of a primary one. There is nothing wrong in doing a particular act, but in being observed and exposed concerning doing it.

Improper exposure and shame are connected to the self experiencing a loss of his capacity to control the basic most rudimentary forms of his appearance. Ongoing forced exposure transforms shame into humiliation since it touches upon a primary sense of helplessness; the inability to decide upon when and how to appear.[2] The practice of forced nakedness as a form of humiliation robs the person of the primary space and power to form a "persona." While secondary shame is about a loss of self-esteem, primary shame is not concerned with such a loss because there was nothing wrong to begin with in the practice of behavior that was exposed, only the exposure itself. We might say that primary shame harms our capacity for any esteem, since self-esteem depends upon our capability of presenting ourselves.

Rousseau mourned the gap between reality and appearance as the essential condition of the human fall. Lack of transparency is the source of mistrust, misunderstanding, and alienation. In the attempt to appear different from who we are and emerge as properly socialized creatures, we pay the price of estrangement from ourselves as from others. The veil between reality and appearance is not only constructed by the self. Costumes are forced on us from the outside as well when we are misinterpreted, and intentions and motivations are attributed falsely to us. It is for this reason that Rousseau yearns for the childlike natural state of transparency, before self-awareness forces upon us the burden of appearance and shame. His *Confessions* serve a redemptive purpose; they are postulated by him as a heroic exemplar of an attempt to bridge the hidden with the revealed.[3] Yet Rousseau's utopia of a community where we are all transparent to one another appears to be a rather harsh, intolerable, and self-defeating state of affairs. Lack of transparency is indeed a source of mistrust and it unravels bonds of friendship, yet the value of trust and friendship would disappear altogether in conditions of full transparency. If there was no interiority and our thoughts, intentions, and desires would emerge written on our forehead, trust would not be a virtue, and intimacy would evaporate altogether. Needless to say our sense of wonder, surprise, and revelation will be diminished, as well as the possibility to indulge privately in what is publicly burdensome and inappropriate.[4]

The concept of internal esotericism enables a deeper grasp of the urge to revelation that is inherent in concealment, a feature that appeared at different moments in the historical material that has been examined. This dialectic of concealment and revelation is connected to the phenomenological juxtaposition of intimacy and shame. Intimacy is reached at the point in which ordinary barriers of shame are shed; it emerges in the domains that are protected by the mechanism of shame. It is therefore impossible to achieve intimacy when such areas do not exist to begin with, as in the case of a shameless person. The connection of intimacy to the domain which is ordinarily protected by shame makes past intimacy susceptible to retroactive shame, when what seems to be at the time a proper disclosure, given a change in perspective or conditions, looks retroactively as a cause for shame. The genuine opposite of shame is not shamelessness but intimacy.

The reversal of shame in intimacy is manifested both in primary and secondary shame. An exposure that might be perceived in relation to another subject as the violation of individuation and transgression of boundaries is experienced in a proper intimate context as an evocation of presence, a way out of isolation. The desire to disappear which accompanies that sense of violation of boundaries is replaced by an acute sense of being, though hesitant. It is for that reason that intimacy cannot be forced since the intimate context is an exposure that does not undermine our capacity to have a persona. In cases of secondary shame as was analyzed above, the observer does not occupy a constitutive role. He is a trigger for a change in self-perception, a transformation that might be achieved without the observer as well. In secondary shame the situation perceived is itself problematic; it is not made as such by the fact of it being perceived. Intimacy, when it relates to the realm of secondary shame, is the capacity to expose a wrong to another person without it causing a harmful change in self-esteem. It is in some circumstances the opposite: self-revelation is done with the expectation of affirmation and trust. The observer, in an intimate circumstance, is supposed to support a change in the opposite direction which is triggered by the shaming eye; his eye might reconstitute a broken self. The quest for affirmation and comfort in areas that might in fact be prone to potential shame is what bonds concealment to revelation.

It is no wonder that concealment and revelation are attached in their primary mode to this non-instrumental internal form, in which improper exposure is onto itself a kind of violation. The internal conception of esotericism which is motivated by the relationship between exposure and violation emerged within the early mystical corpus of the Hekhalot literature, and within the *Zohar*'s conception of the hidden and concealed. In the *Zohar* this internal esoteric conception is developed within the erotic analogy, and in the Hekhalot literature it emerges within the political framework. The *Zohar* perceives the deeper layers of Torah as God's own body uncovered in the interpretative act. The multilayered text that both reveals and conceals is conceived in terms of the erotic subtle movement of intimacy and alienation. In such an outlook the problem of exposure and dissemination of knowledge is not focused on some grave dangers that might result from such acts. The very act of improper exposure is itself a violation and diminishment of the subject and the relationships involved, in similar ways that pornography might be a diminishment of honor and love.

This primary non-instrumental conception of restricting disclosure is enlarged as well into the political realm of authority and power within the Hekhalot structure of concealment. In this body of literature, exposure is diminishment of transcendence and status. In the ethics of vision, which is shaped by the idea of the God who is hidden from the eye, asymmetry in the possibilities of vision gives rise to a relation of authority and sublimity. The more powerful partner may survey the one standing opposite him from head to toe, whereas the weaker one averts his glance, hesitating to create eye contact. The fear of being noticed is immanent to the organization of sight and the hierarchy of power. One of the rules soldiers learn in basic training is to avoid eye contact with their superiors. Being noticed through such eye contact might put the fresh soldier at risk of being picked on, examined, and used as an example for disciplining. It is indeed the case that the awful fate of Job began with one sentence that God uttered to the Satan: "Have you noticed my servant Job, for there is no one like him on earth" (Job 1:8). At the moment Satan was drawn to notice him, Job had been trapped in the net of disaster.

The more a person may see others, without being seen by them, the further his status is elevated; the inverse is also true. Social status is expressed through varying degrees of privacy, for example, through the expanse of space surrounding a person, in which access to others is restricted. A person's status rises in direct proportion to the size of the personal space allotted him. Overrepresentation is therefore a way of dispelling the aura of a subject or object. Walter Benjamin's insight concerning the fate of artistic objects in an age of reproduction applies to political authority as well. Gossip of lower classes serves such a compensatory humanizing role, and malicious exposure of the ruler's embarrassing moments from slipping to mispronouncing might become a real step in lightening his potential gravitas.

It is interesting to note that there are cases in which the opposite structure is manifested. Servants are allowed to observe and listen to extremely intimate matters, and they are not seen at all by their surroundings. In such a case the inferior status of someone is manifested by the fact that his perspective does not make any difference. Losing status as a subject means that in such a case someone is marginalized to a degree that he does not cause another person before him to internalize his perspective, and to become self-aware. It might be said that servants see everything because they are not seen, or more precisely because they are not noticed. Someone's value might be completely diminished when he is no longer a potential source for causing shame, like a piece of furniture in the room.

Such a process, of the erasure of the subjectivity of the other as a source of his capacity to observe without causing shame, takes a similar but subtler form in cases in which an exposure is legitimated given the particular role that the observer is occupying. Physicians who examine an undressed patient, artists who paint a nude model, or therapists who deal with the most intimate details of their patients' lives serve as examples of an exposure that will normally cause shame and yet is legitimated without any recourse to intimacy. In all these cases the full subjectivity of the person who is observing is bracketed by a particular setup. The particular context of role playing defines the observer as "observing as" a physician, painter, or therapist rather than merely observing. (Complete estrangement of the observer might serve the same function as in a confession in front of a random anonymous person, which is so powerfully described in Camus's novel *The Fall*.) Since the exposure was legitimated within the strict bounds of a particular role, a slight shift of perspective and a nuanced change of role might cause shame and humiliation. Imagine the awkwardness of the patient who meets his therapist at a dinner table, or even more so the model who realizes by a shift in the painter's gaze that he does not perceive her any more as a model but rather as a delightful object for his viewing. Encounters that entail exposure that is commonly a source of shame might therefore mistakenly be perceived by one of the parties to be an expression of intimacy, while the exposure is actually legitimated only given a certain bracketing of the subject or even its complete erasure. Within the political and religious sphere one of the main functions of ritual is to serve as a protocol of access that protects such a moment of appeal and encounter from trespassing into violation of exposure. When transcendence and power is connected to concealment in this internal conception of esotericism, there is no wonder that a minute divergence from the protective canopy of the protocol might become dangerously lethal.

The relationship between representation and power are based on two opposing strategies. The one is that nobody has seen the powerful, and the other is that power is seen everywhere. Within segments of the biblical tradition, God's invisibility from human eyes does not derive from His essential formlessness, but rather results from the fact that the exposure of God's form to the human eye blemishes his sublimity. This primary motive of concealment places a severe limitation on the attempt to bridge the fundamental biblical gap between the heard deity and the visible deity. The esoteric is not a body of knowledge that may not be diffused. It is, first and foremost, the creation of a realm that no eye may behold, either in actuality or in its *imagination*. It is the hidden realm in the most literal sense of the word.

This form of esotericism is vulnerable to a certain inner contradiction since power, in order to exist, has to be made visible. As we shall see, such a tension is just one manifestation of an internal problematic with the whole esoteric project. The inner tension breaks open in the Hekhhalot literature devoted to the attempt of the esoteric elite to transgress the boundaries of vision. The daring of this mystical journey is accompanied by an actual desire of the divine to emerge and appear from his isolation. Revelation is forced from that same reason that motivated concealment.

One possible implication for this mode of internal esotericism is connected to democratic politics and its understanding of power. In modern democratic society, the ruler is approachable and visible, and he often appears in the media. The authority of power, according to the concept of transparency, is not supposed to be based on mystery and sublimity, but from argument, conviction, and consent. Every frontal appearance of bearers of power in modern media, however, is a staged and planned performance, and the bearer of power is never seen as he is. The challenge posed by medieval political thought in its conception of esotericism is the relation between truth and society: Can the basic social institutions survive under conditions of transparency? The modern solution presents a profoundly ambiguous approach to the heart of that very question. On the one hand, enlightenment and transparency liberate us from dependence on the esoteric; on the other hand, that very value may create a better-camouflaged and complex secret, in which concealment hides the very fact of its being concealed. I return to this problem below while investigating other modes of esotericism, but it is worthwhile here to point to the problem of exposure and visibility.

II

The second mode of esotericism is the *instrumental*. It focuses on the harmful results of dissemination of knowledge and developed in part as a technique of writing and interpreting authoritative texts in a coded fashion. Leo Strauss focused on this kind of esotericism as an interpretive key to the great texts of the philosophical tradition. Instrumental esotericism has its roots in two different motivations, both problematic from a democratic point of view. It may appear in a totalitarian oppressive situation in which an author has to protect himself, and yet he wishes to communicate a subversive message to the initiate whom he trusts. Coded communication might be supported by another problematic source, this time initiated by the author himself because of elitist considerations. The author adopting esoteric strategy appeals to a divided audience: the initiated enlightened and the masses. By hinting and hiding his genuine intention, he wishes to protect the reader who belongs to the multitude from possibly harmful ideas rather than to protect himself.

Both motivations appear in Maimonides' *Guide of the Perplexed*, which is of great value in understanding interpretative esotericism. Maimonides' esotericism was rooted in an Islamic tradition inspired by Plato, which shared the conviction that myth is a necessity for social order.

Since philosophy is a systematic attempt to examine and criticize myth, the philosopher is in imminent tension with the Polis. For al-Farabi, Maimonides, and ibn Rushed, the main source of such tension lay in the metaphysical attack on the anthropomorphic conception of God, as marshaled both by the Aristotelians and Neoplatonists.

These philosophical doctrines rejected the understanding of God as a personality, and replaced personal attributes of God with attributes of being such as "the unmoved mover," "the necessary being," or "the One." The subverting of the anthropomorphic conception of God as a commanding sovereign who supervises, punishes, and rewards endangers the very existence of society. It enfeebles discipline and obedience to the law, which depends on the belief that there is a judge and a higher judgment, and that the evildoer will get his just deserts, even if he evades the ever-watchful eye of the worldly sovereign at the time that he commits the sin. Such a firm view, that society will collapse under conditions of epistemic transparency, especially in matters of religious beliefs, was common much later than the early medieval period and shared even by Spinoza and Locke. The first thinker to challenge this assumption was Paolo Sapri at the beginning of the seventeenth century, and at his time he was a lonely, original voice that anticipated the claims of later enlightenment figures such as Pierre Bayle, David Hume, and Bernard Mandeville.[5] These figures parted with the previous tradition of instrumental esotericism by claiming that a society of moral atheists is possible, and that a belief in divine providence and retribution is not needed for the sake of social order even in regard to the multitude. The sacred authoritative texts, according to this prior Islamic and Jewish philosophical tradition, address therefore two audiences. The surface anthropomorphic level, which contains necessary beliefs, is directed to the masses; the inner esoteric meaning is directed to the elite. The practice of *instrumental* esotericism gives rise to three internal tensions that put the esoteric project under a constant shadow of self-defeat. These tensions were implicitly articulated in the previous chapters while discussing the historical material, and I would like to bring them into clearer and sharper focus.

The first paradoxical feature of esotericism emerges within medieval schools that claim that Scripture has a hidden coded meaning, which these schools reveal, though secretively. The first commentator to promote such a view was Abraham Ibn Ezra, and it was practiced in various writings, both philosophical and mystical, in the twelfth and thirteenth centuries. According to the esoteric approach, the one who bears a particular scientific knowledge can uncover the hidden meaning of the text. To put it in Mainmonides' terms, the perplexed student who is torn by the conflict between the surface level of the tradition and his philosophical (Aristotelian) convictions will find the harmony in the hidden layer of scripture.

The esoteric realm became a powerful medium of integration of dominating cultural paradigms into the heart of Judaism. It served as well as the breeding ground for the most radical and diverse worldview that Judaism ever produced. In the twelfth and thirteenth centuries the canopy of the concealed shielded a astonishing diversity of astrologists, hermetics, Aristotelians, Neoplatonists, Gnostics, and others. The entry of these approaches into the sacred and precious realm of the secret transformed Judaism from within. The canon of secrecy included the great texts of medieval Jewish thought—Maimonides' *Guide of Perplexed* and Naḥmanides' esoteric hints in his commentary on the Torah, each of them presenting a completely different account of what it is to be a Jew. In that respect the esoteric medium was a mechanism of disintegration as well. These worldviews, essentially hostile to one another, consumed more and more from the surface-shared meaning that kept the community intact.

The addition of an esoteric level expands the text's "receptive capacity to meaning" to almost infinite dimensions. What can be read into it becomes far more varied and extreme. The esoteric idea provides a new and powerful tool for exegesis as a means of receiving ideas and transforming them into an integral part of the tradition. Thus, Maimonides could claim that the Aristotelian worldview, which is, apparently, completely alien to the surface meaning of the text, is in fact the internal meaning of that text.

Esotericism is thus a powerful tool for the reception of a variety of teachings, none of which can claim priority through reference to other written texts or to the revealed tradition. At this point the paradox of esotericism becomes apparent. The initial motivation for esotericism reflects an attempt to preserve particular knowledge in a state of purity, without fault or distortion, as a protected, well-guarded realm not disseminated to the uninitiated. Because, however, the esoteric realm is a closed one, it cannot be effectively controlled. An esotericist may claim that a new body of knowledge is actually the transmission of an ur-ancient esoteric Jewish tradition. In response to those who dispute him, arguing that they had never heard of such a teaching in Jewish tradition, he would claim: "This knowledge was kept secret; consequently, it left no trace in the traditions known to you." Thus, the most guarded realm is also the least restricted. This paradox leaves its surprising marks at the stage at which the esoteric idea reaches its peak of development—in the Jewish works of the Middle Ages.

Indeed, the absorption of widely varied teachings into Jewish tradition through the medium of esotericism lent them not only legitimacy as part of the canonical text, but also primacy. When such doctrines are understood as esoteric and enshrouded with the aura of secrecy, they become accepted as the inner meaning of Judaism, so that they penetrate to the most influential levels of meaning of the tradition. Medieval Jewry was characterized by a tradition of unusual intellectual flexibility as a result of the medium of esotericism. Through this medium, it could digest the worldviews surrounding it, and these worldviews, with all their resultant ramifications, became the inner and deepest meaning of Judaism in the eyes of its defenders.

The paradox of esotericism, in which the most guarded aspect of a tradition or a text becomes the most open-ended (because it was guarded), is thus of enormous importance in understanding a central cultural dynamic concerning the function of secrecy as a powerful uncontrolled medium of integration.[6] This dynamic has important implications concerning the problem of concealment and interpretation at large, and it highlights the second paradoxical aspect of the esoteric project.

The second inherent tension in the esoteric project is connected to a self-defeating feature of the main medium of esoteric transmission—the hint or the sign. The coded sign or hint has to be opaque in order to hide the message from the uninitiated. Yet it has to reveal enough so that it would be noticed by the initiated and properly understood. If it is too opaque, it has no interpretative weight. After all, the hidden layer in the interpretive tradition of the Middle Ages became a placeholder for everything because it is hidden. To hide a secret too well or to bury it too deeply in a text is therefore equivalent to the argument that it does not impact the meaning of the text altogether. If it has no restrictive features on possible meanings, it means nothing. The challenge of coded and concealed texts is therefore to calibrate the hint to such a nuanced degree that it will hide enough from the uninitiated and reveal enough to the initiate.

This fine line is in some ways the deepest problem of such a project altogether. If we take Leo Strauss as our example of the esoteric mode of reading texts, the following example is enlightening. Strauss's claim that Hobbes concealed his atheism is rather plausible and apparent. After all, he was a materialist. Yet Strauss's argument that Locke concealed his Hobbesianism is far more problematic. If it is the case that no reader of Locke realized this until Strauss discovered it, then what does it mean to argue that the secret of Locke's argument is a Hobbesian outlook? The secret is either too apparent or too deeply buried.

This inherent instability of the medium of the hint is manifested in another great historical transformation of an esoteric tradition of Kabbalah. The earliest kabbalists known to us in the middle of the twelfth century in Provence—Avraham ben Yitzḥak and his son-in-law Avraham ben David—were great talmudic scholars but who in relation to their mystical teachings were strict esotericists. The son of Avraham ben David, Isaac the Blind, who wrote an important letter against the dissemination of Kabbalah in books, testified concerning his forefathers: "For my forefathers were the nobles of the land and disseminators of the

Torah among many, and no such thing [secrets of Kabbalah] ever departed from their lips. For they would act toward others as if they were not versed in wisdom [of the Kabbalah]." This tradition of strict esotericism was soon relaxed by the students of Isaac the Blind—Ezra and Azriel of Gerona, who wrote some kabbalistic texts and letters at the beginning of the thirteenth century. The writings of these two mystics outraged their master Isaac the Blind, and he wrote against such practices: "For I have seen the sage and wise and pious who wagged their tongues and stretched out their hands to write of great and awesome things in their books and letters. *But what is written abides in no cabinet;* and the books thus come into the hands of fools and mockers . . . and so it happened through them." These opaque texts which were full of allusions and hints fell in the hands of two groups: the opponents of Kabbalah that blamed the kabbalists for heresy and began a campaign against them, and the supporters and admirers of the kabbalists who were not trained enough and began independently to misinterpret and to expound falsely the meaning of these hints. As a result of this chain of events, the kabbalists were forced to come up with a rather transparent text to clarify their positions. Within the time span of three generations, the esoteric tradition was uncovered by what might be called the dynamics of leaking; Kabbalah was transformed from a well-guarded secret to a literary-exposed corpus. The kabbalist Asher ben David, who was forced to explicate the tradition, blamed the previous authors for beginning to disseminate coded texts. In his bitter words he gave a beautiful formulation of the instability of such a medium of coded text:

> For they have not the ability to speak or write in a way that satiates the instructed while satisfying the needs of the fool, so that one not mislead the other with words that have two faces, by making their words obscure in places where they should not have, or by explaining too much in places where they would do better to conceal their secrets.

Asher ben David raised a profound argument concerning the essential nature of the medium of hinting. This medium, by nature, suffers from an internal problematic: if the hint is too transparent, it betrays its function as a medium of concealment, and if it is too opaque, it does not add to the knowledge of the instructed one, or else it leads to erroneous understandings and false explanations. The hint seems to be fundamentally invalid, and it was better not to hint in writing at all. Once matters had been made public, however, Asher ben David had no choice but to unveil the entire picture and to shatter the barriers of writing entirely: "Thus, I allowed my tongue to wag, and my lips to speak, to make the knowledge of our masters known to the many, for they taught us the paths of life, the ways of God, so that I may be innocent in the eyes of God and man" (*Sefer Hayiḥud*, p. 120).

This inherent instability of the medium of the hint might seem to us to be a problem confined to completely different modes of reading texts within elitist or totalitarian contexts. It might be an intriguing concern for the historians of philosophy or religion, but not for any of us. Yet we are engaged in a daily practice of this mode of interpretation when it comes to psychological explanations. A great deal of the political drama of esotericism as an interpretative strategy is internalized by psychoanalysis toward the self. The interpretative force of the analysis of dreams and symptoms is dependent upon walking this fine line of concealment and revelation. It is no wonder that Freud when seeking an analogue to his technique of dream interpretation points to political censorship: "Where shall we find a parallel to such an event? You need not look far in these days. Take up any political newspaper and you will find that here and there the text is absent."[7] Symbols in dreams, or behavioral symptoms, have to stand in complex relationship to what they represent. They have to be attached enough to make sense, and detached enough to be camouflaged. The failure of some such explanation is often rooted in the lack of capacity to calibrate this fine line.

The instability of the hint points to a larger issue than interpretation, which leads us to the third paradoxical feature of esotericism that emerged from the historical material. In the complicated history of esotericism, transforming something into a secret is not necessarily endowing it with the aura of the more real and precious. This inherent tension in esotericism emerged in the chapter that dealt with the campaign against the spread of philosophy. The Rashba made use of the self-imposed esoteric restrictions on the teaching of philosophy as a tool in his fierce attempt to put it to oblivion. The concealed is also the repressed and the marginalized. It was therefore possible for both the defenders of philosophy as the hidden truth and its opponents who considered it a heresy to agree upon measures for restricting its teaching though from completely different reasons. For the opponents, concealment was at least a way to marginalize its public force and to delay its exposure to the youth until an age when they would be more completely formed and thus protected from its possible poisonous effects. For its supporters, it was the way of maintaining its priviledged position as the core truth of the tradition that only the initiate are allowed to access.

This ambiguity of the concealed between the repressed and the privileged had as well a very constructive role in what I called the coexistence of secrecy in the medieval Jewish world. What was perceived by a certain group as a heretical doctrine was tolerated as long as it was shrouded in secrecy. In concealment, the impact of such doctrine was restricted, with the additional hope that with minimizing its exposure it would make it difficult for this worldview to be sustained indefinitely, that having been repressed and marginalized, it will eventually disappear altogether. For its supporters it was kept in its proper place—the hidden and most exalted. This form of coexistence is rather fragile as we saw, since the first step in the direction of exposure forces other elites of secrecy to assert their position in the public sphere. The fragility of this paradoxical feature of the concealed manifested itself in the cultural war that erupted between the esoteric elites in the thirteenth century, when the coexistence of secrecy fell apart.

Our study of *instrumental esotericism* raised three paradoxical tensions in the medieval esoteric project—the unguarded nature of the most guarded, the inability to properly calibrate the hint between revealing and concealing, and the ambiguity of the esoteric between the culturally repressed or the culturally privileged. These tensions that emerged from the inquiry into a particular historical moment are to my opinion structural to the esoteric project. By structural I mean that the esoteric project as such, even in completely different historical settings, is vulnerable to these tensions. The tensions are structural since they arise from a deeper level than the merely accidental features of medieval Jewish history— they arise from the ontology of the secret.

III

Our ontology and epistemology is, so to speak, in a grip of the "depth metaphor." We distinguish between the apparent and the real, the internal and the merely external. Our epistemology is grounded in such a picture. We "discover" or "uncover" the "underlying" assumption, the depth of the matter and so on. Esotericism is a radical version of such a picture, and it privileges existentially and ontologically the secret and the hidden.[8]

Heidegger's conception of truth is an exemplary case of the centrality of disclosure and the privileged position of the hidden: "To say that an assertion 'is true' signifies that it uncovers the entity as it is in itself. Such an assertion asserts, points out, 'lets' the entity 'be seen' (*apophansis*) in its uncoveredness. The Being-true (truth) of the assertion must be understood as *Being-uncovering*."[9] In his attempt to explicate the notion of truth, Heidegger relies on his understanding of *aletheia*, the Greek word for unconcealment. The function of an assertion is not merely an attempt to represent things in their correctness, as the concept of truth was traditionally understood in correspondence theories of truth. Assertions aim at lightening up a hidden aspect of reality: they uncover being, they make an aspect of it visible.

The equation of truth and uncovering in Heidegger's thought assumes two concepts of hiddenness.[10] The first hidden aspect to be systematically uncovered is reality in its everydayness that lies open before us, and yet we avoid it because we dwell in it, as the fish is unaware of being in water. This notion of hiddenness has little to do with esotericism and concealment in the way in which this work is interested. Uncovering here means attentiveness, turning toward what is wide open or, to be more precise, too wide open to be noticed. Yet Heidegger points throughout his work to a second sense of concealment that privileges the realm which is structurally concealed. This second sense of concealment relates to the way in which humans conceal their own authentic being from themselves. Our authentic way of being in its unsettledness and void is covered by what Heidegger calls the state of fallenness. The primordial concept of anxiety, guilt, and death has to be rescued from its disguised manifestation in the condition in which we find ourselves. In one of the most striking formulations of this notion of concealment and uncovering, Heidegger puts the matter in the following way: "*The entity which is in every case we ourselves are, is ontologically that which is farthest.* . . . The laying-bare of Dasein's primordial Being must rather be *wrested* from Dasein by following the opposite course from that taken by the falling ontico-ontological tendency of interpretation." Following this formulation Heidegger claims: "Dasein's *kind of Being* thus demands that any ontological Interpretation which sets itself the goal of exhibiting the phenomena in their primodiality, *should capture the Being of this entity, in spite of this entity's own tendency to cover things up*. Existential analysis, therefore, constantly has the character of *doing violence*, whether to the claims of everyday interpretation of its complacency and its traquillized obviousness" (359). The project of truth as uncovering, which privileges the concealed and hidden, is in a constant struggle with the ongoing tendency to disguise and mask our genuine reality.

Yet privileging the underlying and the hidden is complicated, especially when the hidden is so deeply buried that it leaves feeble marks. What is not apparent is not real and thus it might literally *disappear*. In rejecting the ontological privilege of the hidden, it is understood that to be is to be visible, to emerge. This sense of being is at the root of the anxiety of secrecy in which the holder of the secret loses his own sense of reality. It is for this reason that self-disclosure threatens spies, for example, who seek to validate who they "really" are by leaving outward signs of their concealed identity. Or secret lovers will seek the space in which they can appear in public as lovers anonymously, just for the sake of attracting simple recognition, and validating the fact that their relationship is not a mere dream. Gamblers, as we know from the technical term "tell," are always at risk of disclosing through subtle body movements some important information concerning their cards, as if their cards do not exist if they are not seen.

The ambiguous ontological position of the concealed, between the privileged and the vanishing, is magnified in another version of esotericism. This magnified version of esotericism is neither *internal* nor *instrumental*, but can be named as *essential esotericism*. This form of esotericism, which has a long history from medieval philosophy and mysticism to modern romanticism, claims that truth is ineffable. Transparency is essentially blocked; we can only intimate the truth by way of symbols and hints. Maimonides, for example, besides his political instrumental esotericism, argues that his text is abrupt, partial, and misleading because the subject matter essentially does not allow full exposure. Matters relating to God are essentially concealed since using language to express such knowledge is a violation of His unity and transcendence. Being imprisoned within the limited medium of language we can only gesture toward the truth rather than fully expose it. The romantics made the distinction between allegory and symbol. Allegory is a mode of representing something that can be articulated in a straightforward, conceptual manner. The symbol is a representation of something which cannot be expressed directly, but only via the symbol. Allegory is the medium for *instrumental* esotericism; the symbol is the medium for *essential* esotericism. *Essential esotericism*, that elevates the concealed sphere to ineffability, is always at risk of vanishing it. As a form of esoteric doctrine it puts into sharp focus the tension inherent in the concealed between privilege and marginality. What cannot be spoken about cannot be thought about and hence might as well vanish altogether. It is no wonder that some scholars interpreted Maimonides' negative theology, which denies the possibility of linguistic articulations of faith, as skepticism about metaphysics altogether.

The ambiguous place of the ineffable appears in Wittgenstein's early philosophy, one of the most complex and bold exercises in essential esotericism in its attempt at carving up the domain of what can be expressed in language and what is beyond such expression. Delimiting this domain is the main aim of the *Tractatus Logico-Philosophicus*, as declared in the introduction: "Thus the aim of the book is to draw a limit to thought, or rather-not to thought, but to the expression of thought: for in order to be able to draw a limit to thought, we should have to find both sides of the limit thinkable (i.e., we should have to be able to think what cannot be thought)." This philosophical work of setting the limit of linguistic expression has to be done from the inside of language, pushing its envelope till one meets the abyss of what cannot be spoken about: "It will therefore only be in language that the limit can be drawn, and what lies on the other side of the limit will simply be nonsense." The *Tractatus*'s main dazzling and disturbing claim is the immense scope of the ineffable which it carves out. It includes propositions not only concerning the transcendental God, as for example was claimed by Maimonidean negative theology, but sentences that seem to be saying something such as "there are objects in the world" or " murder is evil." Even more so, the readers of the work have to struggle with the following problem: in the bold narrowing of what can be said, the claims of the *Tractatus* itself are designated by Wittgenstein as nonsensical.

And yet Wittgenstein's interpreters are puzzled by the following dilemma. Does the limit of expression designate as well the limit of thought, and exhausts for us our experience of the horizon of being? What is beyond linguistic expression has been described as nonsense, though in another paragraph Wittgenstein defined such a realm as the mystical: "There are, indeed, things that cannot be put into words. They make themselves manifest. They are what is mystical" (6.522). What is the ontological status of the mystical? In the last sentence of the *Tractatus* Wittgenstein proclaims the famous call for silence: "What we cannot speak about we must pass over in silence." Is there really something to be silent about; is that silence a pregnant silence? Is Wittgenstein's work the most dramatic case of what we named *essential esotericism*, extending the ineffable to a far larger domain than in its previous formulations in negative theology? Or is the *Tractatus* actually the first grand formulation of logical positivism that empties the domain of the inexpressible altogether? One of the earlier readers of the *Tractatus*, Wittgenstein's friend Paul Engelmann, challenges the positivist reading:

> A whole generation of disciples was able to take Wittgenstein for a positivist because he had something of enormous importance in common with the positivists: he draws the line between what we can speak about and what we must be silent about just as they do. The difference is only that they have nothing to be silent about. Positivism holds—and this is its essence—that what we can speak about is all that really matters in life. Whereas Wittgenstein passionately believes that all that really matters in human life is precisely what, in his view, we must be silent about. When he nevertheless takes immense pain to delimit the unimportant, it is not the coastline of that island which is bent on surveying with such meticulous accuracy but the boundary of the ocean.[11]

Regardless of such rejection of the logical positivist reading, among erudite contemporary readers of the *Tractatus* we find a persistent voice that claims that there is nothing to be silent about, and indeed Wittgenstein is not delimiting the boundary of the ocean but rather points to where the void begins. The nonsense which is beyond language is like mere gibberish, plain nonsense.[12] Given the inherently ambiguous nature of the concealed, the debate as to whether there resides outside of language in the ineffable something meaningful or sheer emptiness is not surprising. Wittgenstein left us with ambiguous formulations concerning the question of whether he is the most exalted and daring essential esotericist, or the forerunner of logical positivism. The question of whether the ineffable is the most privileged or the empty is the sort of question that we cannot answer within a discourse of our language.

The position of the concealed at the twilight point between the privileged and the marginal is part of its deep attraction and defeat. The hidden sphere allows a great degree of freedom, being unrestricted by constraints and friction of the outside rigid world. Concealed from the gaze, control, and restraints of what is "out there," the esoteric becomes the realm of the fantastic. It is no wonder that this realm operated as the breeding ground for the most daring modes of thought that medieval Jews ever produced. Yet such space and freedom is purchased at the price of the ethereal nature of the esoteric and its marginality. It is always under two kinds of pressure: either it evaporates, or if it becomes the focal point of life and consciousness it moves the subject toward estrangement and alienation. When these speculations, fantasies, or actions become increasingly anchored in the visible and the real, they meet the harsh constraints of communal and personal life.

This complex dynamic is present not only in the cultural and personal function of the concealed; it operates in the political sphere as well. With all its efforts of propaganda, oppression cannot fully invade the realm of interiority; the slave is always free to have inner contempt for his master. The oppressed can whisper to himself his loathing of his oppressor. The safety and seclusion of the interior is the root of the Stoic conception of inner freedom. Since such freedom is enclosed within the inner realm of the imagination, it seeks to have some visible resonance through a coded common language developed among the oppressed.[13] Yet such freedom, even if it is shared unseen by the oppressed, is still locked in the realm of the imagined and the esoteric, and it serves as a poor comfort to those who are bonded and humiliated. When the concealed contempt and resistance moves to anchor the inner in the real, it might meet the harshness of conflict and brutality. At its best, the esoteric realm is supposed to act as a point of mediation between the mere empty fantasy and the narrowly constrained realm of the tangible and visible, and because of this it is always under the threat of slipping into either of these zones.

The greatest of all modern esoteric projects, psychoanalysis—which assumes a hidden, censored layer in the self and explains symptoms, dreams, and everyday failures as coded, displaced transformations of unconscious mental activity—rests upon such ambiguity of the concealed. The destructive effectiveness of a symptom is predicated on the fact that its meaning is concealed from the patient. When the symbolic meaning of a symptom is uncovered by the therapist and internalized by the patient, the spell of the symptom evaporates. This therapeutic technique is based upon a firm belief in the redeeming nature of self-transparency. The exposure of the event which is repeated in a camouflaged fashion in compulsive behavior is the key for undermining its grip and power. By breaking the resistance of censorship and shedding light on the unconscious hidden root of the symptom, its power over the patient weakens and disappears. In condition of full repression and concealment, in which unconscious activity would not leave a trace, such exposure would never happen but it is as well unnecessary. Unconscious mental activity in such a case is completely marginalized. Its feeble appearance in the fantasy life of a person such as in dreams is not harmful and even welcome, since it is a way of letting out steam and achieving satisfaction without impacting the real waking life of the patient. In order to achieve efficacy, the mental unconscious material has to leave marks and traces in guiding action and behavior. Yet at that very moment it opens the door to its exposure and annihilation. The possible success of the therapist in his battle with the inner censor is based on the ambiguous ontology of the concealed. When unconscious activity is fully concealed, it is marginalized and therefore has shadowy reality altogether. Its emergence and reality in the life of the patient entails the beginning of disclosure, because what leaves no mark might as well be completely disregarded.

The prevalence of secrecy as a basic mode of operation in totalitarian regimes serves as a fascinating example of the uses of concealment and secrecy in order to diminish the very sense of reality. In her insightful analysis of totalitarianism, Hannah Arendt defines its ultimate goal as obliterating the distinction between truth and falsity altogether, creating at the end a completely fictitious world enclosed within itself.[14] The concept of truth in its direct and raw meaning posits the claim that there is a reality out there, independent of our will. This independent realm threatens the aspiration of complete control. The very idea of reality limits the will, and in some cases it sets a possible independent standard that severs to assess and falsify the regime itself. In order to abolish what seems to be the ultimate obstacle, the totalitarian regime aims at erasing the very distinction between falsity and truth. Such an attempt might be directed at the party's own ideological convictions that are supposedly the objective moral and political basis of its policy, and yet this ideology is a target for obliteration since it might serve as an outside anchor of critique and assessment of the regime itself. Hence the thorough suspicion of such regimes toward the true believers of its own doctrines. The totalitarian project does not stop at propagating a lie; it aims at undermining the very distinction between falsity and truth. Concealment is one among other devices for such a project, and examining its role can teach us a great deal about the connection between isolation and concealment.

In the totalitarian regime there is an inverse relationship between publicity, visibility, and power; the more visible a branch of government, the less powerful it is. Such a mechanism creates an ongoing dependency on the will of the leader, with no capacity to predict it or to ascribe to that will some stable meaning. Yet it aims at something deeper. Our sense of reality depends to a large degree on our capacity to share points of view, to form communal and public experiences and understandings. In a condition of mistrust and suspicion, where everybody is potentially spying on everybody, such public discourse is undermined. The capacity of people to form a shared assessment and understanding of political matters is weakened when they live amidst a power structure that intentionally produces duplications, in which whenever power finds a stable center it is replaced by another inner circle. In a regime that controls public evidence and its manifestations, the private certainty of reality is thoroughly damaged. An innocent prisoner might make the true claim that his past history took a certain course, but if the regime controls and manipulates all the past traces by fabricating and changing documents, by terrorizing witnesses and family members, the innocent prisoner might lose his sense of reality altogether. Such an individual is transposed to a world beyond truth and falseness; he inhabits the realm of madness.

That the possibility of an outward, independent perspective which affirms inner conviction is undermined is rather devastating; only unique individuals can hold on to their version and sustain sanity in such conditions of isolation. Systematic concealment isolates the subject and erodes his sense of reality as well. This is true not only in regard to the person whose information is concealed; it applies as well to the one who is concealing. The concealing party that isolates itself more and more by narrowing the cycle of secrecy causes the shrinking of the horizons of the shared outward world that are constitutive to a sense of reality. The utter condition of isolation in secrecy is the point in which the privileged position of the concealed might turn into a vehicle that undermines the very sense of truth that its privilege rests upon.

The ontological ambiguity of the concealed and the hidden between privilege and marginality is at the core of the inherent tensions we uncovered in the esoteric project. The first tension discussed above revealed that what is most guarded is the most open ended. This paradoxical feature that dominates the history of esotericism is related to the lack of any reality constraints on what is not apparent; since the secret does not appear, there is no way to define it; hence what was supposed to be the most guarded and individuating of all aspects becomes the most open ended and disruptive. The second tension that emerged is the instability of the main medium of esoteric interaction and hermeneutics—the coded hint. The inability to properly calibrate the hint is the reason why esotericism breaks open or banishes. The hidden layer is either too transparent or too deeply buried; it is an immense challenge to achieve the proper balance between depth and oblivion. The fine unstable ontological status of the concealed between what is real and what disappears is at the root as well of the precarious position of the esoteric between privilege and marginality. The esoteric project is inherently paradoxical and its structural tensions are related to the complex ontological status of the concealed.[15]

IV

The inherent contradictions in the esoteric project reveal a far more complex picture of this phenomenon, both historically and conceptually, than what Leo Strauss had in mind when he initiated the study of esotericism. Strauss, who discovered the prevalence of esotericism, began to use it as an interpretative key for understanding the great philosophical texts of the past. Yet for Strauss, the study of esotericism did not limit itself to the purpose of presenting a better understanding of past philosophical texts; esotericism for him was a normatively recommended position. The nihilistic and brutal politics of modernity was, according to Strauss, an outcome of the way in which philosophy lost its esoteric constraints and openly advocated atheism and relativistic views challenging the nature of truth as such, and undermining public morality. Philosophy, which concerns itself with the love of truth, should have been an underground occupation since society cannot survive under complete conditions of transparency. Any political life needs necessary beliefs or noble myths. Pointing to the tensions and self-defeating potential of the esotericism as a whole does not disqualify the project altogether. In order to achieve a full account of the problem there is a need to address the political agenda of esotericism in a more direct fashion.

Liberal democrats tend to two opposing directions in their attitude toward concealment. They aim at protecting concealment in matters relating to the private realm, and they attempt to maximize transparency in relations to the public and political realm. Both tendencies are based on the same impulse of enhancing freedom and autonomy. The protection of the private realm from nonconsensual exposure rests upon the recognition of the privilege and autonomy that individuals have in defining degrees of self-revelation and intimacy. This policy has to be defended independently of instrumental arguments. Sects or other tight groups, who exert social pressure for mutual confession before the community, seem to liberals as intrusive and domineering. Transparency in such occasions works usually to the benefit of the powerful, establishing dependencies and exploiting weaknesses that are based upon information that was innocently revealed. From the liberal perspective, political and social intrusion into the private realm damages our vital concern for individuation and autonomy. On the other hand, the demand for transparency in the political sphere, which rejects the medieval and Straussian picture of the necessary role of myth in politics, is as well an attempt to protect freedom and self-government. Without proper information we are deprived of the capacity to make serious choices, and the manipulation of public opinion through secrecy diminishes our autonomy and self-respect, especially when it is practiced in a paternalistic mode. Public deliberation is perverted in conditions of concealment, and accountability is abolished by secrecy. Transparency is therefore as central to liberal democratic values as equality, freedom, or representation.

The Enlightenment's quest for transparency is based, among other things, upon rejecting the medieval idea of the masses or the multitudes. Truth is accessible in clear and distinct fashion to every thinking human being. Its basic foundation according to the empiricist is in raw sense data, or according to the Cartesians in mental states of self-consciousness that are immediately present to those who are willing to enter the philosophical journey. Political authority ought to be grounded by rational self-interest, manifested in the imagined social contract in which rational human beings move from the state of nature to the political order as a result of a well-calculated reasoned agreement. The capacity to pursue moral obligation is not dependent upon the fear of future punishment in the afterlife, but in internalizing the intrinsic wrong or merit of norms and actions.

It may very well be that Enlightenment and liberal theory is rather naïve in abolishing the political category of the masses. Yet the Straussians are as naïve in believing that genuine elites can be trusted. Trusting the existence of a selected group of wise men who are devoted to the collective good, and who are freed from ambition and self-interest because of their pursuit of truth, is as crude as the belief in a society where masses disappear and deliberation and reason control human's political choices. The rejection of the Platonic noble myth is based upon the suspicion toward the category of the elite rather than the belief in the rationality of society as a whole. The demand of transparency opposes the Platonic faith in the redemptive power of philosophy. Humans, even those who devote themselves to the pursuit of truth, are always embedded within the boundaries of the human condition. The judgment of the most lofty and noble of humans is vulnerable to their quest of power, to their fantasy of glory, to their deepest fears, to their personal hatreds, and to the obstructions stemming from their idiosyncratic love relationships. Over time the elites themselves will believe the noble myth that they spread for the purpose of social stability and political order. Kant expressed this point in his defense of the Enlightenment: "It is very harmful to propagate prejudices, because they finally avenge themselves on the very people who first encouraged them."[16] The permanency of the assumed constrains of humanity is not dependent upon accepting Nietzsche's reductive interpretation of the quest for truth as a manifestation of the will to power. It is enough to view the Platonic claim that the only worthy ruler is the philosopher as a testimony to the vulnerability of the philosopher to the quest for power. Transparency is therefore the only device to avoid false paternalism. Not because none of us adult humans is a child, but because none of us humans can locate himself in the position of the ultimate parent.

Yet, unlike other democratic values, transparency is not shared or internalized by the political elite. Politicians in western democracies do not want to challenge systematically individual rights or freedoms, nor do they aspire to change the electoral system of representation. We can even dare say that most of them actually believe in these values. But many politicians do not believe in transparency, since they ordinarily came to power by ongoing manipulation of public opinion. Even more so, most of them exploit the very means that democracies have to guarantee transparency in order to manipulate and conceal. I am referring to the media, election campaigns, debates, and so on, all of them orchestrated by public relations advisors who make a living out of manipulating public opinion. Successful ongoing manipulation of public opinion through the very means of transparency is the reason for the common contempt that politicians have for their constituencies. (Such contempt is naturally hidden.) The best of them develop self-contempt as well. The struggle for transparency is thus an uphill battle, with no real support from the rulers. It is the most Sisyphean of democratic tasks.

Unlike equality, freedom, or representation, the achievement of transparency is entangled in another particular difficulty. It is clear that a degree of legitimate concealment is necessary to maintain the state and its democratic institutions. Military secrets, techniques for fighting crime, intelligence gathering, and even diplomatic negotiations that will fall apart if they become exposed—all these domains have to stay shrouded in secrecy in order to allow the functioning of ordinary transparency in the other institutions of the state. Our transparent open conversation rests upon a rather extensive dark and hidden domain that insures its flourishing. Democratic theorists insist that there should be at least a second order transparency considering concealment.[17] Secrecy ought to be granted to certain domains only in the context of open deliberation and through the democratic process. Yet even with this second order mechanism, the very existence of a legitimate covert realm creates an ongoing problem to democratic regimes. This most guarded realm becomes the most unguarded and subversive domain, because it is so guarded. Free of the control of public opinion and the political process, the agencies of secrecy gain immense freedom not allowed to any other institution. The temptation to lead a political double life is immense, relegating to these unaccountable domains the dirty work that the public does not want to know about.

There is another important reason for this Sisyphean condition. If we fulfill or approximate the virtues of equality and freedom in our political life, we will know the degree to which we achieved them; it can be measured. We will never know whether we achieved transparency; this is conceptually true. Transparency itself is never transparent. (This intolerable condition is a reason for some psychotic breakdowns.) The proposition "All your secrets are known to me" is an oxymoron. This irresolvable difficulty in transparency is manifested when government officials argue in court against a demand of disclosure in the name of protection of secrecy for the sake of national security. When such an argument is raised, the court itself is prevented from viewing the material in order to render a decision of whether there is a genuine problem of national security involved in disclosure. The best the court can do is to infer from circumstantial evidence whether to force disclosure or to protect secrecy. If the court views the material itself, it is no longer a secret, given the fact that the judges are not part of the agency initiated into secrecy. (Presumably there is a way out of the problem by allowing the court itself to view the material, assuming that the judges themselves are restricted by a commitment to secrecy. Even that solution is vulnerable; after all, serious evidence ought to be disclosed to cross-examination by the defender's lawyers. The cycle of secrecy might be enlarged to include the lawyer as well; in that case he will become mistrusted by his client who cannot view the information himself.)

We can put the matter in the following abstract way. How can the secret life of the state be controlled? If it is controlled by the public, it is no longer a secret, and if it is controlled by another agent who himself is under constraints of secrecy, he is then part of the cycle of secrecy itself. The problem lies in the difficult task of finding the proper calibration of the inside and outside. It is not an easy task to properly design an institutional arrangement of a body or an individual who is both inside the secret domain to have access to the concealed, and is also outside that domain to be trusted by the public as a genuine independent voice. If we come back to psychoanalysis and its political analogy, we are faced with the puzzle that Sartre raised concerning the censor. The censor presumably is an all-knowing element in the economy of psyche. He is both aware of the unconscious material and aware of the conscious potential pain that will be caused if such material eventually emerges into the conscious life of the psyche. As an institution located at the threshold between the conscious and the unconscious, screening what is allowed out and under what proper degree of disclosure, the censor has the privileged position of being omniscience. If this is not the case it would not be able to properly function. But where does the censor belong, inside or outside? And who hides the censor from consciousness? As Sartre was concerned in his argument against the Freudian picture of the psyche, we are in danger of entering into an infinite regression of concealment and censors, where there is a need to censor the censor.

It is important to note that an open-eye recognition, and even anxiety concerning the difficult task of transparency due to the nontransparent nature of transparency, is by no means a collapse into the paranoid conspiratorial worldview. For this shift, from a healthy suspicion of the concealed to the conspiratorial mindset, to occur, other crucial components have to be added. The main one is the search for a kind of providential order that is a constitutive feature of conspiracy theories, in which its believers do not accept the possibility of chance and mere failure. They tend to interpret discrete accidental features as a result of an intentional secret hand. Ordinary failures in planning and execution become signs of malicious intentional plots of the enemy within.

This religious-like quest for order is coupled with a kind of dualistic Manichean division of good and evil in which paranoia and megalomania work in close proximity.[18] The propagator of the claim of the conspiratorial plot endows a certain group—the conspirators—with omnipotent capacities, while placing his own group as the ultimate target that at the end will heroically overcome by disclosing the conspiracy. Groups like Jews or Freemasons were traditionally accused of conspiracies, since they to a certain degree were insular from the rest of society, and yet they were present in it, in a peculiar simultaneous mix of insiders and outsiders. Their dual loyalty to the state and to their own group, a group that usually crosses boarders and is thus universal in scope, makes them the ultimate enemy from within. The presumed disparity between their actual success and status, and their lack of a real power base as foreigners, is filled by projecting onto the Jews a diabolical plot that transcends the recognized and visible seats of power.

Besides these added elements that make the conspiratorial mind, conspiracy theories do not aim at the achievements of transparency; they ordinarily seek to undermine its value and institutions altogether. The prevalence of such modes of thinking (and acting) in both the radical left and right is very revealing. Both camps share a revolutionary ethos claiming that the present state of affairs in its totality is evil and wrong, and it can be cured by a radical political action. Postulating an intentional hidden enemy as responsible for the present calamity becomes necessary for the radical groups who do not accept the inherent limitations and the compromises of actual political life. The illusion of a grand, intentionally planned solution held by radical political groups is thus dependent on constructing the mirror image for the radical action—the diabolical enemy that has to be countered and uprooted. There is yet a more important component of the denial of transparency by conspiratorial modes of thinking. The radical left and right claim that the ordinary democratic means of political deliberation, which they resent, are mere façades of hidden powers who dominate the situation. If so, these groups opt out of the regular deliberative political process, acting as if on a deeper level in order to solve once and for all what they consider the underlying hidden root of the problem. Through propagating a conspiracy theory, they avoid the give and take of the transparent political process and so undermine the institutions of transparency altogether. The conspiratorial mind set must be distinguished from the search for transparency, which is concerned with the Sisyphean qualities of such noble goals.

Yet the obstruction to transparency lies in a deeper aspect of modern politics than the general conceptual problem of the nontransparency of transparency. It is rooted in the complex duality of the function and purpose of the modern centralized state. In its first function the state is dedicated to preserve and ensure the rights of individuals, a function that serves as its main source of legitimation. Individuals, in this picture of the state, are willing to grant the state the right to judge, punish, and even tax in exchange for the security, stability, justice, and freedom that the state ensures. In its second function, the state became a meaning-endowing body, which shapes and structures an all-encompassing identity of its citizens. It achieves this purpose through its public rituals and symbols, but mainly with the aid of a powerful educational system that ensures loyalty and identification to the nation or the state. As a meaning-endowing project its ultimate claim and sovereignty is manifested in the right to conscript. By sending its citizens to war, the state expects self-sacrifice, thus endowing meaning to their deaths.

War as a matter between states shatters the rationality, presumed in the social contract, of moving from the natural state to the political state. The sovereign that was supposed to protect individuals one from the other brought them to a far more problematic position. In the political state there are sovereign, organized bodies that are propagating violence one toward the other without renouncing their right to violence to one shared global sovereign. This sort of violence is far more lethal than the one that Hobbes described in the natural pre-political state. In this political state the means of violence that are recruited through the immense joint efforts of organized states have a far greater destructive power. The shift from the natural to the political state is practically a movement toward a graver and riskier situation, in which the competition between states devours the citizens that they were supposed to protect.

In its attempt to close the gap between its function as the protector of individual rights and its function as the hungriest and most demanding altar of human sacrifice ever created by humans, the state always needs to access myth-making. It appeals to the founding sacrificial act that binds the group together rather than to the social contract that endowed it with legitimacy. It burdens its youth with a heavy sense of betrayal of this primary sacrifice if they do not march forward, and with a great promise of eternal memory if they do. Very few soldiers would show up to the front if the decision-making process that might lead to their deaths had been fully transparent to them. There are exceptions to this, but only exceptions. Could a political body survive under complete transparency? It depends upon the sort of role and function it ascribes to itself. As a pseudo-religious, meaning-endowing project, it will necessarily have a myth. But given the fact that such a function coexists with the social contract function of the state, with its clear demand and assumption of transparency, we might find ourselves in worse conditions than our medieval ancestors. Our myth might be that we do not have a myth.

Notes

1. "Because of his sins, man is unable to know what is the image of what is above; for were it not so, the keys would have been given unto him, and he would know how heaven and earth were created" (*Avot deRabbi Natan*, Version A, chap. 39; Shechter edition, p. 116).

2. We may note that the situation is reversed in societies where literacy is the exception. In such societies, as in Mesopotamia, writing guarantees esotericism, whereas oral transmission is more accessible to a wider public.

3. For a different context of the relationship between esotericism and status, see the interesting observation of Jan Assmann concerning later stages of Egyptian religion in *Moses the Egyptian: The Memory of Egypt in Western Monotheism* (Cambridge, Mass.: Harvard University Press, 1997), p. 109.

4. The expression *mystorin* (*mysterion*) in the Midrash is also used to refer to commandments that are not concealed, but which mark Israel's special status in relation to the Gentiles, like circumcision and the Passover. See M. Bregman, "Mishna as *Mysterion*," *Mehkonei Talmud* 3 (2005): 101–109 (Hebrew).

5. The first to remark and comment extensively on the phenomenon of esotericism from a social point of view was Georg Simmel. On this, see *The Sociology of Georg Simmel*, ed. and trans. K. H. Wolff (New York: Free Press, 1964). For further development of Simmel's ideas, see B. Nedelmann, "Geheimhaltung, Verheimlichung, Geheimnis: einige soziologische Vorüberlegungen," in *Secrecy & Concealment, Studies in the History of Mediterranean & Near Eastern Religions*, ed. H. G. Kippenberg and G. Stroumsa (Leiden: Brill, 1995), pp. 1–16.

6. See L. Strauss, *Persecution and the Art of Writing* (Chicago: University of Chicago Press, 1952).

7. S. Freud, *The Interpretation of Dreams*, trans. J. Strachey (London: HarperCollins, 1988), pp. 223–224; see also p. 661.

8. S. Klein-Breslavy, *King Solomon and Philosophical Esotericism in the Teachings of Maimonides* (Jerusalem: Magnes Press, 1977) (Hebrew).

9. Concepts of an esoteric nature may be found in Second Temple literature. Medieval thought was not exposed to this material; consequently, it remains outside the scope of our discussion. On the idea of the esoteric in Second Temple literature and in the writings of the Dead Sea Sect, see I. Grunewald, *From Apocalypticism to Gnosticism* (Frankfurt am Main: P. Lang, 1988), pp. 53–64. Also, see Gershom Scholem's comments in his *Jewish Gnosticism, Merkabah Mysticism and Talmudic Tradition* (New York: Jewish Theological Seminary, 1960), pp. 3–4.

CHAPTER 1. THE PARADOX OF ESOTERICISM: "AND NOT ON THE CHARIOT ALONE"

1. See Mishna Megilla 4:10.

2. The Talmud defines "the work of creation" as the passages of the creation narrative in the book of Genesis. On the various disputes over which passages are defined as *ma'asei breishit* (the work of creation), see B. Lifshitz, "Expounding the Work of Creation," *Jerusalem Studies in Jewish Thought*, 3, 4 (1984): 513–524 (Hebrew).

3. The examples provided by the Talmud for exposition of matters of incest, which was permitted by Rabbi Ishmael, are entirely conventional. See Talmud Yerushalmi, Hagiga 2:1 (77a).

4. In addition to the passages dealing with the chariot and creation, which may not be expounded publicly, there is a tradition that views the Song of Songs as an esoteric text, which may not be expounded in public. See Scholem, *Jewish Gnosticism*, pp. 38–42, and the comments of Saul Lieberman, "The Tractate of the Song of Songs," Appendix D (Hebrew), in Scholem, *Jewish Gnosticism*, pp. 118–126.

5. Moshe Idel, "The Concept of the Torah in *Hekhalot* and in the Kabbalah," *Jerusalem Studies in Jewish Thought* 1 (1981): 27–30; G. Scholem, *On the Kabbalah and Its Symbolism*, trans. R. Manheim (New York: Schocken, 1996), pp. 37–38.

6. A. Jelinek, *Beit Hamidrash* (Jerusalem: Warmhann Books, 1967).

7. See Y. Heinemann, "On the Development of Technical Terms for Biblical Exegesis, A. *Darash*," *Leshonenu* 14 (1946): 182ff.; Y. Fraenkel, *The Paths of the Midrash and the Aggadah* (Tel Aviv: Masadah Press, 1991), 1: 11–15 (Hebrew).

8. In the Kaufmann and Parma manuscripts, the text reads *hakham v'hevin mida'ato*—a sage who understood of his own knowledge. The title *mevin* refers to a quality of the learner, whereas the expression *hevin* refers to an event. If the Mishna provides instructions for the learner rather than the teacher, the question arises: how does the learner know if he understood on his own if this is a precondition for allowing him to learn? This implies that the knowledge of esotericism begins with the violation of a restriction. The learner knows if he is worthy of learning esoteric teachings only if he attempted to expound them and succeeded; yet the understanding itself is a precondition for being worthy of access to the esoteric teaching. This is what the *Sefer Habahir* means in saying: "Things one cannot discern unless one stumbles over them." For a discussion of this theme, see below, chap. 12.

9. Saul Lieberman, *Tosefta Ki-feshuta* (New York: Jewish Theological Seminary, 1962).

10. Y. Liebes, *Elisha's Sin: The Four Who Entered the Pardes and the Nature of Talmudic Mysticism* (Jerusalem: A. Kademon Press, 1990), pp. 131–139 (Hebrew).

11. Commentary on *Sefer Yetzira* by Rabbi Nasi Yehuda bar Barzilai of Barcelona z"l, ed. Sh. Z. H. Halberstam and D. Kaufmann (Berlin, 1885), p. 268.

12. See Scholem, *Jewish Gnosticism*, pp. 397–398.

13. Liebes, *Elisha's Sin*. This source is also referred to in a long commentary on Hagiga by Saul Lieberman, *Tosefta Ki-feshuta* (New York: Jewish Theological Seminary, 1962), p. 1286.

14. This reading is supported by other sources hinted at in the passage in *Sefer Yetzira*. Liebes, *Elisha's Sin*, discusses them at length. See for example Avot Derabbi Natan: "'And acquire for yourself a friend.' How? This teaches us that a man should acquire for himself a friend and eat with him, drink with him, read with him, study with him, sleep with him, and reveal to him all his secrets, the secrets of the Torah and the secrets of sexual behavior" (Avot Derabbi Natan, Version A, Shechter edition, p. 36).

CHAPTER 2. THE HIDDEN AND THE SUBLIME: VISION AND RESTRICTION IN THE BIBLE AND TALMUDIC LITERATURE

1. See Lieberman in *Tosefta Ki-feshuta*, pp. 1292–1295, on the exchange between Rabbi Yehoshua and Ben Zoma. Apparently, this was the Babylonian Talmud's understanding of the concept *katzatz ban'ti'ot* (cut down the sprouts).

2. See also Babylonian Talmud Megilla 24b, on the internal image created by the blind man: "There it all depends on the discernment of the heart, and the expounder, by concentrating his mind can know."

3. See Lieberman, "Tractate of the Song of Songs," 120–122; D. Boyarin, "The Eye in the Torah: Ocular Desire in the Midrashic Hermeneutic," *Critical Inquiry* 16 (1990): 532–550. For a more extensive discussion of the role of vision in early and medieval mysticism, see E. Wolfson, *Through a Speculum That Shines* (Princeton: Princeton University Press, 1997).

4. It is possible that Rabbi Akiba did not peek, since with respect to him alone, we do not find the word *hetzitz* (peeked), but only *'alah* (arose); consequently, he "left in peace." So explains Rashi on Ḥagiga 16a, *mai darash*. See also E. E. Urbach, "The Tradition on the Secret Teaching in the Tannaitic Period," *Studies in the Kabbalah and the History of Religions Presented to Gershom Scholem* (Jerusalem: Magnes Press, 1968), p. 13 (Hebrew); Liebes, *Elisha's Sin*, p. 90.

5. On the nature of the passage as a parable see Liebes, *Elisha's Sin*, pp. 6–9.

6. The Babylonian Talmud intensifies the focus on vision in its commentary on the mishnaic saying, "'Whoever is inconsiderate of the honor of his Creator, it is fitting that he had never come into the world': What is this? R. Abba says, this is one who looks at a rainbow" (Ḥagiga 16a). Further on in the text, vision of the rainbow is equated with looking at the *Shekhina*, based on the verse (Ezekiel 1:28) "as the appearance of the rainbow in the clouds on a rainy day, so is the appearance of the image of the glory of God" (Ḥagiga 16a). See also the variant reading on the ascent of Rabbi Akiba: "Rabbi Akiba went up unhurt and went down unhurt; and of him Scripture says: 'Draw me, we will run after thee.' And Rabbi Akiba too, the ministering angels sought to thrust away; but the Holy One, blessed be He, said to them: Let this elder be, for he is worthy to avail himself (*l'hishtamesh*) of my glory." Rabbi Ḥananel cites the text version as "he is worthy to look upon (*l'histakel*) my glory" (Ḥagiga 15b). On this variant reading, see below, chap. 4.

7. JT Ḥagiga 2:1, 77c.

8. The greater importance assigned to the act of exposure, rather than the fear of error, is also manifest in the text of the Jerusalem Talmud. Rabbi Yehuda ben

Pazi held that it was permissible to expound the creation narrative in public, and held a long cosmogenic discourse, which began with the sentence: "In the beginning the world was all waters in water." To this exposition, Rabbi Eliezer said unto him, "Your master did not interpret this passage. You ought to compare it to a king who built a palace in a place of sewer pipes, dunghills, and garbage. Whoever comes and says, this palace is in a place of sewer pipes, dunghills and garbage, does he not discredit it? So whoever says, in the beginning the world consisted of waters in water, he too discredits it" (JT Ḥagiga 2:1, 77c). The world, like the king's palace, is built upon dunghills and garbage, but such things may not be expounded in public.

CHAPTER 3. THE ETHICS OF GAZING: THE ATTITUDE OF EARLY JEWISH MYSTICISM TOWARD SEEING THE CHARIOT

1. The Gnostic context has been explored by Gershom Scholem in *Jewish Gnosticism, Merkabah Mysticism and Talmudic Tradition* (New York: Jewish Theological Seminary, 1965), pp. 1–8, 65–74.

2. Scholem, *Jewish Gnosticism*,. and, subsequently, and in much greater detail, I. Grunewald, *Apocalyptic and Merkabah Mysticism* (Leiden-Köln: P. Lang, 1980), claimed that there is a strong link between the esoteric tradition in the Talmud and Hekhalot literature. An opposite view was advanced by Urbach, "Tradition on the Secret Teaching." This view was expanded in D. Halperin, *The Merkabah in Rabbinic Literature* (New Haven: Yale University Press, 1980).

3. On the difference between these two realms of activity, see I. Grunewald, "'Knowledge and Vision,'" *Israel Oriental Studies* 3 (1973): 63–107.

4. For a summary and clarification of the various positions on this issue, see P. Schäfer, *The Hidden and Manifest God: Some Major Themes in Early Jewish Mysticism*, trans. A. Pomerance (Albany: State University of New York Press, 1992), pp. 150–157. On the relation between these aspects in the *Shi'ur Komah* literature, see the comprehensive article of A. Farber-Ginat, "Reflections on the Book *Shi'ur Komah*," *Masu'ot: Studies in Kabbalistic Literature and in Jewish Thought in Memory of Prof. Efraim Gottlieb*, ed. M. Oron and A. Goldreich (Jerusalem: Mossad Bialik, 1984), pp. 361–394 (Hebrew).

5. For a broad analysis of the desire for vision and the internal structure of experience linked to vision, see H. Pedaya, "Seeing, Falling, Song and Longing—Seeing God and the Spiritual Element in Early Jewish Mysticism," *Asufot* 9 (1995): 237–277 (Hebrew).

6. A common motive is the veil of fire stretching in front of the throne of Glory, whose blinding radiance makes even a quick glance impossible: "And if this did not suffice, a pattern of a shining cloak shrouds Him like a radiant light which has no equal among all the luminary bodies in the heights of the *aravot*, such that even the creatures of the *Merkaba* and the cherubim of the *gevura* and the *ofanim* of the *Shekhina* cannot look upon the splendor of the Glory, because of the light that surrounds Him" (*Ma'ase Merkaba*, in *Batei Midrashot*, ed. Wertheimer, vol. 1 [Jerusalem: Mossad Harav Kook, 5712/1952], chap. 3, pp. 56–57). Also: "And if this did not suffice, He enveloped himself as in a pattern of a lamp of

intensely shining splendor, a majesty that has no likeness among all the luminous bodies of *aravot*, so that even the holy creatures of the *Merkaba* and the cherubim of the *gevura* and the *ofanim* of the *Shekhina* cannot look at the splendor of the glory, for it envelops Him. And the splendor of his throne surrounds a vision of brightness around the throne. Thus the Holy One, blessed be He, enveloped Himself in cloud and fog as it is written: 'for he founded the darkness of concealment around his tent,' so that the ministering angels would not nourish themselves from the splendor of the *Shekhina* and the splendor of His throne and the splendor of His glory and the splendor of His kingship" (I. D. Eisenstein, *Otzar Hamidrashim* [New York: Eisenstein Press, 5675/1915], 1: 108).

7. *Midrash Mishlei*, ed. M. Buber (Vilna, 1893).

8. On the various traditions in the literature of the Sages on the angels' struggle with God, against the transmission of secrets to men, see A. Marmorstein, "The Arguments of the Angels with the Creator," *Melila* 3–4 (1950): 93–102 (Hebrew); J. P. Schultz, "Angelic Opposition to the Ascension of Moses and the Revelation of the Law," *Jewish Quarterly Review* 61 (1970–71): 283–307; P. Schäfer, *Rivalität zwischen Engel und Menschen* (Berlin and New York: de Gruyter, 1975). We might mention that in the literature of the Sages, the angels not only block access to contact with God and understanding of His secrets, but also leak His secrets. Bureaucracy, as we know, not only conceals but also leaks information. The midrash seeks to interpret the words of the angels to Lot, "for we shall destroy this place," as an instance of information leakage: " 'For we shall destroy,' Rabbi Levi in the name of Rabbi Naḥman said, 'because the ministering angels revealed God's mystery, they were ousted from their offices for one hundred thirty-eight years' " (*Genesis Rabbah*, pp. 524–525).

9. Version B, chap. 33, ed. Shechter, p. 72; see also emendations, p. 172. For other parallels, see the comments by R. Elior, "Hekhalot Zutarti: New York Manuscript 8218, Critical Edition," *Jerusalem Studies in Jewish Thought*, appendix 1 (5742/1982): 59–61 (Hebrew).

10. See also in *Sefer HaKomah*: "Rabbi Ishma'el said: 'When I said this thing before Rabbi Akiba, he said to me: "Anyone who knows this dimension of his Creator and this praise of the Holy One, blessed be He, is guaranteed (a portion) in this world and in the World to Come. He will live long in this world, and live long and well in the World to Come, he will enjoy the good things of this world and the good things of the World to Come.' " . . . Rabbi Ishma'el said: 'I and Rabbi Akiba are guarantors for this matter, that in this world one will enjoy a good life and in the next world a good name; as long as he repeats this Mishna each and every day' " (M. S. Cohen, *The Shiur Komah: Texts and Recensions* [Tübingen: J. C. B. Mohr, 1985], pp. 151–152). See as well Cohen, *Shiur Komah*, pp. 52, 73.

CHAPTER 4. CONCEALMENT AND POWER: MAGIC AND ESOTERICISM IN THE HEKHALOT LITERATURE

1. See also Avoda Zara 18a.

2. In one sense, esotericism in magical affairs is similar in principle to trade secrets kept by a guild privy to inside knowledge. I. Ta-Shma drew my attention to

the restrictions on the dissemination of professional knowledge, like that denounced at the end of the third chapter of the Mishna Yoma. On this matter, see the inscription found at Ein Gedi, which prohibits by oath and curses the disclosure of the secret of the village. This inscription is linked to restrictions on the dissemination of professional knowledge. See S. Lieberman, "A Preliminary Comment on an Inscription from Ein Gedi," *Studies in the Torah of Eretz Israel* (Jerusalem: Magnes Press, 1991), pp. 399–401 (Hebrew).

3. D. Halperin, *The Faces of the Chariot* (Tübingen: Coronet Books, 1988), p. 385. Moshe Idel does not believe that unschooled circles could create such sophisticated texts. In his opinion, the Hekhalot literature arose among a group that he calls a "secondary elite," which did not belong to the primary elite of the Sages. See M. Idel, "Judaism, Jewish Mysticism and Magic," *Bulletin of the World Association of Jewish Studies* 36 (1996): 39–40 (Hebrew). See also M. D. Swartz, *Scholastic Magic: Ritual and Revelation in Jewish Mysticism* (Princeton: Princeton University Press, 1996).

4. See Y. Dan, *Early Jewish Mysticism* (Tel Aviv: Misrad Habitaḥon, 1989), pp. 118–120 (Hebrew).

5. The references to the passage in Hekhalot cited here are based on the reading of Rabbenu Ḥananel.

6. This passage is an extract from the *Sefer Haḥokhma* of Rabbi Eleazar of Worms. See Y. Dan, "*Sefer Haḥokhma* of Rabbi Elazar of Worms and Its Implications for the History of the Teaching and Literature of the Ḥassidut of Ashkenaz," *Zion* 29 (1964): 171 (Hebrew). For more on the esoteric concept among the Ḥasidim of Ashkenaz and the changes in this tradition introduced by Eleazar of Worms, see D. Abrams, "The *Shekhina* Praying before the Holy One, Blessed Be He—A New Source for the Theosophic Conception of the Pietists of Ashkenaz and Their Understanding of the Transmission of Secrets," *Tarbiz* 63 (1994): 522–527 (Hebrew); see also the reference to the comments of Ivan Marcus concerning this issue in note 69. See also E. E. Urbach, "Sefer Arugat Habosem of Rabbi Abraham ben Rabbi Azriel" (Jerusalem: Mekitzey Nirdamim, 1963), p. 4: introduction, pp. 81–83 (Hebrew).

7. On the perception of crisis as justification for the disclosure of secrets in the consciousness of Maimonides, see below, chap. 8.

8. This idea appears in talmudic literature. See E. E. Urbach, *E. E. Urbach, Haza"l,* (Jerusalem: Magnes Press, 1969), pp. 276–277 (Hebrew). We might note that the calculation of the end time is in itself restricted knowledge. See Tanḥuma, Deuteronomy 4; Ketubot 111a; Genesis Rabbah 96. The revelation of the end time may destabilize the social structure. If the end time is too far off, its disclosure may lead to despair, whereas if it is too close it may lead to social ferment or—if it is in error—to crisis. In medieval Jewish literature, this esoteric realm was often violated by calculators of end times who came from the very heart of the halakhic establishment. In his revelation of the end times in his book *Emunot Vede'ot* (Article 8, 3.4), Rabbi Sa'adia Gaon completely avoids mentioning this limitation; Avraham bar Ḥiyya, in his book *Megillat Ham'galeh* (ed. Poznansky [Berlin, 1923], pp. 2, 12), denies it outright. For an attack on revealers of end times preceding this composition, see Rabbi Abraham Ibn Ezra's commentary on Daniel 11:30. See also Maimonides, *Iggeret Teman*, ed. I. Shilat (Jerusalem: Ma'aliot

Press, 1985), 1: 152–153. See below, chap. 11, n. 11, on Naḥmanides' revelation of the end times and on his justifications for transgressing the boundaries of secrecy.

9. On the messianic element as a force in the printing of the *Zohar*, see I. Tishbi, "The Dispute over the *Zohar* in Sixteenth-Century Italy," *Perakim* 1 (1967): 153–158 (Hebrew).

CHAPTER 5. ESOTERICISM AND COMMENTARY: IBN EZRA AND THE
EXEGETICAL LAYER

1. On the influence of astrology on Ibn Ezra's commentary on the Torah, see R. Yishfe, "Torah and Astrology in R. Abraham Ibn Ezra," *Da'at* 32–33 (1994): 31–52 (Hebrew).

2. See P. Adamson, "Abu Ma'shar, al-Kindi and the Philosophical Defense of Astrology," *Recherches de philosophie et theologie medievales* 69 (2002): 245–270. On the astrological and hermetic elements in the teaching of the Brethren of Purity, see I. R. Netton, *Muslim Neoplatonist: An Introduction to the Thought of the Brethren of Purity* (London: Allan and Unwin, 2002), pp. 50–51. The astrological dimensions in the work of Al-Biruni see S. H. Nasr, *An Introduction to Islamic Cosmological Doctrines* (Albany: State University of New York Press, 1993), pp. 151–165. The entry of the hermetic corpus to the Islamic world might be connected to the Sabian center in Harran; see the remarks of H. Corbin, *History of Islamic Philosophy*, trans. L. Sherrard (London: Routledge and Kegan Paul, 1993), pp. 125–128.

3. See also his commentary on Exodus 25:40: "and he who knows nature shall understand this" (Weiser 2:176). The description of the instructed person may be found in his introduction to *Yesod Mora*: "Only one who knows the wisdom of nature and all its evidences and the wisdom of grammar, knowing the principles that are the guardians of the walls, and the wisdom of astrology in perfect proof from algebra and geometry, and the wisdom of measures—only he can ascend to the higher level to discern the secrets of the soul and the ministering angels and the World to Come from the words of the Torah and the words of the prophets and the words of the sages of the Talmud, and he shall become wise and discern the deep secrets that remain concealed from the eyes of many" (*Yesod Mora* [Jerusalem, 1921]).

4. On the double nature of the public for whom this commentary on the Pentateuch was written, and on the differences between this commentary and the other writings of Ibn Ezra, see U. Simon, "R. Abraham Ibn Ezra—Between the Exegete and His Readers," *Proceedings of the Ninth World Congress for Jewish Studies* (Jerusalem: Ha'igud Ha'olami lemada'ei Hayahadut, 1988), pp. 31–32, n. 20 (Hebrew).

5. See also his commentary on Genesis 3:24. For Ibn Ezra, the immortality of the soul depends on the idea of *d'vekut* (cleaving to God), as described in Ibn Ezra's commentary with reference to esoteric knowledge: "If the soul become wise, it will enter into the secrets of the angels and receive great power from a heavenly power that it may receive through the light of the angels. Then, it will

cleave to the glorious Name" (Weiser 2:34). See also Ibn Ezra's commentary on Enoch (Genesis 5:24; Weiser 1:34, nn. 9, 10). For a similar description of the state of *d'vekut*, see Weiser 2:342.

6. Weiser's edition presents an alternative reading: "Those who add 'to illuminate their eyes,' perhaps the reason is that they know it and do not wish to reveal the secret to their disciples" (Weiser 2:217). The version I cite has been extremely well verified by Shlomo Sela, *Astrology and Biblical Interpratation* (Ramat Gan: Bar Ilan University Press, 1993), pp. 54–62 (Hebrew).

7. On the secret of intercalation, see JT Rosh Hashana 2:5 (58b); Rosh Hashana 20b; Ketubot 112a. In *Pirkei deRabbi Eliezer*, the issue of the secret of intercalation is developed and presented as a continuous tradition that began with God's intercalation of the years. He then transmitted this information to Adam, and it was transmitted continuously down to the High Court sages, who deal with intercalation of the year. See *Pirkei deRabbi Eliezer*, chap. 8. On the source of the tradition about the calculation of Rav Ada see Z. H. Yaffe, *The History of Intercalation* (Jerusalem, 1931), p. 143 (Hebrew).

8. *Sefer Ha'ibur*, third article, chap. 5, ed. Filipovski (London, 1851), p. 94.

9. *Sefer Ha'ibur*, ed. Sh.Z.H. Halberstam (Lajk, 1874), 6b. For more on the calculation of Rav Ada, see Sh. Sela, "Abraham Ibn Ezra and the Unfolding of *Mishp'tei Hamazalot*," *Studies in the Bible and in Exegesis* 5 (2000): 286–287 (Hebrew).

CHAPTER 6. CONCEALMENT AND HERESY: ASTROLOGY AND THE SECRET OF THE TORAH

1. On this matter, see Sela, *Astrology and Biblical Interpretation*.

2. See the comprehensive account of D. Schwartz, *Astrology and Magic in Medieval Jewish Thought* (Ramat Gan, 1999), chap. 2, esp. pp. 74–78. See also M. Idel, "The Magical and Neo-Platonic Exigesis of the Kabbalah during the Renaissance," *Jerusalem Studies in Jewish Thought* 1:4 (1982): 60–120.

3. See also Sela, *Astrology and Biblical Interpretation*, p. 367.

4. The identification of the term *kol* (here translated as "the all") in the thought of Ibn Ezra is a matter of dispute among his exegetes. Elliot Wolfson identifies the *kol* with the first hypostasis of God, which is also identified as the Creator of the world. See E. Wolfson, "God the Demiurge and the Intellect: On the Usage of the Word *Kol* in Abraham Ibn Ezra," *Revue des etudes juives* 149 (1990): 77–111. Hayim Kreisel opposes this view and identifies the word *kol* with the deity. See H. Kreisel, "On the Term *Kol* in Abraham Ibn Ezra: A Reappraisal," *Revue des etudes juives* 153 (1994): 29–66.

5. See Ibn Ezra's comments on Balaam: "For there is no power in creation that can change the deeds of the Creator or His decree. And the secret is that the part cannot change the part; only the decree of the all (*hakol*) can change the decree of the part. But I may not reveal this secret, for it is very profound" (Numbers 22:28; Weiser 3:181). On the talismanic context of the miracle, see the short commentary to Exodus 3:13: "For the triangle has the power to receive and does not

need two. Thus, Moses could demonstrate signs and wonders the like of which had never been created in all the earth, through the power of the Name. For the power of the Name shows signs and creates in the bodies in accordance with the receiver. And he who knows this secret knows the prophecies of 'and He appeared unto him,' and 'A man struggled,' as well as the wonder of the burning bush" (Weiser 2:246).

6. Dov Schwartz clearly demonstrated how Ibn Ezra maintains that idolatry is based on the foundations of the attraction of forces by means of statues. On this, see Schwartz, *Astrology and Magic*, pp. 68–72; also see 31–39, on idolatry and the attraction of forces, and on the astral foundations in the conception of ritual in Rabbi Yehuda Halevi's work.

CHAPTER 7. DOUBLE LANGUAGE AND THE DIVIDED PUBLIC IN
GUIDE OF THE PERPLEXED

1. The idea of the divided public and the layered text first appeared in the period between Ibn Ezra and Maimonides in the writing of the first Jewish Aristotelian thinker, Abraham Ibn Da'ud, in his book *Ha'emunah Haramah*: "It is said that in the books of prophecy, what is achieved by the true philosophy is not stated explicitly, so as not to create difficulties for the understanding of the people, that is the multitudes. Yet, these truths are hinted at, and will awaken the chosen individuals to understand the inner contents of those hints, and know that wisdom is to be found in the books of prophecy, whereas the multitude will be contented with the revealed level in them" (Berlin, 1919, p. 12). See also *Ha'emunah Haramah*, p. 39.

2. Another radical example of the gap between the traditional elite of Torah scholars and the esotericists can be found in Maimonides' parable of the palace in *Guide of the Perplexed* III:51.

3. There is an extensive literature on esotericism in the Aristotelian tradition. For a concise and comprehensive summary, see the article by Robert Lamberton in the anthology *Secrecy and Concealment* (above, Introduction, note 5), pp. 139–152. On esotericism in Islamic philosophy in the writings of Ibn Sina, al-Farabi, and Ibn Bajja, which is linked to Maimonides' sources, see M. Galston, *Politics and Excellence: The Political Philosophy of Alfarabi* (Princeton: Princeton University Press, 1990); A. Z. Berman, "Ibn Bajja and Maimonides—A Chapter in the History of Political Philosophy" (Ph.D. diss., Hebrew University of Jerusalem, 1959); also, the comprehensive summary discussion in Sarah Klein-Breslavy, *King Solomon and Philosophical Esotericism*, pp. 15–27.

4. See Strauss, *Persecution and the Art of Writing*; Klein-Breslavy, *King Solomon and Philosophical Esotericism*.

5. See also Maimonides' words in the introduction to his commentary on the Mishna: "And even to blind the eyes of the fools whose hearts will never be enlightened, for if you show them the truth, they would depart from it, considering it as something tasteless. It is of such people that we say, one should not reveal to them secrets, for their intelligence is not sufficiently perfected to accept the truth

as is" (*Perush Hamishnayot*, ed. Y. Kapah [Jerusalem: Mossad Harav Kook, 1964], p. 19).

6. On the esoteric nature of the doctrine of providence, see *Guide of the Perplexed* III:22. On the doctrine of prophecy as esoteric, see II:33, II:42.

7. *Perush Hamishnayot*, p. 23.

8. See also Maimonides' writings on the obligation of prayer and repentance, which are linked to beliefs that strengthen obedience to the law and the social order—*Guide of the Perplexed* III:36.

9. See also Maimonides' remarks in his commentary on *Mishna Ḥagiga* 2:1: "Since there are matters inscribed in the souls of the most perfect humans, and when we explain them in language and portray them through parables, they lose their sense and they are misconstrued" (*Perush Hamishnayot*, pp. 250–251).

10. Many exegetes of Maimonides were of the opinion that, aside from hinting and scattering of material in the writing of *Guide of the Perplexed*, the contradictions in the book are part of Maimonides' strategy of concealment. This understanding is based on the exegesis of the seventh reason for contradictions enumerated by Maimonides in his introduction to *Guide of the Perplexed*. Recently, Yair Lorberbaum suggested an entirely different reading, which links the contradictions to essential esotericism. According to this reading, the contradictions are not an intentional act of concealment, but stem from the very nature of the metaphysical realm. See Y. Lorberbaum, "The Seventh Reason: On The Contradictions in the Guide of the Perplexed—A Reevaluation," *Tarbiz* 69 (2000). On the role of essential esotericism in Maimonides' understanding, see Y. Lorberbaum, "Maimonides' Conception of Parable," master's thesis, Hebrew University of Jerusalem, 1991.

11. For an extensive discussion on the history of esoteric readings of *Guide of the Perplexed* see A. Ravitzky, "The Secrets of the Guide to the Perplexed: Between the Thirteenth and Twentieth Centuries," in *Studies in Maimonides,* ed. I. Twersky (Cambridge, Mass.: Harvard University Press, 1990), pp. 159–207. For a rejection of any esoteric message in *Guide* see H. D. Davidson, *Moses Maimonides: The Man and His Works* (Oxford: Oxford University Press, 2005), pp. 387–402. If Davidson is correct in his arguments, we still need an explanation for why Maimonides claims that he is hiding the meaning of his text, given that such a statement would naturally draw much suspicion and misunderstanding. He should have put forward his rather conservative approach without such a claim altogether.

12. For examples of leading modern scholars who argue that eternity of the world is Maimonides' esoteric teaching, see A. Nuriel, "Creation or Eternity of the World according to Maimonides," in *Revealed and Hidden* (Jerusalem: Magnes Press, 2000), pp. 40–50 (Hebrew); W. Harvey, "A Third Approach to Maimonides' Cosmogony-Prophetology Puzzle," *Harvard Theological Review* 74 (1981): 287–301; H. Kreisel, "Maimonides," in *History of Jewish Philosophy*, ed. O. Leaman and D. Frank (London: Routledge, 1997), pp. 260–261.

13. S. Pines, "The Limitations of Human Knowledge According to al-Farabi, ibn Bajja and Maimonides," *Studies in Medieval Jewish History and Literature*, ed. I. Twersky (Cambridge, Mass.: Harvard University Press, 1979), pp. 88–109.

CHAPTER 8. THE BREACHING OF THE LIMITS OF THE ESOTERIC:
CONCEALMENT AND DISCLOSURE IN MAIMONIDEAN ESOTERICISM

1. Sarah Klein-Breslavy and Leo Strauss disagree as to whether Maimonides thought that the writing of chapter headings had already been done as part of the writings of the Sages. See Klein-Breslavy, *King Solomon and Philosophical Esotericism*, p.196n.18; Strauss, *Persecution and the Art of Writing*. According to Klein-Breslavy, Maimonides was of the opinion that the writing of chapter headings had a precedent in previous esoteric traditions. It seems to me that the sources cited in Klein-Breslavy's book could be seen as referring to parables rather than to chapter headings. Furthermore, Maimonides claims that such hints are meager and few in number. On the question if, in Maimonides' view, there existed a written esoteric literature, see the contradiction noted by Klein-Breslavy, *King Solomon and Philosophical Esotericism*, p.196n.10.

2. Strauss, *Persecution and the Art of Writing*, p. 49.

3. See also Maimonides' writings on the parallel between the Oral Torah and the secrets of the Torah. Maimonides describes the prohibition against writing down the Oral Torah in light of his conception that writing resulted in great laxity and negligence in the guarding of the reliability and nature of halakhic knowledge: "the multiplicity of opinions, the variety of schools, the confusions occurring in the expression of what is put down in writing, the negligence that accompanies what is written down, the divisions of the people who are separated into sects, and the production of confusion with regard to actions" (*Guide* I:71, p. 176). Later, Maimonides draws a parallel between the Oral Torah and the secrets of the Torah: "Now if there was insistence that the legalistic science of law should not, in view of the harm that would be caused by such a procedure, be perpetuated in a written compilation accessible to all the people, all the more could none of the mysteries of the Torah have been set down in writing and be made accessible to all the people. On the contrary, they were transmitted by a few men belonging to the elite to a few of the same kind" (*Guide* I:71, p. 176).

4. Maimonides thus undermines the basis for potential rivals in esoteric doctrine, who may make claims against him based on the authority of a particular tradition. In his opinion, the transmission of esoteric tradition has ceased, and, as such, he possesses no traditions either.

5. For further writings on the consciousness of crisis, see *Guide* II:11, p. 276: "However, when the wicked from among the ignorant communities ruined our good qualities, destroyed our words of wisdom and our compilations, and caused our men of knowledge to perish, so that we again became ignorant, as we had been threatened because of our sins . . . and their opinions were taken over by us, as were their morals and actions" (*Guide* II:11, p. 276). Another force motivating the disclosure of secrets is linked to the interior drive of the wise man to propagate his words. See *Guide* II:29, II:37.

6. See David Hartman, *Maimonides: Torah and Philosophical Quest* (Philadelphia: Jewish Publication Society, 1976).

7. Maimonides created new literary molds in halakhic literature as well. In his *Mishneh Torah*, Maimonides justifies his deviation from previous forms of organizing halakhic knowledge by means of an innovative concept of the history

of halakhah. He sees his own position within that history as one responding to a deep prevailing crisis. Consequently, he created a work unprecedented in halakhic literature.

Chapter 9. From Transmission to Writing: Hinting, Leaking, and Orthodoxy in Early Kabbalah

1. On the relation between philosophical literature and the disclosure of the Kabbalah, see the final chapter of Moshe Idel's book *Kabbalah: New Perspectives* (New Haven: Yale University Press, 1988).

2. The letter was published and discussed by Gershom Scholem in *Studies in Kabbalah I*, ed. Y. Ben-Shlomo and Moshe Idel (Tel Aviv: Am Oved, 1998), pp. 9–10.

3. Idel is of the opinion that in this letter, Rabbi Isaac the Blind attempts to defend himself against Naḥmanides' criticism. Scholem, and, following him, Yosef Dan, maintained that the instructions of Isaac the Blind are what engendered the esoteric style of Naḥmanides. See M. Idel, "Nahmanides: Kabbalah, Halakha and Spiritual Leadership," in Moshe Idel and Mortimer Ostow, *Jewish Mystical Leaders and Leadership in the Thirteenth Century* (Northvale, N.J.: Jason Aronson, 1998), pp. 15–96.

4. London manuscript 756 reads *sarsur* (a go-between); see *Sefer Hayiḥud: Kol Ketavan ve-Iyunnim be-Kabbalato*, ed. Daniel Abrams (Los Angeles: Keruv Press, 1996), n. 92.

5. On the book of Rabbi Abraham ben Yitzḥak, see G. Scholem, *Origins of the Kabbalah*, trans. A. Arkush (Princeton: Princeton University Press, 1990), pp. 200, 202. See also below, chap. 13.

6. See also *Sefer Hayiḥud*, p. 118: "I have explained and clarified to every wise man and instructed one each and every matter in all its aspects."

Chapter 10. Open Knowledge and Closed Knowledge: The Kabbalists of Gerona — Rabbi Azriel and Rabbi Ya'akov bar Sheshet

1. The work was published as part of *Derekh Emunah*, by Rabbi Meir ben Gabbai (Berlin, 1850).

2. See also the words of Rabbi Azriel in his letter to Burgos: "From the force of the hidden it emanated to the heard, and from the heard to the seen. And we have no dealings with that which is hidden, but with that which was heard, with the ten sayings which were seen in the splendor of the lights. For the force of the heard voice emerges from the thin voice of silence" (G. Scholem, "The Kabbalah of Rabbi Ya'akov and Rabbi Yitzḥak, the Sons of Rabbi Ya'akov Hacohen: Sources for the History of the Kabbalah preceding the Revelation of the *Zohar*," *Jewish Studies* 2 [Jerusalem, 1927]: 233). Although Scholem attributed the letter to the Cohen brothers, it was apparently written by Rabbi Azriel. See also Rabbi Azriel's words in his composition *Derekh Ha'emunah V'derekh Hakfira* (The Way of Faith and the Way of Heresy): "For the language of faith does not apply to what is, that which is seen and conceived, nor to the nothingness that cannot

be seen or conceived, but rather to the place of juncture of nothingness and what is. Being is not separated from nothingness, but being and nothingness together is being . . . and all is one in simple and total evenness. And of the investigation of this thing it was written 'Do not make yourself too wise,' for there is no power in our limited intelligence that can achieve the completeness of investigation which reaches the infinite. And of this it is written 'what is concealed from you do not investigate'" (*Derekh Ha'emunah V'derekh Hakfirah LeRabbi Azriel*, in G. Scholem, "New Fragments of the Writings of Rabbi Azriel of Gerona," *Memorial Volume Dedicated to Asher Gulak and Shmuel Klein* [Jerusalem, 1942], p. 207).

3. See Idel's comments in his *Kabbalah: New Perspectives*, pp. 253–256, on the link between creativity and disclosure.

4. Like Rabbi Azriel, Rabbi Ya'akov bar Sheshet also diverts the restrictions of esotericism to the ineffable domain. See his comments on *sefirat keter*, which he identifies with will: "And it (*Keter*) is the beginning and head of all quantity and measures. Do not expound what is concealed from you, Let not your desire tempt you to come into its camp, for the matter is too difficult for you, you cannot do it; take heed and do not, for he who increases wisdom increases anger. . . . The glory of God is in hidden things. . . . The wonders of knowledge that are too profound for me, I cannot bear" (*Sha'ar Hashamayim*, p. 155).

5. "He who reads in my book knows that everything that I did not write in the name of a Sage or that is not mentioned in two or three of the works of the commentators or mentioned explicitly in the midrashim, is my own opinion and reasoning. I toiled and found in my heart, to drink water of my cistern and my well, liquids of what my hand has attained in each and every matter as is fitting, each one by his own banner. I wrote them down in this composition, whether they be thin or fat. I thus inform all who investigate it that they not think in their hearts that this is authorized by a rabbi or Sage and thus come to reject his own correct opinion in favor of my despised knowledge, or reject his own clear reasoning in favor of my obscure opinion. When he knows that this is a new thing, let him deliberate in private until he attains the depths of the matter with his own good reasoning, and then he should consult his words in secret and what he chooses he should endear" (*Meshiv Devarim Nekhohim*, ed. Y. A. Vajda [Jerusalem: Ha'akademia Hale'umit Ha'yisraelit le'Mada'in, 1969], p. 69).

6. See also his words: "It is true that there are seventy facets to the Law, and these and those are both the words of the living God" (*Kitvei HaRamban* 2:428). See also the disagreements between him and Rabbi Ezra and other kabbalists: "Even though the sages of the Kabbalah do not explain it thus . . ." (*Kitvei HaRamban* 2:358). Compare *Meshiv Devarim Nekhonim*, p. 115. On the various understandings of the expression *elu va'elu* (these and those) in halakhic discourse, see A. Sagi, *Elu Va'elu* (Tel Aviv: Hakibbutz Hameuḥad, 1997).

7. Maimonides presented an opposite model of comparison. He saw the writing of the Oral Law as something forced upon it by reality, which led to the multiplicity of disputations and commentaries. In his opinion, if not for the historical constraints that damaged the uninterrupted transmission, the Oral Law too could better have been preserved as a closed tradition, just like the esoteric teachings. See his remarks in *Guide of the Perplexed* I:71 (pp. 175–176): "You already know that even the legalistic science of law was not put down in writing in the

olden times because of the precept, which is widely known in the nation: 'Words that I have communicated to you orally, you are not allowed to put down on writing.' This precept shows extreme wisdom with regard to the Law. For it was meant to prevent what has ultimately come about in this respect: I mean the multiplicity of opinions, the variety of schools, the confusions occurring in the expression of what is put down in writing, the negligence that accompanies what is written down, the divisions of the people who are separated into sects, and the production of confusion with regard to actions." It is interesting to note that in sixteenth-century Ashkenaz, the opposition to the writing of systematic halakhic works stemmed from a diametrically opposite reason. Halakha was to be preserved as an esoteric occupation, transmitted live from teacher to disciple, in order to enable its local and varied character. The writing of the halakha entailed standardization of norms, the undermining of custom, the changing of its nature as a living tradition, and the weakening of the authority of the rabbi. See the words of Rabbi Ḥaim ben Bezalel in his introduction to the Rama's book *Torat Haḥatat*, whose title is *Viku'aḥ Mayim Ḥayim* (The Dispute of Living Water), on the halakhic literature in Ashkenaz and especially on the composition *Sha'arei Dora* as a text of an esoteric nature. For the introduction, see H. Tchernowitz, *The History of Halakhaists* (New York: Va'ad Hayovel, 1948), pp. 93–100 (Hebrew).

8. Among the kabbalists of Gerona, Rabbi Ezra did not provide a fundamental reason for disclosure. In the introduction to his commentary on the Song of Songs, he justified the writing of Torah secrets in terms akin to the consciousness of crisis in the esoteric tradition of Maimonides. See *Perush Shir Hashirim* (Commentary on the Song of Songs), *Kitvei HaRamban* 2:479. His words also indicate that the philosophical exegesis of the Song of Songs provoked the writing of kabbalistic exegesis. See *Kitvei HaRamban* 2:480.

9. Idel, *Kabbalah: New Perspectives*, pp. 253–254.

CHAPTER 11. TRADITION, CLOSED KNOWLEDGE, AND THE ESOTERIC:
SECRECY AND HINTING IN THE NAḤMANIDES' KABBALAH

1. Naḥmanides sees the answer to Job's complaint in the response of Elihu, which hints at the secrets of intercalation. In speaking of the inner layer of the book, Naḥmanides says: "But in truth there is a great secret in this, one of the greatest of the mysteries of the Torah. A thinking man cannot attain them, only one who is worthy to learn them from a master [who heard it from other masters] going back to our master Moses, of blessed memory, who heard it from the mouth of the Almighty, may He be blessed, and that is what is hinted at in the words of Elihu" (Commentary on the Book of Job, *Kitvei HaRamban* 1:23; see also 1:115). The question that arises from this conception is the following: How is it possible that a kabbalistic secret transmitted only through tradition from one generation to another is brought by Elihu, a character that is difficult to link to the known chain of transmission of the Kabbalah? Naḥmanides himself was troubled by this question, and in his exposition of Ecclesiastes he added Elihu to the chain of transmission of the Kabbalah: "For in truth, the words of Elihu are words received from people of the Torah; thus, I say that he is of the family of

Ram—Abraham" (*Kitvei HaRamban* 1:199). See also his remarks in his commentary on Job, *Kitvei HaRamban* 1:28. Naḥmanides sees the Kabbalah as an internal Jewish tradition, as he writes in his homily on the passage "The Law of the Lord is perfect": "As it is written, 'He tells His words to Jacob, etc. . . . He did not do so for other nations, etc.' For this is the truth, because the Torah contains mysteries like the work of creation, as mentioned by Onkelos, and the secret of the vision of the chariot, and many other secrets that were transmitted from mouth to mouth and are only given unto the pious ones of Israel" (*Kitvei HaRamban* 1:145).

2. An interesting question on the connection between exegesis and tradition is the case of King Solomon. According to Naḥmanides, Solomon acquired his wisdom by expounding Scripture: "[For] everything can be learned from the Torah, and King Solomon, peace upon him, whom God had given wisdom and knowledge, derived it all from the Torah, and from it he studied until he knew the secret of all things created" (*Perush HaRamban*; Chavel 1:12). By contrast, see Naḥmanides' comments in his homily on "the Law of the Lord is perfect": "And from the Torah that he received, King Solomon learned that there was written in it, etc." (162).

3. See I. M. Ta-Shma, *The Revealed in the Hidden* (Tel Aviv: Hakibbutz Hameuḥad, 1995), p. 38 (Hebrew).

4. On the conception of Naḥmanides and his attitude toward the positions of Maimonides and the geonim on the question of disputation, see M. Halbertal, *People of the Book: Canon Meaning and Authority* (Cambridge, Mass.: Harvard University Press, 1997), pp. 54–71.

5. Naḥmanides' attitude toward the place of reasoning in his discussion of kabbalistic explanations becomes clear through the long quote he brings from the writings of Rabbi Ezra in his explanation of Song of Songs. Rabbi Ezra explained a passage of the Book of Job as dealing with the mysteries of the Torah, and on this Naḥmanides testifies: "This is the way [of the kabbalists in their explanation of] these verses; the words themselves should be praised and lauded, but we do not know if the matter supports this explanation. But if it is a kabbalistic tradition, we accept it" (Commentary on the Book of Job, *Kitvei HaRamban* 1:90). Naḥmanides casts doubts on the power of the explanation to withstand the test of reason, but unlike his method in his talmudic innovations, here he is prepared to subordinate reasoning to the dictum of tradition: "But if it is a kabbalistic tradition, we accept it."

6. This issue was discussed at length by Moshe Idel. See M. Idel, "We Have No Kabbalistic Tradition on This," in *Rabbi Moses Nahmanides (Ramban): Explorations in His Religious and Literary Virtuosity*, ed. I. Twersky (Cambridge, Mass.: Harvard University Press, 1983), pp. 31–81.

7. On Naḥmanides' complex relation to Ibn Ezra, see B. Septimus, "Open Rebuke and Concealed Love: Nachmanides and the Andalusian Tradition," in *Rabbi Moses Nahmanides*, pp. 11–34.

8. The disclosure of Torah secrets as a consequence of the dispute with the esoteric conceptions of Ibn Ezra is evident in Naḥmanides' explanations (following *Sefer Habahir*) to the Sages' saying "and the Lord blessed Abraham in all (*bakol*)—Abraham had a daughter whose name was Bakol." At the end of a long passage

Naḥmanides says: "Now, had the commentator who prides himself on his knowledge of the Torah's secrets known this, his lips would be dumb and not deride the words of our Rabbis. Therefore, I have written this in order to silence those who speak arrogantly against the righteous ones" (*Perush HaRamban* 1:134; Chavel 1:293).

9. Such instructions may be found in other hints of Naḥmanides as well. See *Perush HaRamban* on the Pentateuch, pp. 23, 30, 33, 50, 68, 71, 99, 112, 134, 391, and 434–435.

10. On the hermeneutic and kabbalistic conception reflected in this position, see E. Wolfson, "By Way of Truth: Aspects of Nahmanides' Kabbalistic Hermeneutic," *AJS Review* 14 (1989): 103–178.

11. A prominent exception to the general tenor of Naḥmanides' esotericism is *Sefer Hage'ulah*, in which Naḥmanides reveals the end time and fixes its date as 1358. According to Naḥmanides, the immanent messianic age justifies the revelation of end times: "And it has also been made possible since we are close to it, because of the great length of time that has already transpired. Perhaps the decree that demanded that we conceal it (the date of the end time) is annulled, since the reason for its declaration is no longer valid. For it was written that it shall be after many days, then, 'many will run to and fro and knowledge shall increase.' Thus, it was hinted to us that we are permitted to search for the end-time in this book and increase our knowledge. For its meaning, as the instructed will understand, is that when the end-time approaches the instructed shall understand these hints" (*Sefer Hage'ulah, Kitvei HaRamban* 1:290). The coming approach of the end-time enables its precise revelation. See his writings on the study of *gematria* and the end-time in *Sefer Hage'ulah* 1:262–263.

Chapter 12. From Tradition to Literature: Shem Tov Ibn Gaon and the Critique of Kabbalistic Literature

1. On this matter, see M. Verman, *The Book of Contemplation* (Albany: State University of New York Press, 1992), p. 27. On the words of Isaac the Blind, see Scholem, *Studies in Kabbalah*, p. 141.

2. I am thankful to Yoni Garb for pointing to the references from this manuscript of Meir Ibn Sahula, MS Rome Angelika 45/1.

3. In another context, he refers to the relation between Kabbalah and logical reasoning: "I did not receive this from tradition, but I say 'Open my eyes that I may gaze on the wonders of your Law'" (*Sefer Yetzira* 100b).

4. See Y. Liebes, "The Messiah of the *Zohar*—To the Messianic Nature of R. Shimon bar Yohai," *The Messianic Idea in Israel: A Symposium in Honor of Gershom Scholem* (Jerusalem: Ha'akademia Haleumit Ha'israelit l'mada'im, 1982), pp. 132–181 (Hebrew); Liebes, "Eros ve-*Zohar*," *Alpayim* 9 (1994): 67–119. See as well M. Helner, *A River Issues Forth from Eden* (Tel Aviv: Am Oved, 2005), pp. 187–221 (Hebrew).

5. On the centrality of innovation in the *Zohar*, see D. Matt, "'Matnita Dilan: Technique of innovation in the *Zohar*," in *The* Zohar *and Its Generation*, ed. J. Dan, *Jerusalem Studies in Jewish Thought* 8 (1989): 123–146 (Hebrew).

6. On the relation between secrecy, disclosure, and eros, see also E. Wolfson, "Occultation of the Feminine and the Body of Secrecy in Medieval Kabbala, *Rending the Veil: Concealment and Secrecy in the History of Religions,* ed. E. R. Wolfson (New York: Seven Bridges Press, 1999), pp. 113–148.

7. For Shem Tov Ibn Gaon and his works, see D. Sh. Levinger, "Rabbi Shem Ibn Gaon," *Sefunot* (1963): 7–40 (Hebrew).

8. The commitment not to transmit the secret has a judicial dimension as well. See the later example of a contractual commitment of the disciples of the Shlomo Luria, published by Z. Rabinowitz, "From the Geniza Hastolinait," *Zion* 5 (1940): 125–126 (Hebrew). See also G. Scholem, "A Binding Contract of the Ari's Disciples," *Zion* 5 (1940): 133–160. See also Liebes, "Messiah of the *Zohar*," 136n199, 158n251 (Hebrew).

9. On age restrictions for study, see M. Idel, "On the History of the Prohibitions to Study Kabbalah," *AJS Review* 5 (1980): 1–20 (Hebrew).

10. See Idel, *Kabbalah: New Perspectives.*

11. "These hints cannot be understood, except if received from mouth to mouth (going back to) Moses on Mount Sinai." See D. Abrams, "The Book of the Orah of Rabbi Ya'akov ha-Cohen" (Ph.D. diss., New York University, 1993), p. 215; see also p. 236. On the Cohen brothers and Moshe of Burgos, see Gershom Scholem, "The Kabbalah of R. Yitzḥak ben Ya'akov ha-Cohen—R. Moshe of Burgos the Disciple of R. Yitzḥak," *Tarbiz Supplement* 4 (1933) (Hebrew), including, for example, the words of Moshe of Burgos on the Kabbalah: "Far and strange from the eyes of all, without deliberation or reasoning, it is the faithful Kabbalah which is transmitted to all bearers of hidden wisdom" (p. 208).

12. It is of interest to note that the expression "two seeds at the summit of a tall tree," with which Shem Tov describes the Cohen brothers, appears in the writings of Rabbi Yitzḥak Cohen on those who know the secrets of the *sefirot* of the left side: "For this is a path in which, aside from myself, only two or three have trodden. They are seeds at the summit of a tall tree, the ancient wise men, the sages of Sepharad who made used of the palace of Samael" (see Scholem, "Kabbalah of R. Yitzḥak ben Ya'akov ha-Cohen," p. 224). It seems that there is a direct reference, perhaps even ironic, of Shem Tov to the writings of the Cohen brothers themselves.

13. The tension erupted into a full-scale confrontation between Shem Tov's master, the Rashba and Avraham Abulafia. Among other subjects characterizing this tension, we may mention Abulafia's complete liberation from the bonds of esotericism, to the dismay of other kabbalists, as Abulafia himself describes: "Although I know that among the kabbalists are many who did not reach perfection, and thought they had perfected themselves by not revealing esoteric matters, I do not heed their thoughts, even when they condemn me for disclosing things, for in this matter, my opinion is much different from or opposite to theirs" (*Otzar Eden Ganuz,* Oxford manuscript 1580). On this issue, see M. Idel, "The Rashba and Avra'am Abulafia: The History of a Neglected Kabbalistic Polemic," *Atara le Haim: Studies in Talmudic and Rabbinic Literature in Honor of Professor Haim Zalman Dimitrovsky,* ed. D. Boyarin (Jerusalem: Magnes Press, 2000), pp. 231–235 (Hebrew).

CHAPTER 13. "THE WIDENING OF THE APERTURES OF THE SHOWPIECE":
SHMUEL IBN TIBON AND THE END OF THE ERA OF ESOTERICISM

1. It is of interest to note that Ibn Tibon is precise in his description of the different stages in the chain of widening, as opposed to the description of Maimonides. Solomon adds parable to parable, and his parables are a more transparent description of the parables of the Pentateuch and its hints. Maimonides, by contrast, combines chapter headings to each other, and, as we saw above, he rejects the possibility of esoteric writing by means of parables.

2. The formula "widening the apertures of the showpiece" appears frequently in the writings of Ibn Tibon. See *Ma'amar Yikavu Hamayim*, pp. 40, 141, 146, 164. See also his words at the top of p. 123 and on pp. 142–143.

3. The conception of progress in the disclosure of the secrets of the Torah in the thought of Ibn Tibon was pointed out by Avi Ravitzky, "Samuel Ibn Tibon and the Secret of the Guide of the Perplexed," *Da'at* 10 (1983): 19–46 (Hebrew).

4. Ibn Tibon derived his idea of progress from the understanding of the reasons for the commandments in Maimonides' thought. There, Maimonides used the myth of the nations of the Sabeans in order to explain the need to uproot idolatrous beliefs and practices. Maimonides did not, however, use the concept of progress in order to permit the disclosure of Torah secrets.

5. For a broad discussion of esotericism in early Christianity and its later rejection, see G. Stroumsa, *Hidden Wisdom: Esoteric Traditions and the Roots of Christian Mysticism* (Leiden: Brill, 1996).

CHAPTER 14. ESOTERICISM, SERMONS, AND CURRICULA: YA'AKOV ANATOLI
AND THE DISSEMINATION OF THE SECRET

1. Later in his book *Sefer Hamusar* (chap. 15), Ibn Kaspi levies a more severe criticism of talmudic culture, based on Maimonides' words. On the question of the formulation of the curriculum in the Middle Ages and on the different competing elements, see J. Katz, "Halakhah and Kabbalah as Competing Subjects of Study," *Halakhah and Kabbalah* (Jerusalem: Magnes Press, 1986), pp. 70–101 (Hebrew); I. Twersky, "Talmudists, Philosophers, Kabbalists: The Quest for Spirituality in the Sixteenth Century," *Jewish Thought in the Sixteenth Century*, ed. B. Cooperman (Cambridge, Mass.: Harvard University Press, 1983), pp. 431–459. See also my book, *Between Torah and Wisdom: Rabbi Menahem Hameiri and the Maimondean Halakhists in Provence* (Jerusalem: Magnes Press, 2000), pp. 50–62 (Hebrew).

2. The various formulations of Maimonides concerning the *Mishneh Torah* give rise to an ambiguous position, although, in my opinion the weight of evidence supports the more radical approach. In response to the criticism of Rabbi Pinhas Hadayan on the *Mishneh Torah*, Maimonides claimed that he never attempted to precipitate change in the curriculum. See *Igrot HaRambam*, ed. Y. Shilat (Jerusalem: Ma'aliyot Press, 1988), 2:439. In other places, however, he claimed that the *Mishneh Torah* bears the role of replacing the talmudic curriculum,

based on the estimation that the value of talmudic study lies only in its halakhic conclusions. See *Igrot HaRambam* 1:312–313, and also 357, 359.

3. On Maimonides' conception of the canon of learning, and on the inclusion of physics and metaphysics under the category of Torah study, see *Mishneh Torah, Hilkhot Talmud Torah* 1:11–12.

CHAPTER 15. THE AMBIVALENCE OF SECRECY: THE DISPUTE OVER PHILOSOPHY IN THE EARLY FOURTEENTH CENTURY

1. For a broad and reliable picture on the development of the dispute and the positions of the various sides, see G. Stern, "Menachem Ha-Meiri and the Second Controversy over Philosophy" (Ph.D. diss., Harvard University, 1995). I have dealt extensively with this dispute in my book *Between Torah and Wisdom*, chap. 5. This section is a summary of the discussion, focusing on the question of esotericism within the dispute.

2. "For upon that day there was a wedding of one of the renowned, and one of the notables of the land spoke harshly with us; in the presence of the masses, he said of Abraham and Sarah of Scripture that they were matter and form" (*Hoshen Mishpat*, p. 174). See there also for a vivid description of the feast in which the sermon was preached and for other philosophical allegories current among the preachers of Provence. See also *Minḥat Kna'ot*, ed. Haim Zalman Dimitrovsky (Jerusalem: Mossad Harav Kook, 1990), p. 316.

3. According to the Rashba, the Christians too would have punished those expounding such allegories, for they threatened the historical existence of the forefathers: "For the islands of the Cutheans, who are Canaanites, and all the nations would have punished them as heretics, even for one of their words and iniquitous laws that they have inscribed in books. For one who says that Abraham and Sarah are matter and form, they would surround him with faggots and burn him to lime, for all the nations derive their lineage from them. Yet they say that they were naught but parables, they and their sons" (*Minḥat Kna'ot*, pp. 412–413).

4. The accusation that the allegorists intended to empty the commandments of their binding content appears in the letters of the Rashba and the notables of Barcelona: "And their intent is transparent to say that the commandments are not to be understood according to their simple meaning. . . . All is but parable and high words, and they uphold the falsehood to mislead the fools. And through serpentine ways they tend" (*Minḥat Kna'ot*, pp. 411–412).

5. *Minḥat Kna'ot*, p. 724.

6. In chapter 9 of *Minḥat Kna'ot*, Abba Mari identifies himself with the conception that contemplation is the supreme religious goal, and its accomplishment assures divine providence and eternal life: "And for this reason, it was hinted at in the *mezuzah*, as it is written, 'The Lord our God, the Lord is One,' so that one make the effort to know wisdom until he apprehend the existence of the Lord, may He be praised, and his oneness with a proof, and then he should take heed not to serve anyone but Him. Then the providence of God shall cleave unto him so that he may be protected from evil forces, and it shall be more precious to him than all the pearls of the world . . . for the attainment of Him, may He be blessed,

is the true success and salvation and the eternal life, and it is the purpose of the intentions of the Torah" (*Minḥat Kna'ot*, pp. 246–247).

7. For similar formulations, see *Minḥat Kna'ot*, pp. 426–427, ll. 10–15.

8. See also the Rashba's derision of the definition of wisdom as the vision of the chariot: "to the jiggling chariot" (*Minḥat Kna'ot*, p. 378).

9. The tension between the Rashba's attack on wisdom and the formulation of the ban emerged in the comments of Rabbi Ya'akov ben Makhir addressed to the Rashba; see *Minḥat Kna'ot*, p. 507.

10. The Rashba himself changed his tone when addressing his opponents in Provence. In those passages he sounded very close to the position of Abba Mari. See the words addressed to Rabbi Shlomo of Lunel (*Minḥat Kna'ot*, pp. 470–471), to Rabbi Ya'akov ben Makhir (p. 516), to Rabbi Shmuel ben Reuven (pp. 542–543), and to Rabbi Yitzḥak De-Lates (p. 550).

11. Abba Mari sought to suppress HaMeiri's letter to him and not publish it. To his dismay, HaMeiri preceded him and sent the letter to his opponents. The opponents of Abba Mari in Montpelier found in HaMeiri's authority an important source of support, and did all they could to diffuse the letter and utilize it for their own purposes. *Ḥoshen Mishpat*, p. 151.

12. The shifts in loyalty resulting from the ambivalence of the ban is characteristic not only of HaMeiri, but of other persons involved in the dispute as well. See my *Between Torah and Wisdom*, p. 174.

13. Abba Mari truly attempted to anchor his struggle in terms of the Provencal Maimonidean culture, whereas his opponents saw the struggle, especially in response to the Rashba, as a slander against the Provencal tradition and as a questioning of the status of Maimonides himself. Consequently, Abba Mari's opponents saw the dispute as a repetition of the dispute against the writings of Maimonides, which took place in the fourth decade of the thirteenth century in Provence. This dispute, whose violent end left scars on the community, and which resulted in the ascendancy of the supporters of Maimonides, remained as a traumatic memory in the minds of all involved in it: "For it is fitting that we remember the form of the first dispute that we knew and heard of when the books of our master, the teacher of righteousness, arrived here. For who could have predicted the extent of damage, pain, and humiliation which resulted from it" (*Ḥoshen Mishpat*, p. 153).

14. Later on in his writing, Rabbi Shimon ben Yosef disputed the comparison drawn by HaMeiri between the opponents of Maimonides in the dispute over his writings and the faction of Abba Mari, and firmly rejected the comparison: "What is this conjoining that you joined the matter of fury. Reminding us of the sin of the previous dispute. You have compared our deeds to those who spoke against God and Moses. . . . What fault have you found in us and in our deeds? Who envied the revelers who attacked our prince, our lord, the wise Rabbi Moshe and his books? Who gathered this wind of envy in his fist and trampled his enemies underfoot? Who was his aide against his enemies, if not our fathers who came to his assistance? . . . What relevance does that dispute have that you summon up its presence?" (*Ḥoshen Mishpat*, p. 153). According to Rabbi Shimon ben Yosef, Abba Mari and his circle belong to the same tradition that rejected the opponents of Maimonides in Provence, so that no one should attach to them the guilt for "the first dispute."

15. For a fascinating parallel to the metaphor of the uncovering of secrets as the sexual abuse of a maiden in the Neoplatonic literature, see the material analyzed by P. Hadot, *The Veil of Isis: An Essay on the History of the Idea of Nature*, trans. M. Chase (Cambridge, Mass.: Harvard University Press, 2006), pp. 61–62.

CHAPTER 16. ESOTERICISM, DISCONTENT, AND CO-EXISTENCE

1. In his commentary on the Pentateuch, the Rashbam uses the term *maskil* or *maskilim*, and also singles out certain groups among his readers. But the *maskil* does not expose a hidden theological layer of the text. On the contrary, he is oriented toward the surface meaning and deviated from the traditional-authoritative reading of the text. According to Elazar Tuito, the *maskil* is familiar with the readings of the surface meaning developing in the Christian world. See E. Tuito, "The Rashbam's Approach in His Interpretation to the Legal Parts of Torah," *Milet* 2 (1984): 275–288 (Hebrew); on the *maskil*, see n. 4.

2. It is no wonder that Rabbi Moshe Takku, the great polemic defender of talmudic-midrashic faith, attacked the idea that there was a deep allegorical hermeneutic layer to the sacred scriptures or the Talmud. Furthermore, he saw the esoteric canon as an act of deception and trickery.

3. On this broader question, see Z. Griss, "The Copying and Printing of Kabbalistic Books as Source for the Study of Kabbalah," *Mahanaim* 6 (1992): 204–211.

CHAPTER 17. TAXONOMY AND PARADOXES OF ESOTERICISM: CONCEPTUAL CONCLUSION

1. *Being and Nothingness*, trans. Hazel E. Barnes (New York: Philosophical Library, 1956), pp. 261–262.

2. This feature of shame is discussed in J. D. Velleman, "The Genesis of Shame," *Philosophy & Public Affairs* 30:1 (2001): 27–52.

3. For an exposition of transparency in Rousseau's thought see J. Starabinsky, *Transparency and Obstruction* (Chicago: University of Chicago Press, 1988).

4. See T. Nagel, *Concealment and Exposure and Other Essays* (Oxford: Oxford University Press, 2002), chap. 1.

5. See D. Wootton, *Paolo Sapri: Between Renaissance and Enlightenment* (Cambridge: Cambridge University Press, 1983), chap. 1.

6. The open-ended nature of the concealed appears in completely different cultural settings. An interesting example for such a process appears in the attribution of monotheism or deism to early Egyptian mystery cults, claiming that the pagan religion of ancient Egypt was a mere surface that served political needs. See J. Assmann, *Moses the Egyptian: The Memory of Egypt in Western Monotheism* (Cambridge, Mass.: Harvard University Press, 1997), chap. 4, and see his general reflections on secrecy, pp. 212–215.

7. S. Freud, *Introductory Lectures on Psycho-analysis*, trans. J. Stachey (New York: HarperCollins, 1966), p. 171.

8. For an illuminating exposition of the idea of the secret of nature and its complex history, which is based on the privilege of the hidden, see P. Hadot, *The Veil of Isis: An Essay on the History of the Idea of Nature*, trans. M. Chase (Cambridge, Mass.: Harvard University Press, 2006).

9. Martin Heidegger, *Being and Time*, trans. J. Macquarrie and E. Robinson (Oxford: Oxford University Press, 1999), p. 261. All subsequent references are to this editon.

10. See H. L. Dreyfus, *Being-in-the-World: A Commentary on Heidegger's Being and Time, Division I* (Cambridge, Mass.: MIT Press, 1991), pp. 33–38.

11. *Letters from Ludwig Wittgenstein, with a Memoir*, ed. P. Engelmann (Oxford: Blackwell, 1967), p. 97.

12. For such a reading, see C. Diamond, "Throwing Away the Ladder: How to Read the *Tractatus*," in *The Realistic Spirit: Wittgenstein, Philosophy and the Mind* (Cambridge: MIT Press, 1991); J. Conant, "Wittgenstein, Kierkegaard and Nonsense," in *Pursuits of Reasons*, ed. T. Cohen, P. Guyer, and H. Putnam (Lubbock: Texas Tech University Press, 1993), pp. 195–224. For the counterview see P. M. S. Hacker, "Was He Trying to Whistle It?" in *Wittgenstein: Connections and Controversies* (Oxford: Clarendon Press, 2001), pp. 98–140.

13. See J. Scott, *Domination and the Arts of Resistance: Hidden Transcripts* (New Haven: Yale University Press, 1990).

14. See H. Arendt, *Origins of Totalitarianism* (New York: Harcourt Brace Jovanovich, 1973), chap. 12.

15. Some of these tensions are manifested in completely different contexts of classified state information. In his essay "Removing Knowledge" in *Critical Inquiry* (2003), Peter Galison argues that the secret classified material sometimes becomes obsolete because it is not examined by the rest of the scientific community and therefore it might be false and fantastic. Among other problems, the pressure to uncover the secrets comes from the desire for a fuller and enriched use of them in, for example, industry technology. The secret material is thus under a double pressure: if it is effective, it will come out; if it stays concealed, it might be completely nonsensical.

16. *Kant's Political Writings*, ed. Hans Reiis (Cambridge: Cambridge University Press, 1970), p. 55.

17. D. Thompson, *Restoring Responsibility: Ethics in Government, Business, and Healthcare* (Cambridge: Cambridge University Press, 2005), pp. 129–142.

18. See R. Hofstadter, *The Paranoid Style in American Politics and Other Essays* (New York: Knopf, 1966), pp. 29–40.

Index

Aaron, 15, 46
Abba Mari, 121; and Maimonides, 123–24, 125, 126, 127, 132, 188n13; and Menaḥem HaMeiri, 129, 130, 131, 136–37, 188nn11 and 14; *Minḥat Kna'ot*, 120, 129; and philosophical sermons, 134; and Rashba, 126–27, 128, 129, 133, 188n10; and Rosh, 128; *Serer Hayare'aḥ*, 122–25; and Shimon ben Yosef, 132, 133
Abihu, 15
Abraham bar Ḥiyya, 42
Abraham ben Yitzḥak, *Sefer Ha'eshkol*, 74
Abraham Ibn Da'ud, *Ha'emunah Haramah*, 177n1
Abraham Ibn Ezra, 35–43, 44–48, 69, 138, 150, 183n8; commentary on Pentateuch, 92; commentary on the Torah, 5, 6; creativity in, 137; hinting in, 35, 37, 44, 45, 46, 138; and Maimonides, 49; and Naḥmanides, 86–88, 92
Abu Ma'shar al-Balkhi, 38
Ada bar Abba, 42, 43
aggadah, 61, 99
Akiba, Rabbi, 9, 13, 18–19, 25, 28, 31
allegory, 57, 120, 123, 131, 157, 187nn3 and 4
analogy, 79
Andalusia, 49, 105, 106, 128
angels, 9, 18, 22, 25–26, 30–31, 45, 46, 173n8
anthropomorphism, 35, 53, 138–39, 150
Arabic learning: in Abraham Ibn Ezra, 37, 38, 47; causality in, 139; in Maimonides, 49, 52, 55, 60; and Rosh, 128; in Shmuel Ibn Tibon, 105, 106; use of, 43; and Ya'akov Anatoli, 114. *See also* Muslim culture
Arendt, Hannah, 160
Aristotle, 112; in Abba Mari, 125; and Abraham Ibn Ezra, 39; and Christianity, 113; and fourteenth-century dispute over philosophy, 120–21; incorporation of, 140; and Maimonides, 52, 59, 139, 150,

151; in Menaḥem HaMeiri, 130; in Shmuel Ibn Tibon, 106
Aristotlean-Averroesean tradition, 121
Asher ben David, 75–76, 94, 153–54; *Perush Hashevu'ah*, 93; *Perush Shlosh Esreh Middot*, 93; *Sefer Hayiḥud*, 72–76
Ashkenaz, 181n7. *See also* Ḥasidim of Ashkenaz
Assmann, Jan, 169n3
astrology: in Abraham Ibn Ezra, 38, 39, 40, 41–43, 44, 45, 46–47, 92, 138; and anthropomorphism, 138; authenticity of, 4; incorporation of, 140, 151; and instructed persons, 37; in Maimonides, 49; in Menaḥem HaMeiri, 136
astronomy, 37, 127
Augustine, 144
Avot deRabbi Natan, 27
Avraham, Rabbi, 103
Avraham Abulafia, 185n13
Avraham ben David. *See* Ravad (Avraham ben David)
Avraham ben Yitzḥak, 100, 152; *Sefer Ha'eshkol*, 70
Azriel, Rabbi, 70, 71, 73, 81, 85, 93–94, 99, 103, 153, 180n2, 181n4; *Perush Eser Sefirot*, 77–79

Babylonia, 34
Babylonian hegemony, 31
Barcelona, 121, 126, 127, 130
Bayle, Pierre, 150
Benjamin, Walter, 147
al-Biruni, 38
Borges, Jorge Luis, 59
Brethrens of Purity, 38
Buber, Martin, 140
Burgos, 75, 93

Camus, Albert, *The Fall*, 148
canon, 36, 75, 98, 104, 114, 117, 118
Cartesianism, 163
Castile, kabbalists of, 93, 103, 104, 136